LATIN AMERICA
AND THE INDUSTRIAL AGE

Other Works by the Author

THE UNITED STATES AND MEXICO
(F. S. Crofts, 3rd ed., 1931)

LATIN AMERICA IN WORLD POLITICS
(F. S. Crofts, 3rd ed., 1938)

HISTORICAL EVOLUTION OF HISPANIC AMERICA
(F. S. Crofts, 3rd ed., 1940)

THE CARIBBEAN DANGER ZONE
(G. P. Putnam's Sons, 1940)

SOUTH AMERICA AND HEMISPHERE DEFENSE
(University of Louisiana Press, 1941)

LATIN AMERICA AND THE INDUSTRIAL AGE

By

J. FRED RIPPY

Professor of Latin-American History
The University of Chicago

G. P. PUTNAM'S SONS
NEW YORK

Copyright, 1944, 1947, by J. Fred Rippy

*

Second Edition

*

MANUFACTURED IN THE UNITED STATES OF AMERICA
Van Rees Press, New York

TO THE PIONEERS, NORTH AND SOUTH

PREFACE

WITH THE COMING of the present world crisis a good many of our citizens got excited about Latin America. Glib journalists and dapper "movie stars," confident of their ability to probe the intricacies of Hispanic civilization in a rapid tour of three weeks, hurried south to observe, influence, and charm. Emissaries of rich endowments, or of organizations set up to tell them how to spend their money, pocketed dictionaries and boarded Pan American Clippers.

All returned promptly to help build the Pan American front. The journalists informed and misinformed the public, sometimes for handsome fees. The actors employed their art on the screen and over the radio to sway the populace. Agents of the foundations discussed many remote or minute projects of investigation, but framed no comprehensive program of vital research.

Neither the endowments nor the Federal government succeeded in fully mustering the intellectual resources of the Americas. Men appointed to stimulate investigation and focus the light of wisdom on practical affairs seemed at times to be staging a petty revolt against learning. There was no systematic search for fundamentals.

The volume here presented deals with a vital subject which they neglected. It deals with the salient aspects of a grand epic: the joint mastery by Latins and Anglo-Saxons of the Latin-American physical environment, the development of Latin America's resources through science and technology.

Could not this theme be used in art, literature, and diplomacy to cement the Pan American structure? Are not friendships based on memories and anticipations of happy days together, of triumphs over common difficulties, of perils successfully confronted?

At any rate, the fundamental significance of science and technology cannot be doubted. They largely determine the rise and fall of groups and nations. Powerful agencies of social transformation, they are the very essence of social dynamics. They are so important, so basic, that their control, and the distribution of the benefits they create, pose a fundamental problem of our age. The impact of foreign capital, science, and technology upon Latin America is a major episode in modern history which no one who aspires to understand or shape world events can afford to ignore.

The theme is so immense that no single individual could do it justice in a lifetime. What is clearly needed is a research committee, perhaps several, composed of specialists both from Latin America and from the United States, a group of experts adequately financed and equipped to investigate every significant phase of the subject in time to illuminate and influence the present and the immediate future.

The essays included in this volume are mainly introductory. They are intended to call attention to this vital subject, to fix the chronology of salient phases of the technological advance, and to identify some of its agents. Emphasis is placed on contributions of the United States to Latin America's economic development, upon collaborative pioneering, upon promoters, technicians, laborers, and celebrations of technological triumphs. Financial relationships, control and management, and the distribution of goods and profits are given comparatively little attention in spite of my conviction of their profound significance and of the growing demand that such matters be accorded full consideration.

I offer my introductory contribution now because I feel that the times demand it. We seem to be at the threshold of a new era in inter-American affairs.

I am grateful to all who have given me assistance. I am especially indebted to Professor Watt Stewart, Dr. Ella P. Levett, and Mr. David Pletcher. A number of others who aided me are mentioned in the bibliographical notes.

J. Fred Rippy.

PREFACE TO THE SECOND EDITION

SOME OF THE reviewers of the first edition of this work complained, with justice on their side, that it was incomplete because it contained no discussion of manufacturing, the highest form of technological achievement. I did not deal with manufacturing in the first edition because I intended to publish a separate volume on that subject. Since 1944, however, two volumes and several monographs have appeared in the United States on manufacturing in Latin America. Although they do not give sufficient attention to origins and early development, stressing rather the period since 1914, they have filled a large gap; and for this reason I have decided to reduce my projected volume to a careful summary and include it as Chapter XXII in this new edition. The summary is based upon three years of research, financed in part by the Social Science Research Committee of the University of Chicago. I have no doubt that readers who welcomed the first edition with more generosity than I had any right to expect will at least approve of my effort to round out the work, and I hope they will find this new chapter as useful and satisfactory as the rest of the volume.

J. Fred Rippy.

CONTENTS

MAPS

LATIN AMERICA
AND THE INDUSTRIAL AGE

AN INTRODUCTION

INTRODUCTION

IN ITS RECENT efforts to solidify and develop the Pan-American front the government of the United States, although ignoring significant historical background, has placed strong emphasis upon the economic and technological problems of Latin America. More than a score of inter-American committees and bureaus have been established; hundreds of technicians have been sent out; hundreds of millions of dollars have been spent. Propelled by a tremendous war effort, the implements, devices, and processes of the Industrial Age are penetrating the remotest corners of the region. The word "developmental" is heard on every hand and is applied to human as well as material resources. Human welfare is stressed along with increased production in agriculture, forestry, mining, and industry. Mechanization, sanitation, advances in chemistry and all the practical sciences are expected to lift the people to a higher plane of living.

The point may be illustrated by the instructions and attitude of a committee of twenty-one experts sent to South America in 1941 under the joint auspices of the National Research Council and the Council of National Defense. The committee's report describes the state of technology and industry in the neighboring continent and reveals a genuine interest in Latin America's well-being no less than in its capacity to contribute to the global war already confidently anticipated at the time of their visit.

The purpose of the twenty-one business executives was to study at first hand the industrial progress of South America; to exchange ideas with its industrial leaders and government officials; to give advice when requested in matters of research,

engineering, and technology; to establish an enduring association with the Latin-American governments; and to make
available to them the services of the National Research Council
on a basis similar to that accorded the government of the United
States. They were instructed by Co-ordinator Nelson Rockefeller to report on opportunities for collaborative industrial
development through the application of North American skills
and methods to Latin-American raw materials. They were asked
to devote special attention to technical education and research
in the continent to the south.

The investigations of the committee were cursory but energetic. Starting from Miami, they made a 17,000-mile journey by
Pan-American Clipper, spending several days in each of five
South American countries. Venezuela, Ecuador, Bolivia, and
Paraguay were not included in their itinerary, and they tarried
only a short time in Uruguay. Their whole tour lasted only
forty-five days. Nevertheless, they collected a good deal of information and made a number of constructive suggestions.

They discovered immediately the fallacy of thinking of South
America as one country. The continent, they noted, is made up
of ten nations with distinctly different characteristics and in various stages of economic progress. They noted further that South
America is no El Dorado. On the contrary, it is relatively poor
because of its location, climate, and topography. They remarked
that tropical lowlands are an unfavorable environment for the
development of "modern enterprises." They observed, however,
that a good part of the southern continent is situated in a fertile
temperate zone, and they were optimistic regarding the results
that might be achieved by applying in the tropics temperate-
zone driving power in the form of capital and technology.

They found that all the countries they visited were stressing
industrialization. "The pattern varies," they said, "in different
countries, but in every case the desire is the same. All are dis-
playing great enthusiasm." The committee did not fail to note,
however, that the landed gentry of Argentina had misgivings
regarding industrialization. For the emergency it might be
necessary, the big landlords admitted, but it was dangerous. In
the long run the country would have to buy many industrial

products from abroad if it were to continue to find foreign markets for the products of its ranches and farms.

With reference to industrial progress, members of the committee noted that much of South American industry was inefficiently organized and utilizing obsolete procedures because of lack of recourse to advanced technical and industrial experience; that the managers were disposed to welcome North American capital and methods; that means of transportation were inadequate in some of the countries; and that heavy industry hardly existed anywhere, owing, among other things, to scarcity of iron in several of the nations and absence of good coking coal in all of them. They reported, however, that several of the light industries were efficient, especially in cases where foreign experts had been employed in an advisory capacity.

They observed that in the majority of the countries thorough explorations to determine the nature and quantity of natural resources had not yet been effected. Colombia: "Exploration work has not been carried out in a sufficiently systematic or extensive way to lead even tentatively to an accurate evaluation of Colombia's iron ore." Argentina: "Most of Argentina has not been explored mineralogically." Brazil: "Much of the country is unexplored. . . . An area as large as our entire Atlantic seaboard has never had anyone but natives set foot on it." Nor had the raw materials and industrial possibilities of eastern Peru been sufficiently investigated.

The committee reported that technical education and industrial research were inadequate in all the countries, although better in some than in others. Equipment and laboratory ingenuity were meager; research was little stressed and facilities for industrial testing and standardization were undeveloped.

The committee found a number of experts from the United States already in the field. These experts had assisted Colombia with technical studies "in lumber, tanning, fisheries, steel, and rubber." In Peru, they were "studying specific projects" in transportation and helping in the quest for deposits of iron, manganese, limestone, and quicksilver. Chilean leaders were on the point of making requests for capital and "technical brains." The most efficient industrial plant examined in Argentina was under the management of an Argentinian trained in Cornell

University. In Brazil, a technician from the United States Department of Agriculture was helping to develop a tung-oil industry and another Yankee scientist was experimenting with coffee plastics.

"The need for scientifically and technically trained men in the southern countries is great," the committee concluded. "A much increased number of chemists, physicists, biologists, geologists, paleontologists, mineralogists, engineers, and men trained in other specialties" would be required to develop South American resources.

Regarding the policies of some of the governments the committee declared:

Colombia's industrialization is years behind the times, and its government may be trying to close the gap too swiftly.... Peru has a sensible, realistic attitude and its government may be expected to foster industrialization intelligently and properly with the aid of foreign technology. Chilean officials have an intelligent concept of industrialization but must overcome ... low domestic purchasing power, vast distances, and limited knowledge of raw materials. Argentina recognizes that the change from a four-crop agricultural country to an industrial nation will mean an economic revolution, and her officials are divided on the wisdom of promoting this change.... Brazil has the most experience with industrialization ... and its government will doubtless tend to continue a sound policy.

Various members of the committee made a number of recommendations: Selected executives should be sent to the United States for training in factory management. Safety and sanitary engineers should be placed promptly in South American factories. More attention should be given to the testing and standardization of products for export. Mineral and forest-product surveys should be carried out. In view of the scarcity of wood, attempts should be made in Argentina to develop plastics from corn and wheat. Pharmaceutical companies from the United States should be encouraged to establish laboratories in South America for the investigation of medical plants. Experts should be sent down to assist in the development of tung-oil, quinine, flax, and vegetable oil wherever opportunities are favorable. Scientific societies should be founded in South America and similar organizations in the United States should stimulate the efforts of Latin-American scientists and technicians by giving them recognition for their achievements. Technical education and scientific research should be subsidized and encouraged through the improvement of schools and by traveling fellowships for study and observation in the United States.

The attitude of the committee toward Latin-American "backwardness" in science and technology was enlightened and tolerant. Its members informed themselves of the progress of the region in medicine and learned to appreciate the salient characteristics of its civilization. One of them wrote: "The ... educational system in South America is on a plane quite different from the advanced countries of Europe and the United States. The development of education runs toward liberal arts and the law.... The entire culture of the people is one of art rather than of science."

The committee was impressed by the progress the South American nations were making in the development of their resources. In light industries, several of the countries were rapidly approaching the point of self-sufficiency, and committee members seemed to feel that the metal industries, greatly hampered for lack of good coking coal, might be developed by means of water power and electro-metallurgy.

Viewed in the light of history and of the handicaps Latin Americans had confronted, their technological achievements were even more impressive. The proper starting point for the story of their mechanical progress is a consideration of the reception and influence of the Eighteenth-Century Enlightenment in the Spanish and Portuguese colonies. Pioneer studies are being made in that subject by Professor John Tate Lanning of Duke University, and in December 1940, it was considered in one of the sessions of the American Historical Association at New York City.

The tentative conclusions of the historians will startle those who have been taught that eighteenth-century Spain and Portugal were the unmitigated strongholds of obscurantism and intolerance. To a considerable extent the Enlightenment promptly reached both Hispanic countries and their American colonies as well, cracking the foundations of scholasticism and infusing the scientific spirit. In the colonies, experiment began to be substituted for barren speculation during the eighteenth century and advances were made in medicine, metallurgy, and other sciences. Only a generation or two in the Spanish dependencies was required in the middle colonial period to bridge the gap from "European innovator to American academician," and as the decades passed the "gap became less and less." "It was eighty-five years after the death of Descartes before Cartesianism began to be taught openly in the New World, but Newton was an accepted institution a half century after the publication of his *Principia mathematica* and almost within a decade after his death. The pioneer work of Jean Baptiste Lamarck on evolution was published in 1802 and was the subject of academic speculation in [Spanish] America the next year."

Roland D. Hussey concluded that the "proportion of French Enlightenment in the total make-up of Colonial Hispanic Americans was no doubt infinitesimal, but it was large among the groups where it most could count." Lanning remarked that the Spanish Americans "did not so much receive the Enlightenment; they reproduced it from the sources upon which its exponents in Europe depended." At least the ground had been prepared for its reception by the time it arrived from overseas. In Portuguese Brazil, no colonial university was founded, but a number of learned societies sprang up to cherish the spirit of investigation and promote the search for experimental truth. Thus Latin America "inherited some of the zeal for reform, humanitarianism, and useful knowledge that had animated the eighteenth-century philosophers."

All this must be recognized in the interest of truth. Yet the fact remains that progress in science and technology was retarded in the Spanish and Portuguese colonies by the repressions of despotic mother countries. The point that requires emphasis is this: meager colonial heritage in science is but one of several factors which handicapped scientific and technological progress in later Hispanic America. Another is physical environment and resources: tropics, jungle, lofty mountains, bad distribution of rainfall, absence of the best grades of coal. A third is the presence of a multitude of primitive peoples—mainly Indians, mix-bloods, and Negroes—somewhat deficient in aptitude for technological progress and with living standards so low that man-power was often cheaper than mechanical devices. A fourth is the apparently innate traits of the upper classes, who have been far more interested in religion, law, art, and politics than in the techniques of industry. A fifth factor is political insta-

bility, especially during the early national period, and a sixth is the handicap involved in this technological lag itself.

Native capital and skills accumulated slowly. Owners of machinery and processes brought in from the outside siphoned away a large part of the profits from new economic enterprises and gave too little attention to the training of native technicians and managers. Alien investors rarely supported technical schools and for economic reasons were rather remiss in furnishing the natives opportunities for practical technological experience in the upper ranks. A wise policy, from the standpoint of the Latin Americans, would probably have required the foreigners to train the natives more rapidly in the new technology and to accept plans for the gradual nationalization of management and investment. It is doubtful whether such a policy could have been enforced in face of the almost certain resistance of the great powers, but the truth is that it was seldom seriously advocated until recently.

Latin Americans usually welcomed scientific and technological assistance because they realized it was required for the development of their resources. But the demands of the strong nations for raw materials and investment opportunities were so overwhelming that the Latins probably would have been compelled, even if their attitude had been different, to receive the emissaries of the Machine Age. The influence of foreign business in domestic politics, the feeling on the part of Latin Americans that they were being exploited, and their eagerness to obtain a larger share of the income derived from economic activities have given rise in recent years to a rather unfriendly attitude toward foreign capital. To some extent also this attitude may have extended to alien technicians; but, in general, foreign technology is more cordially received than foreign capital, especially in its corporate form. The control of the corporation is a fundamental problem of the Industrial Era and the Latin Americans know it.

Industrialism tended to embrace the whole world in spite of every obstacle; and its influence was felt in Latin America before 1850. Although technological modernization took place there very gradually, it had advanced a long way by the time the delegation of business executives arrived on their mission from the United States in 1941.

It had advanced, in large part, because of the contributions of Englishmen and their kinsmen overseas. The scientific and technological contributions of citizens of the United States to

Latin-American development, the main concern of this volume, began surprisingly early. They began in the time of Benjamin Franklin, that mirror of the Age of Reason whom the Spanish Americans accepted as the "symbol of North American science and democracy." They continued in the early years with Alexander Garden, the South Carolina botanist, whose work on cochineal and tobacco reached Mexico in 1790, and with Benjamin Barton Smith, an eminent physician of the College of Philadelphia.

Present-day journalists and cinema actors would be surprised if they should ever read the early proceedings of the American Philosophical Society, the New York Historical Society, the American Antiquarian Society, and the New York Lyceum of Natural History. As early as 1814 the president of the Antiquarian Society was urging that membership be extended to "gentlemen of distinguished characters in Spanish and Portuguese America." The New York *Medical Repository* for the year 1811 declared: "Nothing has been a more trite and erroneous subject of vulgar remark than the ignorance of the lazy Dons. This silly cant... has been so frequently repeated and so widely proclaimed that many of our honest patriots believe that the Spaniards are... their inferiors. This is a miserable and unworthy prejudice."

The chapters which follow do not pretend to exhaust the history of technological progress in Latin America since the region's independence. Many topics have been omitted for lack of time, space, or information (see Appendix II). The essays deal mainly with transportation and communications, give some attention to electric industries and minerals, and emphasize the contributions of citizens of the United States. The reader will observe that the narrative shifts back and forth between two main bases of organization, the technological-regional and the national-technological. It is hoped that this deliberate confusion of logic, which at times involves slight repetitions, will not be irritating. The shifts have been made with the view of avoiding monotony and suggesting different methods of approach. The main objective of the volume is to sketch and illustrate the background of relationships now rapidly assuming tremendous significance.

ARRIVAL OF THE STEAMBOAT IN
LATIN AMERICA

STEAMBOATS appeared on all the leading rivers of the United States and upon its Great Lakes as well within a little more than a decade after Fulton's *Clermont* began to navigate the Hudson in 1807. The world's first ocean steamer, the *Savannah,* property of citizens of the United States, made the voyage from the Georgia coast to Liverpool by a combination of steam and sail in the year 1819. The *Royal William,* a British vessel propelled entirely by steam, crossed from Quebec to London in 1833. In similar fashion the *Great Western* went from Bristol to New York in 1838. The first regular ocean line of steamers was established by the Englishman Samuel Cunard in 1840, between Liverpool and Boston. Other lines followed rapidly; within twenty years smoke from steam funnels was darkening the waters of almost every sea.

The new means of transport was not long in reaching Latin America. The technological lag was greater, however, in the case of river and lake steamers than in that of ocean liners. Although the first river steamers began to arrive in most of Latin America in the 1820's and 1830's, it was not until the 1850's that regular operations began on Latin America's leading rivers. By that time the important ports of the region had dependable ocean steamer connections with the outside world. Separated in the United States by a period of thirty years, the two types of transportation arrived in Latin America at approximately the same epoch.

In river steamboating much of the pioneering in Latin America was the work of citizens of the United States. In that phase of technology the United States led the world until after the middle of the nineteenth century. But the British were the

pioneers in supplying Latin America with transoceanic steamship connections. Shipowners of the United States were so
proud of their magnificent clippers and Congress was so reluctant to grant mail subsidies that the nation lagged behind in
the transition from sail to steam in the ocean carrying trade,
and the British kept the lead which they had taken in the
1840's. The four or five lines which such Yankee promoters
and operators as Edward Mills, Mortimer Livingston, Edward
K. Collins, and Cornelius Vanderbilt established between the
United States and Europe during the decade following 1847
were soon discontinued. At the end of 1862, less than two years
after the outbreak of the Civil War, not a single line of steamers owned exclusively by citizens of the United States remained
in the trans-Atlantic service.

The first river steamboat, one of the first commercial steamers of any type to reach South America, was the *Fidelidad,*
which arrived at the mouth of the Magdalena River on the
coast of Colombia in 1824. It was imported from Pittsburgh
by a German named Johann Bernard Elbers, who had obtained
a twenty-year monopoly of steamboat navigation on the Magdalena. Elbers imported two more steamers, *General Santander*
and *Bolivar,* in 1825. All three were flatboats built by men who
knew the Ohio, but their drafts were too heavy for the Magdalena. The *Fidelidad* was sent back to the United States at once;
the other two were placed on Colombia's great river, where
they continued to run until both were wrecked in 1829. Profit-
ing by his experience, Elbers had ordered from Pittsburgh in
1828 a vessel of lighter draft named *Libertador,* but he lost his
concession before the boat arrived. Operated by another owner,
the *Libertador* remained alone on the Magdalena until it became a victim of the river's hazards in 1832.

Details regarding the management of these steamers have not
been found. They may have floated down the Ohio and the
Mississippi on their own steam and then crossed the Gulf and
the Caribbean by means of both steam and sail or they may
have been shipped in pieces and assembled after they arrived.
There is little doubt that their captains, engineers, and crews
were citizens of the United States, but the names of these pioneers of the steamboat age in Latin America will remain un-

known until further documents are discovered. The tonnage of the four steamboats ranged from four to five hundred; their drafts, from four to six feet.

For seven years after the destruction of the *Libertador* the natives and alligators along the Magdalena were not disturbed by the steamboat's whistle. Then Francisco Montoya and other Colombians formed a partnership with two Englishmen, Dundas Logan and Julius Plock, and imported the steamer *Unión* from Cork, Ireland. With a British captain and a British crew, it continued to run on the Magdalena until it was blown up by revolutionists in 1841.

No more river steamers arrived until the national government of Colombia, called New Granada at the time, took a hand and subsidized a company formed by residents of Santa Marta. This organization brought down three steamers from the United States, two in 1847 and one in 1852. Their names were *Magdalena, Nueva Granada,* and *Manzanares;* their captains, engineers, and no doubt most of their crews were citizens of the United States or subjects of Great Britain. They encountered an unhappy fate. After two boiler explosions in which a number of people were killed or injured, the *Magdalena* was finally destroyed by a floating tree in 1853. The next year the *Manzanares,* then engaged in transporting government troops sent to suppress a revolution, was stranded on a rock ledge and exploded in an effort to float it off. By that time the Santa Marta company was bankrupt and the *Nueva Granada* had passed into other hands. It continued to run on the river for several years.

In fact, after 1847 steamboats were never again absent from the Magdalena. At the end of 1854 the paddle-wheels of seven steamers were plowing its muddy waters and by 1862 there were twelve. The steamboat age had dawned in Colombia, but most of the capital and technicians were still from foreign lands. Nearly all of the flatboats used there in the early days were manufactured in the United States, and for a quarter of a century the most important organization operating steamers on this river was the United Magdalena Steam Navigation Company, incorporated in New York in 1856.

Although Samuel Glover, a citizen of the United States,

began to operate the first steamboats on Venezuela's Lake Maracaibo and Zulia River in 1826, no regular line of steamers
appeared on the Orinoco until 1849. In May of that year the
Venezuelan government granted Edward A. Turpin and Frederic A. Beelen, recent members of the United States diplomatic
service, the exclusive right to navigate the Orinoco River for a
period of eighteen years. Organizing the Orinoco Steam Navigation Company in New York, they immediately introduced
four steamboats: the *Meta,* the *Apure,* the *Barinas,* and the
Guayana. In spite of political disorders and violence the company continued to run one or more of these steamers until
1865, when the last of them was seized by Venezuelan soldiers
and the company dissolved. They were manned by citizens of
the United States.

This company was succeeded by another New York corporation, the Venezuelan Steam Transport Company, organized by
citizens of the United States and a Venezuelan named Soteldo,
with J. W. Hancox as president. They sent out their first steamers, the *Hero* and the *Nutrias,* in 1869 and placed a third, the
San Fernando, on the Orinoco two years later. As in the case
of the boats of the former company these steamers were run by
North American mechanics and crews. The operations of this
second company were soon terminated because of the seizure of
its vessels by government and insurgent troops; but in 1873
the Caracas authorities granted a third exclusive concession for
the navigation of the Orinoco and its tributaries. This time the
contract went to General Juan F. Pérez, a Venezuelan, and to
William A. Pile, a North American diplomat. They acquired
some of the steamers of the preceding company and imported
others. The era of river steamboats had definitely arrived in
Venezuela.

Citizens of the United States were the first to operate a steamboat on the Amazon. In 1826 they attempted to send a steamer
up that great river to the borders of Peru, but their vessel was
wrecked on the way. The names of the pioneers have not been
ascertained. Between 1826 and 1848 Brazilians made several
unsuccessful attempts to navigate the Amazon with steamers.
In 1853 a citizen of the United States named Whittemore, under
contract with Peru, where he had resided for several years and

engaged in the practice of medicine, brought down to Pará two steam vessels intended for service on the upper Amazon. Their names were *Huallaga* and *Tirado* and they were taken up the mighty river to Iquitos and beyond by Captains Nesbitt and Conely; but the steamers were wooden vessels, none too solidly constructed, and they soon were abandoned and left to rot at the Peruvian port of Nauta.

Credit for establishing the first regular line of steamers on the Amazon belongs mainly to the Brazilians, who had obtained a good deal of experience by the operation of coasting vessels. The government of Emperor Pedro II subsidized an important steamship enterprise which was organized in 1852 by Ireneo Evangelista de Souza, Baron de Mauá. It was called the Amazon Navigation and Commercial Company, and the line of steamers was established on the great river late in 1853. English and Portuguese capital as well as Brazilian was invested in the company, whose concession—later modified—was exclusive for a period of thirty years. By 1856 the organization had seven steamers in operation on the river. The captains, technicians, and crews were probably Brazilians in the main. It should be noted, however, that the first careful survey ever made of the Amazon with reference to its navigability for steamboats was conducted by two officers of the United States Navy, Herndon and Gibbon, before this line of steamers was established. In 1873 it was taken over by the British, who dominated the Amazon steamboat traffic until after 1900.

The first merchant steamer to navigate the Plata river system was probably the *Potomac,* sent out to Buenos Aires in 1833 by the Homers of Boston. A vessel of less than three hundred tons, its first captain was a North American named Richard Sutton. Having changed its name to *Federación* and acquired another captain, a Yankee named Richard Thorne, this steamboat was the first to ascend the Uruguay River.

The first merchant steamers went up the Paraguay River to Asunción in 1853. The first to arrive there may have been the *Manuelita Rosas,* with David Bruce, a citizen of the United States, as captain. It is certain that steamers were sent up to the Paraguayan capital late in 1853 and in 1854 by the United States and Paraguay Navigation Company, a corporation organized in Rhode Island in 1852 by Edward Augustus Hopkins, Samuel G. Arnold, and associates. Hopkins was an amateur diplomat and Arnold was a Rhode Island merchant and politician. During the two years of the company's existence it placed four or five steamers on the Paraguay River: *Fanny, Asunción, Yerba, Riachuela,* and perhaps the *C. B. Stevens.* Hopkins, who represented the company in Paraguay and served at the same time as United States consul, soon had serious trouble with Carlos Antonio López, the dictator of Paraguay, trouble which caused the bankruptcy of the enterprise. In the meantime, Thomas Jefferson Page, an officer of the United States Navy, had begun his extensive explorations of the Plata River system. But here, as in the case of the Amazon, the harvest was not for the pioneers. Permanent steamboat traffic on these rivers was established by the British and citizens of Argentina. Of the some thirteen or fourteen steamers plying up and down the Paraguay, the Paraná, and the Uruguay and across the Plata Estuary in 1863, perhaps there was only one which was the property of a citizen of the United States. These merchant vessels were owned and operated mainly by the English and the Argentines.

Elisha Lee of Chicago, Matthew P. Game of Philadelphia, and other citizens of the United States organized the first line of steamers on Ecuador's leading river system in 1858-1859. These boats suffered the vicissitudes of many revolutions; but they were still under the management of Captain Lee in 1867, and twenty years later it was reported that a United States company was running a line of paddle-wheel steamers on the Guayas, the Daule, and other rivers flowing into the Gulf of Guayaquil.

Cornelius Vanderbilt was the first to place steamers on the San Juan River and on Lake Nicaragua, in Central America, operating a regular line along this route for five years following 1851. Thereafter traffic was often interrupted by political disorders, sometimes for almost a decade at a time. Citizens of the United States appear also to have been the first to send steamers up Mexico's larger rivers but steam navigation on these streams was never very significant.

The first ocean steamers appeared along the coasts of Latin

America in the 1820's, and the first lines furnishing regular communications between Latin-American ports and the world overseas were established in 1840. That year witnessed the beginning of both the Royal Mail Steam Packet Company and the Pacific Steam Navigation Company. The former, which was wholly British, furnished steamship connections between Southampton and the ports of Havana, Vera Cruz, San Juan (Nicaragua), Aspinwall (Colón, Panama), La Guayra (Venezuela), and Puerto Cabello (Venezuela). The latter, organized by William Wheelwright of Massachusetts but financed by British capital, connected the principal ports of South America's Pacific coast with Panama, whence passengers and freight could be transferred to the Royal Mail steamers and transported to the West Indies and England. Later, some of the vessels of the Wheelwright company steamed regularly through the Straits of Magellan to Europe.

In 1848 two steamship lines to northern Latin America were founded in the United States. They were the Pacific Mail Steamship Company, organized by William H. Aspinwall, George G. Howland, and others, and the United States Mail Steamship Company, organized by George Law and his associates. The first connected Panama with San Francisco and, directly or through subsidiary companies, soon furnished steamboat accommodations for the Pacific ports of Central America and Mexico. The second operated a line of steamers between New York and Aspinwall (Colón). Both were granted mail subsidies by the United States government. In 1850-1851 Cornelius Vanderbilt, in connection with his transportation venture in Nicaragua, began to operate steamboats between New York and San Juan, Nicaragua, and between San Francisco and San Juan del Sur.

In the meantime, the Atlantic Coast of South America was being supplied with overseas steamboat transportation by the British and other Europeans. In 1850 the Royal Mail Steam Packet Company, detaching a few vessels from its West Indies fleet, began to send them southward to Pernambuco, Bahía, Rio de Janeiro, Montevideo, and Buenos Aires, thus furnishing these ports connections with Southampton and Europe. Three years later a Liverpool company initiated a line of steamers between that port and the South American East Coast from Pernambuco to Buenos Aires. Other lines followed rapidly. By 1857 there were eight in operation between Europe and eastern South America. In addition to the British Southampton and Liverpool lines, there were two French lines—one starting from Havre and the other from Marseilles—a Sardinian line running from Genoa, a German line operating from Bremen, a Belgian line from Antwerp, and a Luzo-Brazilian line from Lisbon.

By the early 1860's the steamboat facilities of the Gulf and Caribbean ports of Latin America had greatly expanded. The British had added the steamers of the West India and Pacific Steam Navigation Company to those of the Royal Mail Steam Packet Company, and the French were operating a line between Saint Nazaire and the main ports of the region. The Germans, who had established three lines across the Atlantic to the United States, one from Hamburg and two from Bremen, in competition with the Cunard, the Inman, and other British lines, would soon be sending their steamers to the ports of Mexico, Central America, the West Indies, and northern South America. And already, through the Pacific Mail Steamship Company and through the Panama, New Zealand, and Australian Royal Mail Steam Packet Company, the Latin Americans were furnished rapid communications with the South Pacific and with China and Japan.

The steamboat age had come to Latin America. But citizens of the United States were not running a single line between their country and the ports of South America. In ocean transportation they had fallen behind even in the Western Hemisphere, in the region of their special interest. During the last quarter of the nineteenth century their position was strengthened through the efforts of Charles Morgan, James E. Ward, F. A. Dallett, William P. Clyde, and W. R. Grace.

For the Latin Americans, the coming of the steamboats, accompanied by steam railways and the telegraph, was an event of great significance regardless of who brought them. These important inventions of the new technology stimulated their economic and cultural development, brought the people into closer contact with the rapidly-flowing thought currents of the time, and linked them inextricably with the growing capitalism and industrialism of Europe and the United States. Their dependence on the overseas world increased, their isolation diminished, and they became inevitably a part of that complex, mechanized cultural pattern which was spreading so rapidly over the world.

THE FIRST RAILWAYS

ALTHOUGH THE EPOCH of steam railways dawned slowly in
Latin America, projects for this new type of transportation began to be considered with surprising promptness. Peru's
first contract for the construction of a steam railway was signed
in 1834, Cuba's in 1835, Colombia's in 1836, Mexico's in 1837,
and Brazil's in 1839—and it will be recalled that the world's
first steam railroads began operation in 1829 (England) and
1830 (United States). Contracts were signed for the building of
such railways in five more Latin-American countries—Chile,
Honduras, Argentina, Paraguay, and Venezuela—during the
twenty years following 1839; but actual construction was begun
in only two countries of the region before 1850, and by 1860
railway building had been initiated in only eight. In 1860
the United States had more than 30,000 miles of railroad in
operation, while the British Isles had more than 10,000. The
majority of the world's railways were built by engineers and
other technicians of these two nations, and many of their activities were centered in Latin America.

The first steam railways of Latin America were built in Cuba.
That colony, which in many respects was abused and exploited
by Spain, had in operation almost three hundred miles of railroad before a single mile was built elsewhere in the region—a
fact which may be explained by the splendid adaptation of
Cuban soil and climate to the growth of sugar cane, coffee, and
tobacco and by the deep interest of the United States and Great
Britain in the island. At the end of 1859 some 425 miles of
railway were in operation in Cuba, more mileage than existed
in all the rest of Latin America at that date.

Cuba's first steam railroad was the Havana Railway, and its

construction was begun under the auspices of the Spanish colonial government in 1835. It was opened to the public with a big celebration in Bejucal, which it reached before the end of 1837. Then seventeen miles long, it arrived at Güines, forty-five miles from Havana, the next year. By 1849 it had reached Unión, seventy-seven miles southeast of the Cuban capital; and, by that time, two branches with a total length of some thirty-five additional miles had been completed. This railroad was financed by British capital, but it was constructed under the supervision of Alfred Cruger, a civil engineer from the United States. The labor crews consisted mainly of Irish and Spanish immigrants (*Gallegos*) and Negro slaves. In 1842 the road was sold by the Spanish government to residents of Havana.

Pioneer efforts to build railroads in Mexico achieved little success. Naturally enough, a railway from Vera Cruz to Mexico City was the first to be attempted. Hall J. Kelly, an eccentric Boston schoolmaster, was the first to suggest such a railway. He discussed the subject in 1833 with the United States consul and others in the Mexican capital while there on his way to Oregon. The contract of 1837, signed by the Mexican government with Francisco Arrillaga, a Vera Cruz merchant, proved futile. Concessions made to other Mexicans in 1842 and following resulted in the construction of only some ten miles by the end of the 1850's. Begun at Vera Cruz, this railroad did not reach Mexico City until 1873. Most of it was built by British and United States engineers. Two other short lines were constructed in Mexico before 1860. One was begun by Mexican promoters under a contract dated August 2, 1855, and was intended to be an interoceanic railway running from Vera Cruz to Acapulco. Starting work in Mexico City, the promoters managed to build only three and a half miles extending from the capital to Guadalupe-Hidalgo. This line was opened to traffic on January 11, 1857. Its construction was supervised by Robert B. Gorsuch, a New York engineer. The third pioneer railway linked Mexico City with Tacubaya, only four miles away. Built by George L. Hammaken, a citizen of the United States, it was formally opened on January 1, 1858.

The pioneer Honduras contract of 1853, with a Yankee diplomat named Ephraim George Squier, required the building of a railway across that country from the Caribbean to the Pacific; but Squier lost his concession a few years later after having made an expensive survey. He was unable either in England or the United States to raise the funds necessary for construction.

Colombia's first railroad, and Panama's as well, was a line some forty-seven miles long across the Isthmus of Panama. It was begun in May 1850 under a contract granted two years before to the Panama Railway Company, a New York corporation organized by William H. Aspinwall, Samuel Chauncey, and John L. Stephens. The initial contract for the road, the one of 1836 assigned to Charles Biddle of Philadelphia—brother of the more famous Nicholas Biddle—had turned out to be futile. The railroad was opened in sections, the first of them, eight miles, in November 1851. Begun at Colón (then called Aspinwall), it finally reached Panama City on January 27, 1855. George M. Totten, John C. Trautwine, J. L. Baldwin, and J. C. Campbell were the construction engineers. The common laborers, who suffered severely from humid heat, insect plagues, and tropical fevers, were brought in from Colombia's Magdalena Valley and from China, Hindustan, and Jamaica. The death rate was enormous.

In Peru, three railways were completed during the 1850's. First to be finished was the line from Callao to Lima, a little less than nine miles long. The contract of 1834, already mentioned, had been awarded to an Englishman named Thomas Gill. Another went to William Wheelwright of Massachusetts in 1847; but the railway was finally built under the management of a Chilean named Pedro Gonzales Candamo and a Peruvian named Vicente Oyague, who employed English engineers and prison labor. Construction started in June, 1850, the first locomotive reached Lima on May 17, 1851, and the railroad was opened to public traffic in July following. Peru's second railway, the line between Arica and Tacna, in the far south, was built under the management of an English merchant by the name of Joseph Hegan; but the construction engineer was Walton Evans of New York. This railroad, about thirty-nine miles long, was finished on June 30, 1856, and formally opened to traffic on January 1, 1857. Apparently Chinese labor was employed in grading and in laying the ties and rails. The third Peruvian line of the 1850's ran from Lima to Chorillos, a coastal settlement some eight miles from the capital. It was constructed by English engineers and Chinese contract labor. Initiated late in 1856 under the management of Barreda Brothers, a Peruvian firm, it was opened to traffic on November 7, 1858.

Chile was the first of the independent countries of Latin America to evince genuine enthusiasm for railways. One Chilean railroad was finished and two were initiated by 1860. The first railway of any length in South America was the line between the Chilean seaport of Caldera and the mining village of Copiapó, a little over fifty miles inland. Its leading promoter was William Wheelright, who imported his technicians from the United States, Allan and Alexander Campbell prominent among them. The contract for this pioneer road was dated November 20, 1849; construction was begun in March the next year, and the road was formally opened to traffic as far as Copiapó at the beginning of 1852. Further extensions were made by the Campbells and Walton Evans in 1854-1855, so that the railway was almost a hundred miles long at the close of the latter year.

In the meantime, Allan Campbell had been employed by the remarkable Wheelright to make surveys for a railroad between Valparaíso and Santiago; but Wheelright did not succeed in building this line. He obtained a contract from the Chilean government but was unable to raise the funds. Construction was started under Chilean management in 1852—and after nine years of effort only the thirty-five miles between Valparaíso and Quillota were opened to traffic. The chief construction engineers were George Maughan and, after his death, William Lloyd, both Englishmen.

The second of the Chilean railroads begun but not completed during this decade was the line running southward from Santiago to the Maule River. Its construction was begun under the management of a company organized in 1855 and composed of Chileans. Most of the engineers employed were citizens of the United States: Walton Evans, Joseph A. Bernard, Edward C. Dubois, Charles F. Hillman, and several others. The road reached the Maipó River, a little more than seventeen miles from Santiago, in 1858; then a remarkable Yankee railway builder named Henry Meiggs took charge, finishing thirty-five miles in less than two years and extending the road to San Fernando, eighty-five miles from Santiago, by 1862. Obtaining a contract on September 14, 1861, to complete the Valparaíso-Santiago line, he also finished that road, which was formally opened to the public on September 14, 1863, Meiggs having built and equipped over eighty miles of this railway in two years! At the end of 1862 he had under his direction a working force of 9151 men, more than 9000 of them Chileans and the rest mainly technical experts from the United States, England, France, Germany, and even Italy. Sixty-two were citizens of the United States, five of them construction engineers. Meiggs had made himself famous by his energy, tact, and ability to dramatize the importance of railroads. A few years later he won eternal renown by his railway achievements in Peru.

Argentina's first railroad, and the only one started there before 1860, was a short line of some fifteen miles extending from Buenos Aires to Morón. The concession for this railway was awarded by the Province of Buenos Aires to Argentine and British residents of that city in January, 1854. Construction was begun early the next year under the supervision of an English civil engineer named William Bragg; most of the manual laborers were imported from the British Isles. The first seven miles were opened to traffic in August, 1857; the rest, two years later. At least two other Argentine railroad contracts were negotiated during this decade, both with citizens of the United States. In 1854 Edward A. Hopkins, then conspicuous because of his steamships on the Río de la Plata system and his industrial enterprises in Paraguay, was commissioned to build a railway from Buenos Aires through the suburbs of Palermo, Belgrano, and San Fernando; but little or nothing was accomplished. The next year William Wheelwright received the first railway concession granted by the national government of Argentina, a concession authorizing him to build a long railroad extending all the way from Rosario to Córdoba. Although Allan Campbell made surveys for the line, lack of capital delayed construction until after 1860. Wheelwright already was dreaming of a railway across the lofty Andes, extending from the end of the Caldera-Copiapó Railway through Córdoba to Rosario, and had employed North American surveyors to examine the route! Statues have been erected to his memory in Chile and an Argentine writer has praised him in an enthusiastic biography.

Work was initiated in 1854 on the first railway that was to be built in Paraguay for many years. Surveys were made by British experts employed by President Carlos Antonio López, and construction was begun under the supervision of a British engineer by the name of Padison in 1859. Starting at Asunción, the rails reached Paraguari, forty-five miles away, in 1861—and there the road stopped until 1885.

Construction was begun on five Brazilian railroads during the 1850's. The first to be planned was the Dom Pedro Segundo Railway designed to connect Rio de Janerio with the important provinces of São Paulo and Minas Geraes. The first contract for its construction was awarded to Thomas Cochrane, a British subject, on June 1, 1839. He associated with himself in the enterprise another Englishman by the name of Charles Pentland and a few Brazilians; but he held the contract for nearly fourteen years without building a mile of railroad. Construction was not actually begun until June 11, 1855, under the auspices of a Brazilian company organized by the efforts of Viscount Rio Bonito, Caetano de Almeida, and others who obtained a contract which included a government guaranty of 7 per cent interest on the capital invested. The first thirty miles, built under the supervision of a British engineer named Whittaker, were opened to the public in 1858; and then engineers—Charles F. M. Garrett and the Ellison brothers—were called in from the United States to continue construction through the mountains.

This was not, however, Brazil's pioneer railway. The first railroad actually opened to traffic in Brazil was a part of the line intended to connect the nation's capital with the royal mountain resort of Petropolis, a little more than fifteen miles away. The first section, built across the swampy coastal jungle at great cost in lives of workers, began operation in April 1854. Only nine miles long at that time, it had been constructed under the management of the brilliant Brazilian promoter Ireneo Evangelista de Souza, Baron and later Viscount Mauá, with the Englishman William Bragg as chief engineer. It was many years before the track was laid up the mountainside to Petropolis.

The other three Brazilian railroads of the 1850's were in the provinces of Pernambuco, Bahía, and Rio de Janeiro. Although small sums of Brazilian money were invested in them and a few Brazilian engineers took part in their construction, they were built mainly by British capital and British engineers.

The total length of Brazilian railroads in 1863 was hardly more than 180 miles; but, even so, Brazil ranked next to Cuba and Chile in railway mileage in 1860. Englishmen made surveys for the famous Santos Railway in the late 1850's; but construction on this line was not started until 1862.

In Venezuela, the British had started to build a short industrial railroad to the Aroa copper mines in the 1830's, but it did not become a public carrier until forty years later. In 1859 the United States firm of Flanagan, Bradley, and Clark was awarded a contract to build a public railway from Caracas to Petare, a town some seven miles to the southeast. Although the line, or most of it, was constructed, it was soon abandoned. This was a very disorderly period in Venezuelan history.

The railway epoch did not begin until the 1870's in Uruguay, Ecuador, and Colombia (excluding the Isthmus of Panama) or in Honduras, Nicaragua, Costa Rica, and Guatemala. In El Salvador, the Dominican Republic, Haiti, and Bolivia, it did not arrive until the 1880's and 1890's. In these countries, however, the story was the same as in those where the iron roads made their appearance earlier: their railways were built mainly by the British and the Yankees, with occasional contributions by Germans, Frenchmen, and other Europeans. Even as late as the 1940's the railroad systems of most Latin-American countries—the total for the whole region was only some 83,000 miles —were still inadequate; but they were being supplemented by highways—not discussed in this volume—and airlines.

The building of the early steam railways of Latin America was an important episode in the migration of capital and technology. Although the short line in Paraguay was financed entirely by the Paraguayan government and small sums of native capital were invested in a few of the other lines, most of the capital came from abroad. The surveyors, the construction engineers, the locomotive engineers, and the train crews were composed at first almost entirely of foreigners; and even the common laborers employed in grading and laying the tracks were often immigrants. Latin Americans, however, made some progress during the period in railway finance and in the building and operation of railroads. Later, of course, they would make further progress; but many years would pass before they would own, manage, and operate their railway systems, although a few would make much more rapid advances than the rest.

Because of topography or tropical climate and disease some of the early Latin-American railroads were difficult to build. In the construction of others—such as those of Cuba, Argentina, and Paraguay, the short railroads around Lima, and the line running southward from Santiago, Chile—no serious obstacles were confronted. Lack of coal for fuel was a problem in all the countries; in Argentina, as well as in parts of Chile and Peru, wood also was scarce. Many of the early railways were narrow gauge with light equipment.

The cultural aspects of the new transport technology were not fully evident in Latin America in the 1850's. Except in Cuba and perhaps in Chile, the mileage was still too limited to have much effect on the life of the people. It was already becoming clear, however, that the new means of transportation, in spite of the heavy work required in construction, would lighten the burdens of both men and beasts, save time, lower travel and shipping costs, and stimulate the development of natural resources. Although owners of oxcarts and baggage mules and those in control of the labor of *peon* porters might denounce the new machines, many people of influence in Latin America were becoming convinced of the benefits of the Machine Age.

The moving of the first spade of dirt on each line and the opening of each section to traffic were usually accompanied by feasts, oratory, music, poetry, and dancing. Latin Americans, like most other peoples, were devoted to ceremonies and celebrations, which were readily supported by promoters because they liked them too, and because ceremonies and celebrations were effective means of advertising. The greatest railway dramatist in Latin America during the early railroad epoch was Henry Meiggs. The elaborate processions and banquets which he provided became famous, and his oratory, as well as that of his collaborators, went ringing down the century.

ARRIVAL OF THE TELEGRAPH

FIVE OF THE Latin-American countries were not much behind the United States and Europe in erecting their first telegraph lines. The 1840's and 1850's witnessed the full dawning of the telegraphic era in the United States, England, and practically all the European nations; the 1850's witnessed the building of the first lines in Mexico, Cuba, Chile, Argentina, and Brazil. During the next decade the telegraph arrived in Peru, Colombia, Uruguay, and Costa Rica. It arrived in Guatemala, El Salvador, Nicaragua, and Venezuela in the 1870's, but did not reach the rest of the countries until the 1880's—perhaps in one or two instances not until shortly after 1890.

Thus, in the case of the telegraph, there was a rather long lag in several of the Latin-American nations. In fact, there was a considerable lag in the *spread* of the new system of communication even in the five countries which were so prompt in establishing their first lines. It is hardly necessary to point out that this lag was caused by lack of technological skill, scarcity of capital, low living standards among the masses, political disorders in most countries, absence of timber for telegraph poles in some sections, and jungle and mountain barriers in a good part of the whole region.

One may state with confidence that telegraphic facilities were inadequate in the majority of the Latin-American nations even as late as 1913. But inadequate is a vague and relative term. Concrete details are necessary to convey a proper understanding of the situation. The following table, which includes the countries with the most limited telegraphic services in 1913, should be illuminating:

Countries	Area (sq. mi.)	Population	Telegraph Wire (mi.)	Offices
Colombia	444,100	5,472,600	11,860	579
Peru	524,800	4,500,000	9,315	317
Bolivia	514,600	2,800,000	5,979	133
Venezuela	352,143	2,764,200	5,450	209
Ecuador	110,000	1,500,000	3,952	163
Paraguay	176,000	800,000	4,367	80
Haiti	10,204	2,000,000	723	—
Dominican R.	19,332	700,000	353	16
Panama	28,575	419,000	1,309	57
Nicaragua	49,500	600,000	2,947	116

Here were 21,000,000 people scattered over an area of more than 2,200,000 square miles with hardly more than 46,000 miles of telegraph wire and less than 1700 telegraph offices! Huge Brazil, with an area of over 3,286,000 square miles and a population of approximately 24,000,000 in 1913, had only 38,304 miles of telegraph wire and 1543 offices; but, since the bulk of its national domain was very sparsely inhabited, this broad statement may give an incorrect impression of the accommodations available to the majority of its people. All Latin America, with an area of over 8,000,000 square miles and a population of more than 80,000,000, had approximately 330,000 miles of telegraph wire and less than 8600 telegraph offices at the end of 1913. The United States proper, with an area of slightly over 3,000,000 square miles and with 92,000,000 people, had well over 1,800,000 miles of telegraph wire and nearly 31,000 offices. Only Argentina, among the Latin-American nations, could be classed with the United States in the adequacy of its telegraphic facilities in 1913.

The story of the construction of the Latin-American telegraph lines, through the jungles, across the scorching deserts, across the bleak plateaus, and over the giant mountains, has many thrilling episodes; and more excitement is added by the activities of vandals, bandits, and revolutionists, who often cut and destroyed the wires, insulators, and poles. But the story cannot be elaborated here. A broad outline must suffice until a more opportune occasion is presented.

Before the era of the telegraph was well under way in Latin

America nearly all of the leading countries of the world, including the British Isles and a good part of the British Empire,
had concluded that this new method of communication should
belong to governments and not to individuals and corporations.
The United States was the only important exception, and strong
opposition to private ownership was frequently expressed here.
Owing to this general trend and the obvious strategic significance of the telegraph in regions often harried by revolution,
as most of the Latin-American nations were, the politicians in
the majority of the countries promptly adopted the policy of
state ownership and operation. Governmental expansion into
the realm of the telegraph was limited, however, by administrative policy with respect to railways and cables.

While several countries—notably Chile, Argentina, Brazil,
Mexico, and Colombia—revealed decided tendencies toward state
ownership and management of railroads, progress in that direction was slow and often vacillating; and privately-owned railways
practically always included privately-owned telegraphs in connection with the various railway lines. Cables, which will be
discussed at some length later, were left in private hands, mainly,
one may presume, because of the heavy expense and the high
degree of skill required in construction and operation. Nevertheless, opportunities for private profit from purely telegraphic
enterprises in Latin America were considerably restricted by the
policy of state ownership and management. They were confined
to the laying and operation of cables, to privately-owned land
lines in areas where these were permitted, to the sale of equipment, to construction contracts for government lines, and salaries
and wages paid by governments for technicians and common
laborers.

Aside from contriving the instruments and wires and manufacturing both on a large-scale basis, contributions from the
outside in this type of technology, with the exception of the
cable systems, were smaller than in many other types; and they
were restricted mainly to the early years of the telegraph in
Latin America. The people of the region learned the art of telegraphy rapidly and were soon able to construct and operate their
own land lines, although they continued to depend on foreign

manufacturers for equipment and occasionally called upon foreign technicians for advice.

The most important contributions made by foreigners to the telegraphic systems of these nations were those of Englishmen and their kinsmen in the United States. William Wheelwright brought the telegraph to Chile, connecting Valparaíso and Santiago in 1853. William Lee Styles of New York built the first line in Colombia in 1865. A citizen of the United States named Lyman Reynolds constructed the first one in Costa Rica in 1868; Charles H. Billings, likewise a citizen of the United States, was the pioneer in El Salvador; and the Central and South American Telegraph Company of New York erected the first line in Ecuador. Citizens of the United States were among the pioneers in Mexico, where they later built many of the telegraph lines, and probably in two or three other countries besides. The British carried the telegraph to Uruguay and to Argentina, where an Englishman named Charles Burton was for several years the director of the national system. John and Matthew Clark, also of British descent, pushed the first telegraph line across the Andes, linking Santiago and Buenos Aires; and a Canadian named Stanley McNider not only introduced the telegraph into Guatemala but also did a good deal of pioneering in El Salvador and Ecuador. Moreover, wherever the Anglo-Saxons, or any other foreigners for that matter, built railways, they also constructed telegraphs as an inseparable adjunct of the railroad systems.

It was in the laying and operation of cables, however, that the two Anglo-Saxon nations made their largest contributions to the telegraphic facilities of Latin America as a whole. Starting with the English, John Proudfoot and Matthew Gray, organizing the River Plate Telegraph Company, linked Buenos Aires and Montevideo in 1866 by laying a cable under the Plata Estuary and continuing overland to the Uruguayan capital; and thirty years later the Amazon Telegraph Company, Limited, connected Pará and Manáos by means of a cable under the Amazon.

The Latin-American countries began to be connected by ocean cables with the world outside also in the year 1866, but it was nearly thirty years before the process was completed. In fact, *direct* connection with the Orient was not provided until

1906, when the cable across the Pacific from San Francisco to the vicinity of China and Japan was finished by citizens of the United States.

In furnishing this new means of long-distance communication the British pioneered on South America's Atlantic coast as well as on its Pacific coast as far north as Chorillos, Peru. Yankees led the way down the eastern coast of Mexico and the western coast of Central and South America to the point the British reached on their way north. In the Caribbean, the pioneering was divided between the two groups, although the British made the larger contribution. The cables across the Atlantic from South America to Europe and Africa were the work of the Germans, as well as of the British.

Five English companies and three corporations organized in the United States took part in establishing and operating the early overseas cable connections of the Latin-American countries. The British firms were: The Cuba Submarine Telegraph Company and the West India and Panama Telegraph Company, each founded in 1869; the Brazilian Submarine Telegraph Company and the Western and Brazilian Telegraph Company, both organized in 1873; and the West Coast of America Telegraph Company, established in 1876. At the outset two others participated to some extent, namely, the India-Rubber, Gutta-Percha and Telegraph Works Company and the Telegraph Construction and Maintenance Company; but these corporations were engaged mainly in manufacturing, laying, and repairing submarine cables. The three Yankee corporations were the International Ocean Telegraph Company, organized in 1866; the Mexican Cable Company, founded in 1878; and the Central and South American Cable Company, organized in 1879. The word "Telegraph" was soon substituted for "Cable" in the titles of the second and third.

In spite of the fact that Cyrus W. Field of New York had been the pioneer in laying the first cables across the Atlantic, the British clearly had the advantage over their kinsmen in capital, experience, and prestige. Not only were British organizations—among which the India-Rubber and Gutta-Percha Company, the Telegraph Construction and Maintenance Company, and Siemens Brothers were the most important—practically the exclusive manufacturers of submarine cables for more than half a century following the 1850's; British cable technicians for many years were more skilled than those of any other nation, and Englishmen had manufactured and laid many thousand miles of cables in various parts of the world before any were landed on the coasts of a single Latin-American country with the exception of Cuba.

Getting down to individuals, the pioneer British promoters in South America were John Proudfoot, Matthew Gray, Sir William Thomson (Lord Kelvin), Charles T. Bright, and William F. Jones on the Atlantic side and C. S. Stokes on the Pacific. Among the Yankee pioneers were James Alexander Scrymser, Alfred Pell, Theodore J. de Sabla, who was a native of French Guadeloupe but a naturalized citizen of the United States, Major General William F. Smith, and Jonathan Edwards. Scrymser stands out above the rest. He became interested in cables for Latin America in 1865, at the early age of twenty-six, gained the support of others, organized all three of the American companies, and made cables his major life work. After 1879 he obtained the backing of J. P. Morgan and Morgan's banking associates.

Scrymser's collaborators in the organization of the International Ocean Telegraph Company were Alfred Pell, Alexander Hamilton, Jr., Oliver K. King, M. L. Delafield, Major General William F. Smith, and James M. Digges. Smith was Scrymser's commander during the Civil War, Pell was Scrymser's close personal friend, and Digges was Scrymser's brother-in-law. With the aid of Horatio Perry, secretary of the United States Legation in Madrid, Smith obtained from the Spanish government an exclusive concession for a cable linking Cuba and Florida, while Scrymser secured a landing and operating license from the United States. The cable, which was purchased from the British India-Rubber and Gutta-Percha Company, connected Punta Russa, Florida, with Key West and Havana and was opened to the public in December 1866.

The next enterprise was that of the Cuba Submarine Telegraph Company, Limited, which linked Santiago with Batabanó and built a land line on to Havana in 1870. This was followed immediately by the laying of cables between Santiago, Jamaica, and Colón, and from Santiago to Puerto Rico, the main British colonies in the eastern Caribbean, Trinidad, and British Guiana. These were laid between 1870 and 1872 by the West India and Panama Telegraph Company, Limited.

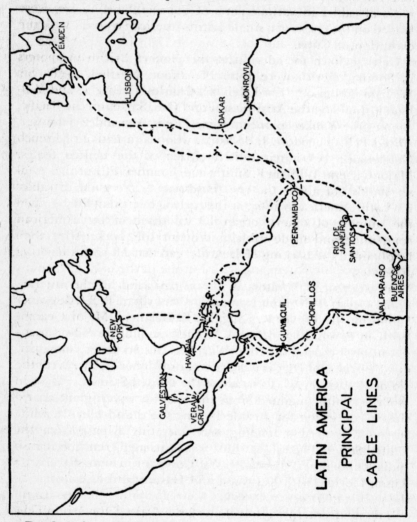

LATIN AMERICA
PRINCIPAL
CABLE LINES

By that time the British were soliciting cable concessions in South America. The Panama and South Pacific Telegraph Company, Limited, made an unsuccessful effort to secure a contract for a line connecting Panama, Colombia, and Ecuador, and then apparently dissolved. The Brazilian Submarine Telegraph Company, Limited, and the Telegraph Construction and Maintenance Company, Limited, were more fortunate. Through Baron Mauá, Charles T. Bright, William F. Jones, and E. B. Webb, they obtained in 1873 exclusive contracts for sixty years covering the whole coast of Brazil and including the right to connect Brazil with Portugal. These concessions were soon transferred to the Western and Brazilian Telegraph Company, Limited, and later to the Western Telegraph Company, Limited. In the 1870's and following cables were laid both along the Brazilian coast from Pará to Rio Grande do Sul and from Pernambuco (Recife) by way of the Cape Verde and Madeira Islands to Lisbon. Service was inaugurated on the Pernambuco-Lisbon line in July 1874, thus giving South America its first connection with Europe.

Late in 1882 a direct cable connection between the United States and South America was provided, but this will be discussed in connection with the cables along the western side of the continent. Continuing with the story of the lines on the eastern side: Uruguay and Argentina were linked with the Brazilian telegraphic system and with Europe in the middle 1870's; and so likewise were Chile, by means of a land line across the Andes, and Peru, by the same route and through a cable extending up the Pacific to Chorillos. It was not until the early 1890's, however, that Brazil, Uruguay, Argentina, and Chile were connected by direct lines with the United States, and it is interesting to observe that they were provided with direct cable communications with Africa almost at the same time.

On February 22, 1890, the Brazilian government granted an exclusive concession for twenty-five years to the *Société Français des Télégraphes Sous-Marins* authorizing the laying of a cable from Salinas, State of Pará, northward through French Guiana and the French West Indies. With the permission of Spain, this cable was landed on the coast of Cuba and thus connected with the lines already in existence there, including the one from Cuba to Florida. This French line was opened for service in 1892 and was soon extended to the Dominican Republic, Haiti, and Venezuela. Meantime, in April 1891, the India-Rubber, Gutta-Percha, and Telegraph Works Company, Limited, had obtained from Brazil a contract for a cable linking Pernambuco with the Brazilian island of Fernando Noronha and Dakar, Africa, but had transferred its concession to the South American Cable Company, Limited. This line was opened to the public in 1892 and was taken over by French interests several years later.

Finally, in 1908, Brazil granted a concession to a German firm for a cable connecting the island of Borkum, a few miles from Emden, Germany, with the Canary Islands, African Liberia, and the coast of Pernambuco. The concession was transferred immediately to the *Deutsch-Südamerikanische Telegraphengesellschaft* and service was inaugurated on March 29, 1911.

On the western side of South America, the India-Rubber and Gutta-Percha Company and the West Coast of America Telegraph Company, Limited, laid a cable between Valparaíso, Chile, and Chorillos, Peru, with a number of intervening landings, in 1875 and 1876; and the latter company, which soon took over this line, connected Valparaíso and Talcahuano in 1893.

Returning to the activities of Scrymser, it may be noted that he withdrew from the International Ocean Telegraph Company in 1878 after this corporation was taken over by the Western Union Telegraph Company, which was then dominated by Jay Gould. Scrymser determined immediately to establish cable connections between Galveston, Texas, and the Latin countries to the south. Organizing the Mexican Telegraph Company and the Central and South American Telegraph Company and obtaining the backing of Morgan and other capitalists of the United States, he began at once to negotiate for exclusive long-term contracts. Between 1879 and 1882 he obtained them from Mexico, Guatemala, El Salvador, Nicaragua, Costa Rica, Colombia, Ecuador, and Peru; and by the end of 1882 he and his companies had submerged cables along the eastern edge of the Gulf of Mexico to Coatzacoalcos and down the Pacific from Salina Cruz, Mexico, to Chorillos, Peru, with a connecting land line across the Isthmus of Tehuantepec and numerous intermediate landing points. Three of the contracts ran for twenty-five years; the rest were fifty-year concessions.

The cable of the Scrymser companies was not carried beyond

Chorillos for nearly a decade. Then, in 1890-1891, it was extended to Valparaíso and at the same time a land line was purchased across the Andes to Buenos Aires. An even longer pause followed this expansion, for it was not until 1919-1920 that Scrymser and his group laid cables from Atalaya, Argentina, to Santos and Rio de Janeiro. By that time the cables to Mexico and down the Pacific coast of South America had been duplicated and double cables had been laid between New York and Colón by way of Cuba. A few years later these lines were triplicated; branch lines were laid to Haiti, the Dominican Republic, and Puerto Rico; Bolivia was connected with the system; and other cables flared out across the Caribbean to Limon, Costa Rica, and Barranquilla, Colombia. In 1927 the Western Union Telegraph Company, which still retained the properties acquired from Scrymser's International Ocean Telegraph Company, took control of the Mexican Telegraph Company; and during the same year the Central and South American Company, which had changed its name to All America Cables in 1920, was taken over by the International Telephone and Telegraph Corporation.

Such, in brief, is the history of the laying of the Latin-American cables. In the early years, cable communications among these nations and between them and foreign countries were very expensive; but the tariffs began to be reduced in the 1890's because of competition between the British and Yankee rivals. And rates were forced down to much lower levels with the appearance of the various systems of wireless (see Chapter XVII) early the next century. In the 1940's, rates were probably as cheap and the services as efficient as the rates and services of most other cable systems.

The engineers in charge of submerging these cables deserve to be better known. Among the British engineers were Sir William Thomson, Sir Samuel Canning, Everhard Holmes, Edward Nelson, and three others known to this writer only as Clark and Forde and Felstead. Even less information has been found regarding the Yankee technicians. Scrymser, in his *Personal Reminiscences,* makes no reference to them. Nor does the commemorative volume published by All America Cables in 1928 do them justice. This work is filled with portraits and biographical sketches of promoters and speculators, but the actual builders and operators of the system receive only one sentence of tribute on the last page. "It is regretted," says the editor, "that ... personal reference could not be made to the hundreds of station managers, department heads, engineers and others who have shared in no small measure in the success of the Company." Thus it has ever been in this imperfect world. In a cemetery in Frankfort, Kentucky, stands a monument erected to the memory of James Francis Leonard, a skillful young operator of early telegraphic instruments. The world contains too few of its kind. Two centuries ago Sir Thomas Browne, a distinguished English scientist, posed a pertinent question: "Who knows whether the best of men be known, or whether there may not be more important persons forgotten than any that stand remembered ... ?"

HENRY MEIGGS AND THE EARLY
PERUVIAN RAILWAYS

Henry Meiggs was perhaps the most remarkable railroad builder who ever appeared upon the Latin-American scene. Landing in Chile early in 1855, a stranger and "like a thief in the night," he obtained his first railway contract three years later, and by the end of 1867 had managed the construction of nearly 200 miles, a good part of it across the Chilean coastal range. In 1868 he went to Peru, where the railway era was at its dawn, with less than 60 miles in operation. At his death in Lima on September 30, 1877, Peru had approximately 1200 miles of track, more than 700 miles of which had been built under Meiggs's direction.

The major part of the Peruvian railways he constructed ran over difficult ground. One of the lines ascended the Andes and passed through a tunnel nearly 16,000 feet above the sea. One went like a serpent through the tall *mesas* and sands of a desert cordillera. A third continued this line along the plateau toward Bolivia and to the shores of Lake Titicaca. A fourth aspired to connect this mountain lake with the ancient capital of the Incas. Three more linked Pacific ports of Peru—two in the north and one in the far south—with inland mining and agricultural regions.

As early as 1862 the Peruvian minister in Chile had urged that Meiggs should be induced to come to Peru and build its railroads. Five years later Meiggs sent his first proposals to the Peruvian government; but his first railway contract in Peru was not awarded until April 30, 1868, three months after his arrival in Lima. A few weeks afterward he set his engineers and labor crews to work on the Arequipa line.

Already his fame was so great that no further evidence of his capacity was required. Three additional contracts were almost thrust upon him before the Arequipa road was finished. By the end of 1871 the total of his contracts mounted to seven, which required the construction of some 990 miles of railway. The aggregate contract price, in cash and in bonds taken by Meiggs at considerably below par, was more than 130,000,000 Peruvian *soles;* and at that time a Peruvian *sol* was almost the equivalent of a United States gold dollar.

Not only did nearly all the Meiggs railways in Peru run up steep canyons into the giant Andes or along lofty plateaus higher than the highest passes of the North American Sierras and Rockies; floods or scarcity of water accentuated these baffling topographical barriers. The seven railroads, their length, and the dates of the contracts signed with Meiggs are as follows:

1. Mollendo to Arequipa, 107 miles, April 30, 1868.
2. Callao to Oroya, 136 miles, December 18, 1869.
3. Arequipa to Puno, 218 miles, December 18, 1869.
4. Pacasmayo to Magdalena, 91 miles, December 13 and 24, 1870.
5. Ilo to Moquegua, 63 miles, January 12, 1871.
6. Chimbote to Huaraz, 166 miles, October 31, 1871.
7. Juliaca to Cuzco, 210 miles, December 2, 1871.

On February 3, 1877, Meiggs was awarded his eighth and last railway contract. It provided for the construction of a railroad from Oroya to the Cerro de Pasco silver and copper mines, a distance of some 85 miles.

Meiggs did not live to complete these railways. Only the Arequipa, the Puno, and the Ilo-Moquegua lines were finished at his death. He had managed, however, to build the major part of the others, except the Juliaca to Cuzco and the Oroya to Cerro de Pasco roads. No doubt he would have built them all if the national finances had not failed. He made a tremendous attack on the formidable Andes; and often he dreamed of laying rails down their rugged eastern slopes to the mighty Amazon.

The most difficult of the Meiggs railroads to build were the lines from Mollendo to Arequipa and from Callao to Oroya. The longest was the line from Arequipa to Puno, with hardly a mile of its 218 lower than 7500 feet above the sea and with two passes at an altitude of more than 14,500 feet—higher than Pikes Peak or Mount Evans. But the terrain, in this case, was comparatively smooth and the climate fairly healthful.

Most of the Mollendo-Arequipa line had to be pushed through desert and mountains. The cost of providing a water supply for the railway after it was finished was nearly two million *soles,* to say nothing of the expense of transporting it during the period of construction. The mountains and canyons required, of course, many fills, excavations, curves, bridges, and culverts. On one stretch tons of drifting sand were confronted and mastered. Disease and accidents took a heavy toll of the laborers—2,000, it is said—and bloody fights sometimes occurred between the Chilean and Peruvian workers.

The Oroya Railway arouses the admiration of all who see it. After a journey over the road in the 1930's Christopher Morley declared that Meiggs was "one of the world's great poets," for he "built a rhyme loftier than Lycidas." A Peruvian journalist, many years before, had called the enterprise a great hymn with notes running all the tones from "the dull blow of the pickaxe . . . to the shrillest whistle of the locomotive." Some have called it the "railway to the moon." It is, to say the least, a marvelous railroad. The first thirty miles or so run over a gradually rising coastal plain; but the railway then enters the narrow, deep gorge of the River Rímac, as formidable as any on earth. There are 61 bridges, 65 tunnels, and 26 switch-backs; the passenger hardly knows whether he is coming or going. The towering, artistic Verrugas bridge, destroyed years later by an avalanche, was the pride of Peru. The Galera Tunnel runs under Mount Meiggs at an elevation of 15,645 feet. The construction of the road is said to have cost ten thousand lives. Fatal accidents were numerous; mortal fever swept repeatedly through the ranks of the workmen. Only 87 miles were in operation at Meiggs's death.

The gauge of all the Meiggs roads except the Chimbote line was standard: four feet, eight and a half inches. Yet he sent the locomotives higher than they ever had gone before.

Meiggs was the last man to claim exclusive credit for what he did. He was not a trained engineer; he was merely a great executive and a dynamic personality. He imported his experts from all the skillful nations of the world, but mostly from the United States. Some of the managers and technicians were his kinsmen, his brother John G. Meiggs and his nephew Henry Meiggs Keith among them. Prominent among his construction engineers were John L. Thorndike and William H. Cilley. He also employed a few Peruvian technicians who had learned how to build railways. Among his physicians were George A. Ward, Juan Martínez Rosas (a Peruvian), Henry Kinney, Isaac T. Coates, and Edwin R. Heath, who was later to make himself famous by his explorations in the Amazonian jungle. The hard labor was done mostly by Peruvians, Chileans, Bolivians, and Chinese coolies—all employed on a scale seldom witnessed in Latin America. As many as twenty or twenty-five thousand were working for Meiggs at the height of his construction enterprises in 1872.

Meiggs paid his laborers well and was seldom indifferent about their welfare. They were exposed, of course, to the hazards of precipices, landslides, rolling boulders, falling stones, and work trains, as well as to those of climate and disease; but their food was better than they had been accustomed to, and while the medical service was often clearly inadequate it was superior to any they had known before. Of the Chilean *rotos* whom he employed both in their home country and in Peru, Meiggs once said: "I have treated them like men and not like dogs, as is the custom, for they are good if one knows how to direct them." Sometimes his peons were roughly handled by labor bosses or Peruvian soldiers; but that was almost unavoidable in view of the Latin-American attitude toward the lower classes at the time. Criticized in some quarters because of the high death rate among the men working on the Oroya, Meiggs once remarked that people were accustomed to die in Peru as elsewhere. The remark did not signify, however, that he was not grieved. He was careful regarding the food of even the Chinese.

Meiggs had to import nearly everything he used in building his railroads. Peru furnished only the powder for blasting, the rights-of-way, rock for ballast, and a part of the food, medicines, and clothing for the workers. Purchasing agents were located both in England and the United States; but all of the rolling stock and most of the tools, machinery, and materials for construction came from the United States. The bulk of the ties and lumber was shipped in from Washington, Oregon, and California.

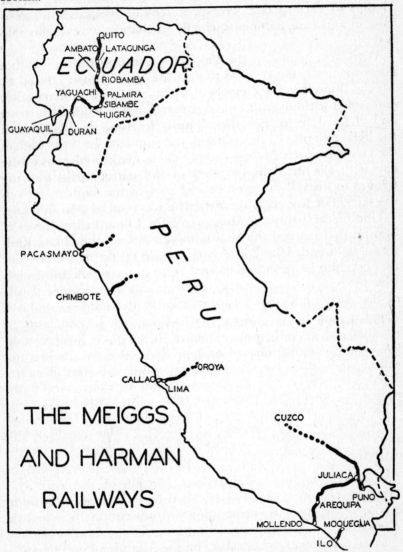

Meiggs knew how to win Latin-American sympathies. He was a great dramatist and a great orator. His banquets, celebrations, and charities were long remembered both in Chile and Peru. A Chilean declared that he was a true philanthropist. He distributed thousands of *pesos* and *soles* among the poor and the victims of earthquakes. He spent tens of thousands on ceremonies and entertainments, chiefly in connection with his railways.

Work was begun on the Valparaíso-Santiago Railway with a gorgeous fiesta; interrupted to dedicate a monument erected by Meiggs himself to the memory of a Chilean Revolutionary hero; concluded with magnificent ceremonies that extended from one end of the line to the other. Trains received the blessings of the higher clergy; Chileans drank toasts to Don Enrique Meiggs the Great Builder; Meiggs compared the Chilean officials of the day with the intrepid founders of the nation, paid glowing tribute to his railway experts, and praised the Chilean *roto* to the skies. For five years thereafter he was a social lion in Chile.

One of the banquets Meiggs gave in Lima during the celebration that marked the beginning of work on the Oroya Railway was attended by 800 of the double cream of society. On that occasion he promised eternal fame to the top-flight officials who were soon to collaborate in unlocking the treasure vaults of the nation and expanding its rôle in history:

This happy event proclaims...a great social revolution whose triumph and whose benefits are entrusted to the locomotive, that irresistible battering ram of modern civilization. At its pressure will fall those granite masses which physical nature until today has opposed to the...aggrandizement of the Peruvian nation. Its whistle will awaken the native race from...[its] lethargy....

Peru, ever noble and generous, will...inscribe in the book of its glorious history, at the head of its lofty benefactors, the names of all the illustrious citizens to whose indefatigable exertions and patriotism is due the establishment of this iron road.

The Peruvians called Meiggs the "Messiah of the Railway." After the elaborate ceremonies ended he published an apology in the newspapers to those whom "unintentionally" he had failed to invite to the feast.

The initiation of construction on the Arequipa-Puno line was punctuated by a celebration only a little less impressive. Meiggs's oratorical flights were barely excelled by the eloquent

Peruvian aristocrats themselves. "The work which we are initiating," he said, "opens to Peru a horizon of well-being so vast that the mind can hardly encompass it." Economically railways stimulated production and consumption, banished isolation, facilitated immigration, and uncovered new elements for science and industry. Socially they made "practical the spirit of Divine Christianity, the essence of which is fraternity." The lofty Andes were "bending their proud crests" before the "civilizing banner of steam." "Gentlemen," said Meiggs, facing Arequipa's far-famed conical peak, "I drink to Arequipa and Puno; I drink to the proud Misti which, more enduring than human aspirations, will . . . [forever] witness the benefits of industry and power."

Meiggs chose July 28, 1870, Peru's Independence Day, for the opening of the first section of the Oroya Railroad. President Balta and his cabinet and a large group of distinguished people were taken down to Callao for breakfast and then brought back on the special train to Lima and beyond to rails' end while 50,000 enthusiastic witnesses lined the banks of the Rímac and looked on.

Two weeks of celebration marked the opening of the Arequipa Railway to public traffic late in 1870. Four steamers were required to transport Meiggs's guests to Mollendo and five trains were employed to haul them up to Arequipa. The president and all the members of the cabinet and Congress were in the party. The locomotives received a sprinkling of holy water from the bishop. Many speeches were made at both ends of the line.

At Mollendo, Meiggs spoke with deep emotion of the cost of his technological triumph. "I do not refer to money," he said. "I speak of the blood and the lives poured out by hundreds of Chileans, Peruvians, Bolivians, Frenchmen, Irishmen, and even Anglo-Americans who have died on this work. Let us drink here in silence to the memory of those who died. . . ." The Bolivian minister called Meiggs a "colossus of fortune and credit," a "contractor without fear," a wizard who had come to Latin America to erase the word "impossible" from all the dictionaries, a miracle-man who had joined Valparaíso and Santiago and brought Arequipa down to the sea, and who would on the morrow place Puno, Cuzco, Oroya, perhaps even distant Potosí and "dear" Sucre "close to the breakers of the Pacific." After the banquet was over the guests began to dance. They spent the night in Mollendo, their temporary abode the railway buildings; they were provided by Meiggs with food, drinks, good mattresses, pillows, sheets, and—for the ladies— even mosquito nets.

In Arequipa, which recently had been gravely damaged by an earthquake, the railway was described as a "present from heaven to compensate for the sufferings of the past." Almighty God, President José Balta, and Henry Meiggs were praised and thanked. Handing Balta the hammer and the last spike, Meiggs declared:

Be certain, most excellent sir, that as you place the last rail... the civilized nations will look upon you as the collaborator of Newton, Fulton, and Humboldt in science, and that the history of the fatherland will open to you its pages alongside those which Bolívar and San Martín occupy, because the steam and the iron with which you are endowing your country affirm also the liberty and independence of nations.

Always less fluent than most Latins, Balta was almost speechless with elation. He gazed about for a moment in silence, then spoke a few words and drove home the golden spike that completed the first of Meiggs's Peruvian railroads. After more feasting, oratory, poetry, and dancing the party returned to Lima, where they left with Meiggs many souvenirs of their profound appreciation.

Such pageantry was never surpassed even in the glittering days of the colonial viceroys. Much of the Latin temperament seems to have entered Meiggs's soul. He was welcomed into the best social circles of Peru.

The closing scene of the Meiggs drama was most impressive. He died poor. The debts he left behind probably exceeded the value of his mortgaged property. He could build no more railways and there was no more money for charity. But twenty or thirty thousand people, the majority of them Peruvian peons, came to witness the last rites. The ceremony took place in La Merced, a Catholic church in Lima, and the body was buried in a private cemetery on the Meiggs estate. As the corpse was being transferred from the church to the flower-covered hearse drawn by four white horses a great crowd of humble people surged forward. They demanded the privilege of bearing the metal casket to the open grave, two or three miles away, and took the heavy burden on their tired shoulders. "Harry" Meiggs must have enjoyed his funeral.

Meiggs's spectacular career is not free from the stain of dishonesty and corruption. Having overspeculated in California real estate, he sold forged warrants and issued unauthorized stock in an effort to save himself and his friends. When his crime was about to be discovered he fled to Chile to avoid prosecution—perhaps even execution—by irate citizens determined to take "justice" into their hands. Although his record in Chile is untainted and it is said that he later made amends for his financial sins in California, he has been accused of resorting to large-scale bribery in Peru. He is also charged with major responsibility for bankrupting the nation.

The millions spent on his railways and others of the period did bring Peru at least to the very brink of bankruptcy; and the unsuccessful war with Chile that followed in 1879-1883 sent the country over the precipice. In 1890 the Peruvian Corporation, an English enterprise organized to bail out European bondholders and salvage the wreck of Peruvian finances, took over most of the railways of the nation. And the Peruvian railways are still dominated by this English corporation. In the midst of their calamities it was natural for the Peruvians to search for a scapegoat, and some of them found one in Henry Meiggs.

Meiggs probably bribed several politicians. Bribery seems to have been the custom in those days, not only in Peru but in a number of other countries. It is likely that Meiggs had to buy some of the Peruvians in order to obtain permission to build the railways. And the drive for bribes, along with the Meiggs pageantry, no doubt contributed to the railway boom. But other factors were involved. The earning capacity of railroads and their power to stimulate economic development were vastly overestimated—perhaps honestly so by many—and enthusiasm for the new means of transportation was already tremendous among the members of the ruling class before Meiggs reached

Lima. It is doubtful whether he originated a single railway project upon which he actually began construction. Certainly most of the lines he finished or started had been discussed for years before he arrived in Peru.

The conclusion seems clear. Peruvian leaders must share much of the blame for the nation's calamities. At times Henry Meiggs was a scoundrel; but he had his good traits and he built some remarkable railways. Few have ever accused him of shoddy workmanship or the use of any but the best of materials. His iron roads may not last as long as the Inca palaces; but they are sure to endure for many years.

THE WAY TO BOGOTÁ

T HE MAGDALENA RIVER is the way to Bogotá. There are other
routes to Colombia's capital, of course, but this has been
the main one for centuries. The Indians swarmed on the river
before the Spaniards came and the Spaniards used it for three
centuries without greatly improving the means of transportation. Their boats were only a little better than the dugout
canoes of the natives. The Magdalena is still the most important
trade route of Colombia.

This route to Bogotá is by no means easy. Travel and transportation by the Magdalena is hampered by alternating floods
and drought; by sandbanks, rocky shallows, shifting channels,
swirling rapids, floating trees, scorching heat, ravenous insects,
and exposure to mortal disease. Moreover, Bogotá is not located
on the Magdalena or any of its navigable tributaries. It stands
on a high plateau, the Plateau of Cundinamarca, between eight
and nine thousand feet above the sea and seventy or eighty
miles from the nearest approaches on the river—three or four
days by mountain trail and mule or, in recent years, six or seven
hours by mountain railroad. Yet the best way to Bogotá from
the Caribbean coast, until the arrival of the airplane in 1919,
was up the river by boat for some six hundred miles and then
up the Andes by mule or railway.

The *bongos* and *champanes,* the river craft used by the Spaniards of the long colonial period and by the Colombians until
the steamboat lines were established, were adaptations and re-
finements of the Indian canoe. The *bongo* was twenty or thirty
feet long and three or four feet wide, its deck usually exposed
to the sun and rain. The *champan* was likely to be twice as
large; with roof of palm-leaf thatch supported by bamboo poles

bent into an arch, it resembled the covered wagons of the North American prairies. Travel by either type of boat was a great hardship. Even the *champanes* were very uncomfortable because of the limited space and the spiders, bugs, fleas, and mosquitoes that found their rendezvous in the roof. Sails, as well as oars and poles and ropes, were used on both types of craft, but the winds along the Magdalena were rare and uncertain. Usually the boats had to be pulled and punted up the river against the current at a speed of only two or three miles an hour. Progress down stream was easier, of course, and swifter, although not free from the perils of whirlpools, rapids, and floating timber.

These boats were managed by crews called *bogas:* Negroes and mix-bloods of Negro and Indian or white parentage, whose life —and this is not strange in view of the tropical climate and primitive conditions—was not far removed from that of the savage. They wore almost no clothing, slept in floorless huts or along the beaches exposed to the alligators and aggressive insects, and spent their idle time in orgies in the river villages. Their food consisted of plantains, cassava, fish, and occasionally tough beef and rice. Their drink was strong liquor and the muddy water of the Magdalena. Their religion was a mixture of Roman Catholicism, superstition, blasphemy, and profanity. Slaves for the most part until after 1800, they bore hardships which few other men could have endured; and they were bound in a sort of peonage for years after their liberation from slavery. They were noisy, stubborn, vulgar, and pugnacious; but they were indispensable.

The aggregate tonnage of cargo moving up and down the Magdalena River during the colonial period was small; it could hardly have been otherwise given the poverty of the region and the very inadequate means of transportation. Passenger traffic, particularly through traffic, was also small. The population of New Granada, as Colombia was then called, was never dense— it was less than a million and a quarter as late as 1825, although it was nine million by 1940—and not many of its inhabitants had funds or disposition to travel in distant lands. Departure for the trip up or down the river was preceded by the writing of wills, fervent prayers, and fond farewells.

Conditions were greatly improved by the arrival of the steamboats. But permanent steamer traffic was not established on the river until 1847, as we have observed, although steamboats began to navigate the Magdalena as early as 1824 or 1825, with citizens of the United States prominent among the pioneers.

Seven steamers were afloat on the Magdalena in 1854, all of them built either in the United States or the British Isles. Practically all the engineers and mechanics manning them were citizens of the United States or subjects of Great Britain; but the deck hands were mostly Colombians. Such Colombians as were employed as pursers and traffic agents were usually able to speak English. In 1855 the New Granada Canal and Steam Navigation Company was organized in New York, with Henry Wells of that city as president. The word "canal" in the title of the company referred to an arm of the river, called the "Dique" by Colombians, which flowed into the Caribbean near Cartagena. Recently this had been dredged by George M. Totten, a North American engineer then at the beginning of a notable career in the tropics. This company soon placed two steamers on the river; and a British company organized in 1854 was operating four steamboats. In 1856 Robert A. Joy, likewise an Englishman, added another steamer to the river flotilla and two Germans brought in still another during the same year. Steamboats were multiplying on Colombia's leading trade artery in spite of revolutions, rocky rapids, sandbanks, and drifting debris.

The idea of consolidation occurred at once and the United Magdalena Steam Navigation Company was organized before the end of 1856. Although the leading spirit in the combination was the Englishman Robert Joy, this company soon received a charter from the State of New York. It took over all the steamboats on the river, imported several others, and purchased a good many more as they were introduced from time to time by rival enterprises. Although unable to monopolize steamer traffic on the Magdalena, it nevertheless held a dominant position for almost thirty years. Citizens of the United States were large investors in the United Company from the outset, and they owned nearly half of its capital in the early 1880's. The share of the British was not quite so large; Germans and Colombians held the rest. The majority of its boats flew the Stars and Stripes or the Union Jack. Its captains, engineers, and mechanics were mostly from the United States and Great Britain; its pursers, crews, and agents were mainly Colombians.

In 1862 there were twelve steamboats on the Magdalena, all except two or three owned by the United Company. In 1883 there were twenty-seven, with only six the property of this company. Strong rivals had appeared, but a citizen of the United States was among them. An international company, *Compañia Internacional,* owned mainly by Colombians and Brazilians, was running three steamers and transporting more passengers, although less freight, than the United Company. Third place in the river steamboat traffic was held by a company owned mainly by Francisco J. Cisneros. This company was operating eight steamers; but all except one of them were quite small. Cisneros, then famous as a railway builder in Colombia, was a Cuban exile who had acquired citizenship in the United States. The remainder of the twenty-seven river steamers of 1883 belonged to the Germans and the British; but in spite of the decline in the United Company's relative position, corporations owned and managed largely by citizens of the United States were still carrying most of the steamboat traffic on the Magdalena.

In 1884-1885 Colombia was harried by a bloody civil war which gravely injured shipping on its leading river. In 1889 there were only twenty-five steamboats on the Magdalena, with five belonging to the United Magdalena Company. The next year this corporation sold out to the Colombian Transport Company, *Compañía Colombiana de Transportes,* another attempt at consolidation—a merger of the International Company with the Cisneros and German interests. The consolidation had occurred in 1886 and the new enterprise was dominant for a time after the purchase of the five steamboats from the United Magdalena Company. In 1892, for instance, the Colombian Transport Company owned all but three of the nineteen steamers plying on the river. As in the case of the combination of 1856, however, this new consolidation was not long free from effective competition. A number of rival companies, British, North American, Colombian, and German, soon sprang up.

Travel and transportation by steamer on Colombia's great river was never very cheap; but this was not often the result of lack of competition. Fares and shipping costs had to be high if the steamboat companies were to make any profits. Revolutions and the natural hazards of the river made the life of a Magdalena steamboat short. The twenty-five steamers on the river in 1889, for instance, were all that were left of the some seventy that had floated there since the beginning.

In 1908, the vigorous Rafael Reyes, then dictator of Colombia, declared that competition on the river was ruinous to the owners of the steamboats and injurious to the national interest. He intervened and effected a partial consolidation but the arrangement did not last long. By 1915 some eight or ten companies were running forty-two steamers.

The first World War prevented expansion; in fact, in 1920 there were only forty-two steamers on the Magdalena. Thereafter, however, another period of rapid development took place, caused by expansion in coffee culture, the new petroleum industry, and a vast construction program. An official report of 1935 contained a list of seventy-six steamers plying on the Magdalena and its tributaries. The list included seven steamboats belonging to the national government; the sixty-nine privately operated were owned by more than twenty companies. No single company owned more than eleven, and at least half of them possessed only one steamer each. Although British and probably other foreign capital was still invested in the 1930's in the Magdalena River steamboats, shipping on the Magdalena and its tributaries was by then pretty thoroughly nationalized.

The importance of the *bongos* and *champanes* declined with the multiplication of the river steamers, but these reminders of vanished centuries lingered for many years. A few of them could still be seen even after 1900.

The river steamers were little flatboats. They had to be small and of light draft because of shallows, shoals, sandbanks, and rapids. Their tonnage seldom exceeded 400; the average ranged between 150 and 200 tons, and many were not that big. Drafts varied from two to five feet. As late as the 1930's hundreds of small craft were still engaged in transportation on the Magdalena. In Colombian official statistics they were classed as motor boats, motor launches, wooden boats, wooden sailboats, and canoes. For a stretch of three or four hundred miles along the

lower reaches of the river, the cargo of the steamers was supplemented by two loaded barges, one on each side.

Steamboats reduced costs and saved time; but the river jour-

THE WAY
TO BOGOTÁ

ney was still far from rapid or cheap. It cost the traveler almost
as much as a voyage from Colombia's northern coast to Europe
and often required more time. The life of a stevedore or a

steamer deck hand was somewhat less primitive and strenuous than that of the *boga* of an earlier day, but it was still a life of grinding toil and a good deal of misery.

Until the late 1930's it was usually impossible for river steamers to go all the way down to the Caribbean or for ocean steamers to enter the mouth of the Magdalena. The approach to the flatboats from the seacoast might be made from three points of departure: from Santa Marta by rowboat or canoe through sixty or seventy miles of lakes, channels, and swamps; from a landing near the Magdalena's mouth overland to Barranquilla, some sixteen or eighteen miles away, by horse or mule or—after the 1870's—by train; and from Cartagena through the Dique or across country on horseback or—after the early 1890's—by rail to Calamar, which was some eighty miles above the river's mouth.

It is not to be supposed that these river steamers of the late nineteenth and early twentieth century were luxurious or even comfortable. Although some were designed more exclusively for passengers than were others, and made fewer stops, nearly all were heavily loaded with freight and baggage. Wood-burners altogether until the 1920's, they had to spend hours each day tied up at the river's bank while sweating crews carried aboard huge piles of fuel.

The steamers customarily contained three decks, especially after the turn of the last century; but the top and the bottom decks were almost unbearably hot. The boats contained *camarotes,* some of them more than others: *camarote* being the word used in Colombia to describe a berth, a cabin, or a stateroom; but these compartments were several degrees hotter than the blistering decks themselves. The *camarotes* were furnished with a washstand and basin, a cane-bottom chair, and a cot. The passengers had to supply the sheets, pillows, towels, and mosquito nets. Food on board consisted mainly of tough beef, rice, and bread, with soup and occasionally some kind of dessert. Coffee was plentiful; but there was no milk to drink, only a little of the canned article for the coffee. One dared not drink the water until it had been boiled. Usually the decks were not screened; flies and other small creatures swarmed continuously around the table. Ice was seldom to be had even after 1911 when electricity and convenient means of refrigeration began to appear on the river steamers. The arrival of electricity made possible the installation of fans in the *camarotes,* but the fans were often out of order. Since there were showers on the steamers, a bath could be taken in the tepid, muddy fluid of the Magdalena provided the paddle-wheels lifted it high enough for the purpose. The bathrooms and toilets were seldom clean.

Until the 1880's a good many vessels had the paddle-wheels located at the side; then the side-wheelers disappeared, giving way to the stern-wheelers, which were better adapted to the river and more comfortable for the passengers because they left the decks open to the wind. The trip by steamer from near the Caribbean coast to the vicinity of Honda required from a week to more than a month, depending on the vicissitudes of the voyage. Sometimes the steamers were stranded for days on the sandbanks or gravely injured by jutting rocks or drifting trees. Then one had the choice of hiring a *champan* or some other small craft or waiting for another steamer while praying for a rise in the river. For the first three hundred miles or so the steamers usually ran both day and night; beyond that point night travel was dangerous, and the boats anchored shortly after sunset to the great delight of hungry insects eager for prey. Throughout the whole course of the river as far up as Honda, mosquitoes, stinging gnats, and other flying plagues attacked the passengers in relays and unceasingly except at rare intervals when a lively breeze blew them away. Subjected to all these vexations and hardships, the traveler was often too depressed to appreciate the primeval tropical forests and the magnificent mountain scenery.

The last lap of the journey taken by most travelers on the way from the Caribbean coast to Bogotá until well after 1900 was the ancient trail across the river from Honda. The trail led over four mountain ridges to the Cundinamarca Plateau and thence across the plateau to the Colombian capital. A distance of seventy miles or more, the journey was usually made during the rainy season because of the dangers and uncertainties confronted on the Magdalena during periods of drought.

The slippery mountain path was most disagreeable, and hazardous as well. From the east bank of the Magdalena the

saddle-mule—horses were seldom used here—climbed slowly up
the first ridge to Alto de Sargento, from which a sublime view
could be obtained of the river valley to the rear. A descent was
made from Sargento before starting the second climb up to Alto
de Raizal; then another slippery descent before beginning the
longer and steeper climb to Alto de Trigo, from which the trail
descended again, rapidly, to Villeta, a village scarcely 1800 feet
above the starting point at Honda. At Villeta began the most
dangerous climb of all; the trail up the fourth ridge to Alto
de Roble, at the edge of the great tableland, was nearly per-
pendicular. Some thirty miles still lay between Roble and Bogotá; but the country from Roble on was almost level, sloping
gently down toward the capital with two giant peaks towering
behind it. After the middle of the nineteenth century the traveler might change from saddle-mule to coach a few miles beyond
Roble; and after 1889 he might make two-thirds of the distance
from Roble on a railway which extended out from Bogotá.
Whatever the means chosen, the journey from Honda up to the
capital was likely to require from three to five days, with nights
spent at miserable inns.

The old trail from Honda was virtually abandoned after the
completion of the Girardot Railway in 1909. In recent years
travelers and goods have gone by steamer from Barranquilla or
Calamar to La Dorada, thirty-five miles below Honda; by rail
from La Dorada to Beltrán, forty miles above Honda; by
steamer again from Beltrán to Girardot; and by train from
Girardot to Bogotá. Since the 1930's, in fact, it has been possible to make the entire journey from La Dorada to Bogotá by
rail, although a change of trains was still required at Girardot
in the 1940's. No iron road links the Caribbean coast with the
national capital, and none is likely to any time soon. The building of such a road would be a tremendous task; its maintenance
almost impossible.

In the 1920's another means of transport from the seacoast to
Bogotá was provided. Since that time those who could afford to
travel by air have been able to make the journey in a few hours,
avoiding the withering heat and the insects except while waiting
for the planes and during the brief landings at the river ports.
Established by Germans, this airline was later acquired and

operated by the Colombians. After the late 1930's one could also go to Bogotá by highway and auto from the Venezuelan coast, speeding along the eastern range of the Andes, or by train and auto from Colombia's Pacific port of Buenaventura. The Magdalena and its steamboats are comparatively less significant than they used to be; but this way to Bogotá is still important, especially for freight and baggage. The story of steamboats on the river is a story of international collaboration; and in large measure it is a story of Yankee and British pioneering in the tropics.

The life of Colombians has centered on their main river as completely as the lives of the Assyrians, Babylonians, and Egyptians ever converged on the Tigris, the Euphrates, and the Nile. It has centered there because of geographical factors and the location of its foreign markets in Europe and the United States. Three lofty mountain ranges, with the Magdalena and its Cauca tributary flowing between them, cross the country from southwest to northeast. Except for a few stretches along these rivers, Colombia's hot and humid lowlands are sparsely settled and always have been. The vast majority of Colombians always have lived on the cool plateaus and slopes of the three Andean cordilleras. By geographical decree they are mainly a mountain people compelled to face toward the Caribbean, and compelled until recently to reach the northern coast by the difficult Magdalena. That they have increased and prospered in spite of these enormous handicaps is a high tribute to their vigor and industry. Their achievements cannot be fully appreciated without taking into account the geographical barriers which they have confronted.

DAWN OF THE RAILWAY ERA
IN COLOMBIA

THE BUILDING of Colombia's railways was a very slow process. The first railway in Colombia, the line across the Isthmus of Panama, was begun, as we have seen, in 1850 and completed five years later. The second was started in 1869 and finished early in 1871. In the 1870's, construction was begun on four more Colombian railways; but none of the four was finished during the next few years. In fact, one of them, a railroad designed to connect Bogotá with the Magdalena at a point across the river from the town of Honda, was abandoned after five miles had been built. Work was initiated on five other railways during the 1880's; but one of these, a line intended to connect Bucaramanga in northeastern Colombia with a port (Puerto Wilches) on the Magdalena River, was soon surrendered to the jungle. In the 1890's, four additional railroads were started, and the year 1909 witnessed the beginning of Colombia's sixteenth railway. The railroad connection between Bogotá and the Magdalena was not completed until that year, and, even then, it consisted of two divisions of different gauge. The railway between Cali, an important town in the fertile Cauca River valley, and the Pacific port of Buenaventura was not completed until 1914. The first steam locomotive puffed into the city of Medellín, capital of the large Department of Antioquia, the same year; but the railway connecting that city with the Magdalena River at Puerto Berrío consisted of two parts, which were not joined until a tunnel through the mountains was finished in 1929. Even as late as the early 1940's it was still impossible to go by rail from Colombia's capital to either of its seacoasts, although only a gap of sixty-eight miles interrupted the railway lines between Bogotá and the Pacific port of Buenaventura.

The total length of the thirteen railways existing in Colombia at the beginning of 1915 was less than 700 miles (1,082 kilometers). The Panama Railroad was not among the thirteen; its

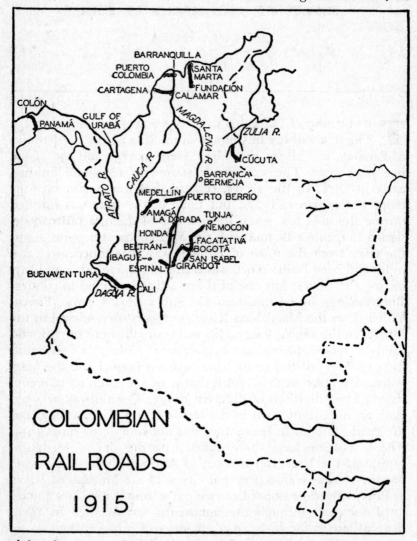

right-of-way ceased to be a part of Colombian domain with the secession of Panama in 1903. Omitting that line, some 80 kilometers long, which, as we have seen, was built at great cost in money and life by the Panama Railway Company of New York, with J. L. Baldwin, John C. Trautwine, and George M. Totten as engineers in charge of construction, the achievements of the railroad builders in Colombia down to the end of the year 1914 were, in summary, as follows:

1. The Bolívar Railway, connecting Barranquilla with Puerto Colombia on the Caribbean, was 27 kilometers in length. Started by British promoters in 1869 and constructed by German engineers, most of the road was opened to traffic in January 1871.

2. The Antioquia Railway, intended to link Puerto Berrío on the Magdalena with the mountain city of Medellín, was 169 kilometers long. But it consisted of two divisions connected by a cart road over a mountain pass. Construction was begun in 1874 under the management of Francisco Javier Cisneros. Prominent among his construction engineers were George M. Totten and J. D. Thayer, both citizens of the United States. The major part of the railway was constructed, however, under the management of Colombians, with the assistance of several foreign engineers. Among the latter was a North American named John B. Dougherty. The leading Colombian engineers connected with the road were Camilo Restrepo, Arturo Acebedo, Jorge Páez, and Pablo E. Pérez. It embraced only 47 kilometers of track when Cisneros severed his connection with it in 1885.

3. The Cúcuta Railway measured 71 kilometers. The main line linked San José de Cúcuta with the head of navigation on the Zulia River in northeastern Colombia; a branch extended to the Venezuelan border. The trunk line was initiated in 1878 under Colombian management, and was completed in 1888; the spur was opened to the public in 1897. Among the promoters of the Cúcuta road were Marco A. Estrada, Alejandro Galvis, and Elías Luzán Ruiz. The leading construction engineers were Juan N. Gonzáles Vásquez, Enrique Morales, and Lobo Guerrero. Perhaps they received assistance from foreign experts.

4. The Pacific Railway, formerly called the Cauca, extended from the Pacific port of Buenaventura to Cali in the Cauca valley, a distance of 174 kilometers. Construction was begun at

Buenaventura under the management of Cisneros in 1878, with J. D. Thayer and other North American engineers supervising the work. Cisneros surrendered his contract in 1885 after building 27 kilometers, but this short line was operated by Colombians for several years. In the early 1870's David R. Smith, Frank B. Modica, Charles S. Brown, and Barton C. Smith had tried to build this railway, organizing the Cauca Valley Mining and Construction Company of Illinois and the Cauca Valley Railroad Company of New York; but they had lost their contracts because of failure to begin construction within the time limit. Between 1891 and 1897 James Cherry of California constructed eight kilometers, but was then deprived of his contract. Afterwards two Colombians managed the construction of another stretch of 12 kilometers. In 1905 Alfred and Edward Mason of the Chicago engineering firm of Mason and Bishop took charge of the railway, organizing the Colombian Pacific Railroad Company, repairing the old line, and adding 8 kilometers before this corporation collapsed. (Two of the engineers employed by Mason and Bishop—W. B. Perkins and W. E. Hardenburg—later went to the rubber region of the upper Amazon and exposed the enslavement of the Indians). The remainder of the railway, some 118 kilometers, was built largely under the supervision of Rafael Álvarez Salas and Lobo Guerrero, Colombian engineers.

5. The railroad around the rapids and whirlpools of the Magdalena, called La Dorada Railway, was begun by Cisneros in 1881, and the first section, 15 or 20 kilometers, was opened to the public the next year. Under the management of a British company, the road was extended to Ambalema (Beltrán) by 1907, the total length of the line then being 111 kilometers. In 1879 Frank B. Modica had obtained a contract to build this railway and had organized the Magdalena Railroad Company, but had lost his contract because of inability to secure funds.

6. The Girardot Railway, planned to link Bogotá with the Magdalena River, was initiated in 1881 by Cisneros, who opened 33 kilometers to traffic by 1885. J. B. Dougherty and five other engineers from the United States had charge of construction. Several other individuals and companies later assumed the task of completing the line. A North American named John H. Pen-

nington held a contract for two years, apparently without beginning construction. Samuel B. McConnico, a citizen of the United States once connected with the Illinois Central Railway, secured a contract in 1895 and turned it over to the Great Colombian Railway Company of New York; but this company accomplished little before transferring the concession to a Colombian. Engineers from the United States continued to help with the construction, at least until 1900, when two of them died of yellow fever. In that year the railway, then 49 kilometers in length, was taken over by a British company. Under English management it reached Facatativá, on the Cundinamarca Plateau, in September 1909. The length of the railway was then 132 kilometers, and it was still 40 kilometers from Bogotá.

7. The Santa Marta Railway, a line planned to connect that coastal town with the Magdalena River, was begun by the British in 1882; but it never reached its original destination. By 1906 it had arrived at the banana town of Fundación, 94 kilometers from Santa Marta; and that was as near as it ever approached to the Magdalena. It became primarily a banana railroad.

8. The Sabana Railway, begun at Facatativá in 1882, reached Bogotá seven years later. Forty kilometers long, it was constructed largely, if not entirely, by Colombian engineers. One of its promoters was Carlos Tanco; the chief construction engineer was Manuel Peña.

9. The Cartagena Railway, running between Cartagena and Calamar, on the Magdalena River, consisted of 105 kilometers of track. Begun in 1891 and finished in 1894, it was constructed under a contract obtained by Samuel B. McConnico and under the management of the Cartagena-Magdalena Railway Company of Boston, Massachusetts.

10. The Colombian Northern Railway was intended to furnish transportation between Bogotá and the centers of population to the north and the northeast. Construction on this line was initiated in 1891, and the line reached Zipaquirá in 1898, from which point it was extended to Nemocón, 62 kilometers from Bogotá, by 1907. It was begun by a Colombia company under contracts obtained by Carlos Tanco and Juan M. Dávila; but it passed into the hands of the English in 1898. The con-

struction of the entire road was supervised by Alejo Morales, a Colombian engineer. The first contract to build the railway had been assigned in 1882 by the State (later the Department) of Cundinamarca to Charles S. Brown and Charles Rodgers, both citizens of the United States; but they had failed to raise the requisite capital.

11. The Tolima Railway, which was intended to connect Ibagué, the capital of the Department of Tolima, with the Magdalena River at a point near Girardot, was begun in 1893 under Colombian management, Carlos Tanco being the promoter. By July 1914 about 30 kilometers had been constructed by native engineers. The railroad did not reach Ibagué, only 77 miles from the Magdalena, until 1921.

12. The Southern Railway, designed to afford an improved means of transportation between Colombia's capital and the southern part of the Cundinamarca Plateau, was initiated under the management of Guillermo Torres and Juan M. Dávila. Begun in 1896, it reached San Isabel, 30 kilometers from Bogotá, in 1906; and there it stopped for a decade in spite of the fact that it was taken over by an English company the year it reached San Isabel.

13. The Amagá Railway, intended to furnish the Department of Antioquia a western outlet to the Cauca River, was started at Medillín in 1909. It arrived at Amagá, 37 kilometers away, in 1914. It was constructed by Colombians. Its leading promoter was Alejandro Angel; among the construction engineers who built it were Luis A. Isaza, Jorge Escobar, and Juan de Dios Vásquez.

Such, in brief, is the story of railroad building in Colombia down to the beginning of 1915—a little less than 1200 kilometers, not quite 750 miles, including the Panama Railway, in 65 years! But there were good reasons for this slow rate of progress.

In the first place, Colombia's population was small. With an area of approximately 450,000 square miles after the loss of Panama—about the equivalent of that of Arizona, New Mexico, Nevada, and Colorado combined—its inhabitants numbered a little less than two million and a quarter in 1851 and slightly more than five million in 1912. In the latter year more than half of the national domain was still virtually empty. Only the mountains and plateaus and a few sections along the Cauca valley and the Caribbean were fairly densely settled. Shipment by rail of the commodities produced and required by this meager population would not be a very profitable business. Earnings would be small; rates would tend to be high.

In the second place, Colombians as a whole were poor. They had borne the brunt of the bloody struggle for independence from Spain, a war which dragged on for fifteen years. They had fought not merely for their own independence; they had helped to liberate the Venezuelans, the Ecuadorians, the Peruvians, and the Bolivians. The total national debt of Colombia, most of which was contracted during these wars for independence, amounted to nearly fifty-two million *pesos* in 1839. The Colombians had almost no revenues for railway building and their credit was not good.

In the third place, economic conditions were made worse by the turbulence of the Colombian people. At the beginning of their national independence they had no training or experience in self-government. The population of the new nation was composed of whites of Spanish descent, Indians, Africans, and mixtures of the three races, with the primitive, mixed, and servile elements making up the majority. National unity and social harmony were hard to achieve. Agreement on political policies and personnel could not be reached by peaceful procedures. Civil wars were frequent. The worst of them occurred after the railway era began to dawn; the last started in 1899 and continued for three years. During these internecine conflicts the railways were seized and abused or demolished.

Fourth, the administrative organization of Colombia was for many years a handicap to railway building. The nation began to drift toward an extremely loose federal system in the 1850's, and between 1863 and 1886 the nine states into which the nation was divided were practically independent. Neither these small states nor the weak national government at Bogotá could muster sufficient funds to build many kilometers of railroad. The extent to which the resources of the country were scattered is impressively indicated by the state of the railways in 1885. Nine railroads had been initiated, two already had been abandoned, and only the Panama Railway and the short Bolívar line had been completed. The situation was chaotic.

Fifth, Colombians, as a rule, had comparatively little training or interest in science and technology. They were far more devoted to theology, philosophy, literature, and law. Members of the upper class were little disposed to manual labor. The lower classes were for the most part undernourished, afflicted by disease, and lacking in energy and ambition. It required a good many years for Colombians to become moderately skillful in the construction and operation of railways. Expert assistance as well as capital had to be imported from the United States and Europe.

Sixth, Colombia's topography and climate made railway construction, repair, and preservation a tremendous task. The mountains—three lofty Andean ranges running across the country from southwest to northeast, with the Magdalena and the Cauca rivers flowing between them—were not merely steep; they were traversed by numerous deep valleys which required many excavations, fills, viaducts, bridges, and tunnels, and at certain seasons the rainfall was torrential. The heavy rolling stock and a good part of the steel rails for the 132 kilometers of railroad built on the Cundinamarca Plateau before the Girardot Railway joined the Sabana line at Facatativá in 1909 had to be dragged or hauled up the precipitous slippery slopes of the eastern cordillera by human drudges and oxen; and the weighty materials of a considerable portion of the Antioquia and Amagá railroads were brought over the central cordillera in the same way. The Colombian lowlands were hot and humid, covered in the main by dense tropical vegetation or swamps, and infested by insects and disease. The heat, humidity, and pests of these lowlands can be fully realized only by those who have suffered them. In such regions, at a time when modern remedies and sanitary precautions were unknown, railway laborers were often the victims of intestinal parasites, malaria, yellow fever, and other plagues.

The some 700 miles of railway existing in Colombia at the begining of 1915 could not have been built without the financial and technical assistance of foreigners. These railways were the result of international collaboration. Most of the mountain railroads were built under the supervision of Colombian engineers; and the humble toilers of the nation did most of the drudgery on all the lines, digging, shoveling, straining, and sweating for long hours each day. Of the 1082 kilometers of railway in operation in 1915, some 495 kilometers had been built under the management of Colombian governments or companies, with Colombian engineers supervising a good part of the construction. British companies had managed the construction of about 310 kilometers, employing United States, Colombian, and (in one instance: the Bolívar Railway) German, as well as British, engineers. Citizens of the United States, employing occasionally a few Colombian engineers, had managed the construction of 277 kilometers. They had also constructed the Panama Railway, which was no longer in Colombian domain, as well as a then abandoned stretch of some eight kilometers across the river from Honda—a total of 365 kilometers. The Colombian railways were financed by private investment, cash subsidies, government guaranties of interest on capital expended, and public lands. Cash subsidies and interest payments were drawn in the main from the proceeds of bond sales in England and not immediately from Colombian revenues.

Citizens of the United States were the pioneers. They constructed at least 189 kilometers by 1885 and 330 or more, including the Panama road, by the end of the century, without taking into account the length of track laid under the supervision of North American engineers employed by Colombian and British railway organizations. The significance of this contribution becomes apparent when one observes that there were only some 289 kilometers of railroad in Colombia in 1885 and only 645 kilometers, including the Panama line, in 1904.

Achievements of North Americans in Colombia would have been greater during this period if they could have secured more capital. Accumulations in the United States for foreign investment were comparatively small until after 1910. The loss of a number of railroad contracts by North Americans because of failure to raise funds already has been noted. It would be easy to extend the list: the J. T. O'Bryan and Charles L. Wright contract of 1903, for instance, for the construction of a railway from Medellín down the Porce valley to Santa Lucía on the Lower

Cauca, and the Henry Granger contract of 1905 for a railroad from Medellín to the Gulf of Urabá.

Although these Colombian railways were narrow-gauged and poorly equipped, having few diners and no Pullman cars, their construction in most cases had been very expensive. In some instances, perhaps, the cost was greater even than Colombia's difficult climate and terrain would justify. Owing to the prolonged and rather haphazard process of building, as well as to oscillations in Colombian currency and land values, only a financial wizard could ascertain construction costs on many of the roads. It is certain that the bonds of the country were sold at heavy discounts in the London market in spite of fairly high interest rates; but this was largely a reflection of Colombian political and financial disorders.

Whatever their cost, these railways were an immense improvement over previous means of transportation in regions lacking navigable rivers or where fluvial navigation was dangerous, as was the case with the treacherous and turbulent Dagua, rushing down the Pacific slope, and with the Magdalena in the vicinity of Honda. Travel and shipping rates were still high; but they were by no means as expensive as in the days of the pack animal and the human porter. And by the end of the 1930's Colombians were to become the owners and operators of all except two or three of their railroads. In 1940 the total length of the railways in Colombia was 2190 kilometers.

During the half century or so following 1850 the leaders of this South American nation were eager to attract foreign capital and foreign technology. Their attitude toward the government and experts of the United States, in particular, was generally quite cordial, until Colombians were embittered by the Panama episode of 1903-1904. Many *Colombianos* spoke of Francisco Javier Cisneros in terms of warm appreciation. Two railway stations were named in his honor, and in 1907 the National Congress ordered his portrait to be hung in the office of the Ministry of Fomento. Years later, no less a figure than Rafael Reyes —explorer, warrior, and ex-president of Colombia—urged that a monument be erected to Cisneros's memory. Although these honors may have been bestowed in part because Cisneros was a Latin, the relations of Colombian leaders with George M.

Totten, J. D. Thayer, John B. Dougherty, and other American engineers of Anglo-Saxon descent seem to have been characterized by friendship and esteem. James Cherry came to be disliked in Colombia because of a long legal battle which he finally won, collecting a large sum of money from the national government; and Alfredo Ortega, the historian of Colombia's railways, expressed the view that Samuel B. McConnico and his Boston company made more money than they were entitled to from the construction of the Cartagena-Calamar line; but at least two distinguished Colombians referred to Charles S. Brown with appreciation and sympathy.

Brown's career in Colombia, because of his misfortunes and his tenacity, may well evoke both pity and admiration. He spent more than fifteen years in the country, negotiated numerous contracts, and was connected at one time or another with various railways which he tried to lengthen or build entirely. He succeeded in constructing only five miles through the jungle across the river from Honda. He introduced a locomotive and a few cars, but the railway did not prosper and his funds were soon exhausted. He sold out his interest to Charles Rodgers for a thousand *pesos* (which were more than it was worth, for the railroad never resumed operations). Obtaining his last contract in 1888, a contract to complete the Antioquia railway, Brown died shortly afterward and was buried near the abandoned engine and rusty rails of the jungle road he failed to finish. His grave and the rotting remnants of his railway could still be dimly seen as late as 1920. They were almost hidden by the tall grass and lusty trees. Amidst all his hardships and failures he never lost faith in Colombia or his determination to master its steaming tropics and its rugged mountains.

THE TECHNOLOGICAL MODERNIZATION
OF ECUADOR

NEAR THE END of 1853 Courtland Cushing, minister of the United States in Ecuador, declared: "There is not a carriage nor a wagon and not more than a dozen carts in the whole Republic. Everything is transported on the shoulders of men or the backs of beasts." He noted further that Ecuador had only one foundry and a single sawmill run by steam.

The picture of the state of mechanical progress in Ecuador was a little too dark. Cushing failed to observe a few flour and sugar mills and a cotton mill which Englishmen had built at Chillo in 1842. He might have added, however, that there were no ice plants, tramways, or telegraph lines; and, of course, there were no telephones or electric lights because these had not been invented.

A Baltimore mechanic named Kuhn, with the backing of Matthew P. Game and Horace Cox, citizens of the United States, had brought in the sawmill, which incidentally may have been the second instead of the first of its kind introduced. Kuhn also built the foundry and introduced a sugar mill, a flour mill, and machinery for spinning and weaving, while Game and Cox collaborated with Vicente Rocafuerte, recently president of Ecuador, in constructing a shipyard at Guayaquil. This pioneering had occurred in the 1840's.

In spite of grave political disorders, the next decade witnessed the arrival of the first fire engine, manufactured in Baltimore, and the installation of the first gas plant, which was the work of Baltimore businessmen who organized the Baltimore and Guayaquil Gas Company in 1859. During the 1850's, likewise, citizens of Paterson, New Jersey, built a cotton mill at Otavalo and Matthew P. Game, formerly of Philadelphia, joined Elisha

Lee of Chicago, who acted from time to time as United States consul, in establishing, in 1858-1859, the first line of steamers on the Guayas, the Daule, and other rivers flowing into the Gulf of Guayaquil.

The political dominance of Gabriel García Moreno, 1860-1875, was marked by great strides in modernization. This vigorous statesman's religious zeal and intolerance did not prevent him from appreciating the remarkable inventions of the Machine Age. The technological advancement of the period in Ecuador was limited only by political turbulence and Ecuador's poverty.

Before taking charge of the government of his country, García Moreno, himself a rather noted scientist, had visited the United States and resided for some time in the leading countries of Europe. Having witnessed the technological progress of other nations, he had returned home with the determination to improve the material as well as the moral condition of his own. He promptly equipped his army with Winchester rifles, and it was not long before he began to import engineers, mechanics, and other skilled artisans from France, England, Germany, and the United States. At least twenty citizens from the United States were residing in Ecuador by 1867 and there must have been twice as many by 1875.

García Moreno started the great highway from Quito to the coast in 1862, and it reached Sibambe, nearly 200 miles on the way to Guayaquil, by 1873. A mountain highway running along an avenue bordered by lofty peaks and volcanic domes, its numerous stone bridges, culverts, and viaducts called forth the admiration of all who saw it. Gradients were easy, curves were gradual, and the width of the boulevard varied from twenty-four to twenty-eight feet. Designed to accommodate coaches, carriages, and carts, it was opened section by section with great solemnity—by official journeys, prayer, and thanksgiving. Europeans served as chief engineers, but they were assisted by a number of experts from the United States. Several other roads were built by García Moreno, but none was so magnificent as this central highway.

The energetic Ecuadorian ruler intended to have a railway constructed from the vicinity of Guayaquil to the end of the paved highway at Sibambe, but he did not live to complete it. The railroad was begun at Yaguachi in 1872, but was only some twenty-seven miles long at the death of the dictator three years later. Construction was initiated under the supervision of engineers from the United States, who continued operations until they were interrupted by political disorders and exhaustion of funds.

To supervise the construction of school buildings and other public edifices, García Moreno employed Europeans in the main, although at least one Yankee was assigned the task of rebuilding the town of Ibarra, recently destroyed by an earthquake. It was the skill of citizens of the United States in constructing means of communication that most aroused the dictator's admiration.

Diplomats and consuls of the United States, while lamenting this ruler's despotism and bigotry, were deeply impressed by his constructive statesmanship and his warm admiration for the United States. Rumsey Wing and Thomas Biddle served as ministers during the most fruitful period of García Moreno's administration.

"He is the moving spirit in every work of skill and science now in course of perfection in the country," declared Wing in 1870. Later the minister reported that Arthur A. Rogers was engaged in rebuilding Ibarra; that Henry G. McClellan had made a "gallant" survey for a road from Quito down the mountains and across the jungle to Esmeraldas; that Rogers had explored "on foot" the country between Quito and Manabí; that Rogers and Albert Millet had surveyed a road from Quito to the Bay of Caraquez, a third outlet on the Pacific coast; that a New York engineer named Salter was supervising the building of the Quito-Esmeraldas highway; that John Curtis and Francis Merrill of New York were assisting McClellan with the railroad; and that "Americans" had constructed and were managing "several fine wheat and corn mills." (The minister might have added that McClellan was purchasing agent of the railway and that he had helped to build the National Observatory.) Wing was delighted with this collaboration between his countrymen and Ecuador's determined chief executive, and looked forward to an epoch of prosperity and stability.

Thomas Biddle was greatly impressed by an interview which he had with the dictator shortly before the latter's death. "He said... there was no foreign land which he loved so well as ours," wrote Biddle. García Moreno then alluded to the services of several citizens of the United States and "complimented their efficiency and fidelity, particularizing... Arthur Rogers, Albert Millet, Henry G. McClellan, and John Curtis." Preparations for the Centennial celebration at Philadelphia were then in progress, and García Moreno promised that Ecuador should be adequately represented. "Of all things," he said, "I should like to attend its inauguration."

The period of political and financial disorder that followed the dictator's assassination in August 1875 hampered Ecuador's technological progress. Yet, during the next twenty years a few advances were made. In the early 1880's James A. Scrymser of the Central and South American Telegraph Company, a corporation of the United States, furnished Ecuador a cable connection with the outside world and built a telegraph line from Santa Elena Peninsula to Guayaquil. Other lines soon followed, and during the same period citizens of the United States built Ecuador's first ice plant and tramways and installed its first telephones, all of them at Guayaquil. By the end of the next decade streetcars and telephones were operating in Quito, and electric lights were beginning to appear in Ecuador's leading towns.

Railway progress during the twenty-year period was slow. Efforts were concentrated mainly on the line between Yaguachi and Sibambe, but little was constructed in spite of numerous contracts. In 1897 the railroad was only some fifty-six miles long, extending from Durán, across the river from Guayaquil, to Chimbo, at the foot of the Andes. A gap of forty miles still separated the end of the rails from the end of the highway, and both were in bad condition. The greatest achievements on this difficult railroad during the epoch were made under the supervision of Mark J. Kelly, a British subject with experience in engineering acquired in the United States and Central America. In the late 1880's, with the assistance of Yankee engineers, Kelly laid the track through the "succession of marshes" between Durán and Yaguachi, a distance of some fourteen miles, and added a section of approximately the same length at the other end of the line. The railway was carrying only a part of the traffic destined for Quito, however, and was being operated at a loss. The government had taken it over again in 1895 (see map on page 45).

Two years later, June 14, 1897, an important contract was signed with Archer Harman of Virginia and New York. By its terms Harman agreed to reconstruct the old line and complete the railway to Quito. In return, he was granted the right to operate the road for a period of seventy-five years and was to be provided with capital by the flotation of securities guaranteed by the Ecuadorian government. The new organization, the Guayaquil and Quito Railway Company, was incorporated in New Jersey in September 1897. Besides two Ecuadorians, fifteen citizens of the United States and four British subjects were members of the original board of directors. Most of the securities were sold in Europe; among New York capitalists backing Harman were Robert M. Thompson, George Hoadley, Charles R. Sherrill, and Charles R. Lee. The term granted for the completion of the railroad was six years, later extended to ten.

The new company took charge in 1898 and began construction at once; but while work continued without much interruption, the line did not advance rapidly. Perplexing topographical and financial obstacles were confronted along with tropical diseases and one or two revolutions. Ties, rails, steel for bridges and trestles, rolling stock, and supplies and provisions of almost every sort had to be imported, and shipments were often delayed by yellow fever in Guayaquil. The ties came from California, Oregon, and Washington; the rest of the materials were imported from the eastern industrial centers of the United States. The renovation of the old road was no small task. Bridges and culverts had to be rebuilt and ties replaced. The roadbed had to be raised through the swampy section and the track was finally relaid in order to widen the gauge. The new line must climb the lofty Andes and continue along the high plateau flanked by volcano-crowned cordilleras and crossed by a number of transverse ridges or *nudos*. Although the distance from Durán to Quito by the route followed by the railway was only some

290 miles, its construction was one of the world's remarkable feats of engineering.

William F. Shunk, a noted North American engineer, was chief of Harman's surveying corps. The chiefs of construction were Henry Davis and John Harman, Archer's brother and a graduate of West Point. F. W. Bennet was assistant chief; R. R. Hancock was superintendent of the old section between Durán and the mountains. By 1901 eighty-four engineers, thirty mining and blasting experts, ten physicians and surgeons, and several other technicians were at work on the road. The total of common laborers at that time was 8500, composed of 4000 natives of Ecuador, 3500 Jamaicans, more than 300 Barbadians, and several hundred Puerto Ricans.

In 1904, John Harman surveyed for *Engineering News* the obstacles confronted and achievements up to that time. Although hardly more than fifty miles of new track had been laid in five years, the railhead was already high up in the Andes. Jungle, swamp, and torrential rains had been very "trying" in the lowlands; climate improved after an elevation of some four thousand feet had been reached, and, with it, the health of the workers. But from there on vast mountain gorges and slippery precipices had to be mastered. Many culverts, viaducts, and bridges were necessary; a "switchback" had to be built along the giant "Devil's Nose" and beyond that a dizzy loop. Summing up the enormous difficulties encountered, Harman listed lack of funds and credit; Ecuadorian skepticism; severe climate: sweltering heat and tropical rains in the lowland, tremendous floods and numbing cold in the mountains; absence of records on annual precipitation; scarcity of labor; treacherous landslides; and shifting sands around Palmira, 10,600 feet above the sea.

Already Henry Davis had died of sunstroke, and others became the victims both of the climate and its diseases and of the enormous landslides in a region but recently shaken by volcanoes. John Harman died of malignant fever early in 1907 and was buried near the railroad track at Huigra, his enduring monument the railway itself.

But the work went on. Riobamba was reached by the middle of 1905; and soon rails surmounted the highest point at Urbina, at an elevation of 11,841 feet. Thereafter, construction was somewhat easier, but progress was delayed by shortage of funds. Some of the final section was built by moonlight. On June 17, 1908, the last spike was driven by América Alfaro, daughter of President Eloy Alfaro; the first train reached Quito on June 25.

More than a week was devoted to feasting and celebration. The nights were noisy with the clanging of the church-bells of the world's most pious city. There were many speeches, of course. Among them was one by Archer Harman, who referred sadly to the large expenditures required and the "great sacrifice of life." "I have only carried out, to the best of my ability, your government's instructions," he said with Virginia tact. "I feel that I have had great honor in being your servant in performing this work." He was addressing this part of his speech to Eloy Alfaro, whom many Ecuadorians rate as their greatest statesman. Certainly Alfaro and García Moreno deserve much credit for the building of Ecuador's most important railway; but it was the result of the hard work and sacrifices of many men from many countries.

As the festivities approached their climax, a telegram from President Theodore Roosevelt to President Alfaro was read. "Be pleased to accept my earnest congratulations on the completion of the railway to Quito," Roosevelt said. "May this great achievement enhance the prosperity of Ecuador." Alfaro promptly replied: "I am deeply grateful to you for your sincere ...congratulation. We are following here, to the extent of our powers, the handsome example of the great nation you are governing...."

But Archer Harman and Eloy Alfaro did not live to reap the rewards of their railway enterprise. In October 1911, near Hot Springs, Virginia, Harman, then only fifty-three, was thrown from his horse and killed. A few months later, January 28, 1912, Alfaro, who had dominated Ecuador since 1895 and tried to liberalize the country, was hacked to pieces by a Quito mob. But the locomotives still move up and down the lofty Andes, along the magnificent avenue with smoking volcanoes on each side, and few who ride the coaches have not heard of Alfaro and the Harmans.

By the 1940's Ecuador had in operation eight other railways, but most of them were short lines extending, or branching off from, the iron road from Guayaquil to Quito. The longest of the eight ran from Quito toward the Colombian frontier and from Guayaquil to the Pacific. The others started inland from the Pacific ports or nosed out slowly from the great trunk line toward the tributaries of the Amazon or southward toward the Peruvian border. The aggregate length of the eight was considerably less than thrice the mileage of the Guayaquil-Quito road. Citizens of the United States had taken some part in the construction of most of them. The Ecuadorians, the English, the French, and the Germans built the rest.

Concrete, asphalt, and other types of hard-surfaced highways were being built also. In fact, the highway era began its gradual dawn around 1920 and there were hundreds of miles of automobile roads in Ecuador by 1940. They followed in general the pattern of the railways. A grand trunk boulevard—Ecuador's part of the Pan-American Highway—started at the Colombian border near Tulcán, continued through Ibarra and Quito to Sibambe, and then on south toward Peru. Another paved road left the trunk route at Ambato and descended the Andes to Guaranda and Babahoyo on its way to Guayaquil. Other highways, under construction or planned, ran, or would run, from the leading towns along the great central boulevard to the tributaries of the Amazon on the east and the Pacific ports on the west. The system was by no means complete; road-building through these high mountains and down their rugged slopes was a difficult task, which became even more difficult through the rain forests to the west and the east. But a good deal had been accomplished and much more was under way; and, once again, contributions by citizens of the United States were large. The Foundation Company of New York and other Yankee organizations, equipped with modern machinery, had built the major part of the automobile roads and would continue their work. Some were constructed by Ecuadorian laborers with pick and shovel and wheelbarrow.

In the meantime, progress was being registered in the mining, petroleum, and electric industries as well as in sanitation. In mining and sanitation, citizens of the United States were taking the lead in collaborating with leaders of Ecuador; in the extraction of petroleum, the British and the Canadians were in the vanguard.

The only mining region of much significance in Ecuador until recently was in the Province of El Oro, southeast of Guayaquil. The South American Development Company, a United States corporation, acquired it from the British in 1897 after the British had worked it for seventeen years. Another rich area in the Province of Cotopaxi was being exploited, since 1938, by the Cotopaxi Exploration Company, controlled by the English, the Canadians, and the Yankees but managed by citizens of the United States, who have formed several other organizations to search for Ecuador's minerals since the outbreak of the second World War. Some of the mining companies were also building roads.

Modern techniques began to be used in producing petroleum in Ecuador during the first World War. They were introduced by the British and, on a smaller scale, by the Ecuadorians themselves. English companies—Anglo-Ecuadorian Oilfields, Limited; Ecuador Oilfields, Limited; and other corporations—were still dominant in the 1940's; but Canadians had been participating for some time, and companies from the United States seemed likely soon to expand their operations. Like the mining organizations, the oil companies were building roads. They were also making rapid explorations by means of airplanes.

The utilization of electricity had expanded gradually but steadily since electric lights began to appear on the streets of Ecuador's cities in the 1890's. The tramways of Guayaquil were electrified shortly after 1900 and those of Quito ten years later, both by citizens of the United States. All the leading towns had electric light plants by 1917 and the number of central power plants had reached twenty-three by 1927. A United States Department of Commerce survey made at the end of 1940 listed fifty-four urban centers with electric utilities. The survey disclosed an impressive trend toward municipal ownership, with forty towns owning their plants. The majority of the electric utilities in private hands belonged to Ecuadorians themselves, but the largest systems were foreign-owned. A subsidiary of American and Foreign Power Company owned the big plant at Guayaquil and a smaller one at Riobamba. A subsidiary of the

Ecuadorian Corporation, Limited, an Anglo-Canadian company, owned both the power plant and the tramway of Quito. The tramways of Guayaquil had finally been acquired by a native company. The combined capacity of these three power plants amounted to nearly half of the total developed capacity of the nation. Its potential capacity was estimated in 1931 at a million horsepower for its rivers alone. Most of the stations are hydro-electric; and because of ample water resources and scarcity of coal, future plants will be of this type. The percentage of Ecuador's some three million inhabitants making use of electricity in one way or another is uncertain. Electricity is probably being utilized (1943) by all of the residents of the mining and petroleum settlements, but it is not likely that half of the inhabitants of the fifty-four towns are able to appropriate the benefits of the new commodity. The majority of the people are certainly too poor to bear the expense of electric appliances such as stoves, refrigerators, and washing machines. The electric age is only beginning in Ecuador.

In sanitation, the country made almost no progress until well after 1900. Sewer and plumbing systems are for the most part improvements of the twentieth century, although some steps were taken to provide these facilities in Guayaquil and Quito at an earlier date. In the late 1880's Guayaquil employed engineers from the United States to pipe pure water from the mountains fifty-three miles away and to install sewers; two of the engineers—Thomas M. Cleeman and William B. Tobey—lost their lives while engaged in the task. James C. Hallock, employed by the national government in 1903 as director of public works, made some improvements in the sewerage and plumbing of Quito; but as late as the 1940's the facilities of the capital were defective.

Ecuador's major efforts in public health and sanitation centered on Guayaquil, where the inhabitants had suffered from the terrible scourge of yellow fever intermittently since 1740. As soon as the cause of the dreaded disease had been identified in Cuba and Panama, agitation for its eradication at Guayaquil began. It was not until 1916, however, that the International Health Board of the Rockefeller Foundation sent its scientists to make a thorough investigation, and not until 1918 that an agent of the board, Michael E. Connor, in co-operation with native physicians, began the attack on the deadly mosquitoes. At the same time, J. G. White and Company of New York and London inaugurated, at the expense of the national government of Ecuador, a vast program of improvement in the sewerage and water supply. The public health campaign was successful. Yellow fever was exterminated by the end of 1919 and Guayaquil soon became as free from dangerous tropical diseases as any other city of tropical Latin America.

Albert B. Franklin, who spent the year 1941 in Ecuador and traveled widely about the country, witnessed numerous instances of co-operation between the United States and Ecuador. Frederick A. McGonigle, graduate of the Idaho School of Mines, was the tactful and efficient manager of the mines in El Oro. "Swede" Holmgren had charge of the mining enterprise at Machuchi, in the Province of Cotopaxi. Arthur Fried, who had been employed by the national government at Quito in 1936 to help set up agricultural co-operatives, was supervising a colony of Spanish exiles. Engineers Rasmussen and Seversen were building highways. Skillful employees of Pan American Grace Airways were managing the airlines, which had been inaugurated by the Germans a few years before. The Ecuador Development Corporation, owned and managed jointly by Ecuadorians and Yankees, was initiating numerous enterprises in public works, agriculture, and industry. Ecuador had received a loan of $1,250,000 from the United States government. Collaboration between the two nations was rounding out a century and economic and technological ties were stronger than ever. A more striking example of practical Pan Americanism would be hard to find.

RAILROAD TO EL DORADO

IT IS ASTONISHING that supposedly hard-headed citizens of the United States should have expected to find El Dorado somewhere in the vast basin of an immense jungle river. This, however, is exactly what they did repeatedly, like Spaniards of the credulous sixteenth century.

El Dorado, which originally meant "The Gilded Man" and referred to a legendary Andean Indian chief who was accustomed to anoint himself with oil, sprinkle his body with gold dust, and take ceremonial baths in a mountain lake, eventually came to signify any region containing abundant riches easy to acquire. At least three times in less than a century not a few people in the United States envisaged such a bonanza land in eastern Bolivia or somewhere else in the immense jungle basin of the Amazon, while others who may have known it was not there pretended to see it for speculative purposes. Men in Washington, Philadelphia, New York, and London poured out glamorous propaganda, emptied the pockets of unwary investors, and sent adventurous workers to die in dank tropical forests.

The first period of enthusiasm was largely the creation of a scientist named Matthew F. Maury, native of Virginia, adopted son of Tennessee, and head of the National Observatory at Washington, who turned his eyes away from the ocean currents and the planets and fixed them on South America. Maury began in 1849 to fill newspapers and magazines with glowing accounts of the Amazon and its tributaries and borderlands. He introduced the subject into a number of commercial conventions, where his exaggerated memorials were adopted and sent to the United States Congress. In the Memphis Commercial Convention of 1853 Maury's Amazonian dreams were championed by the eloquence of Bishop James H. Otey of Tennessee.

Mainly as the result of this agitation, the United States sent two stalwart naval officers, Lieutenants Lardner Gibbon and Lewis Herndon, to spy out the land, examine its resources, and explore its mighty river system in order to discover its potentialities for steam navigation. One of the special advantages of this selection arose from the fact that Herndon was Maury's kinsman.

Quoting, perhaps, his own contribution from Herndon's report, Maury declared that the vast basin of South America's huge river was the "most enchanting" and potentially the richest region on earth:

From its mountains you may dig silver, iron, coal, copper, quicksilver, zinc, and tin; from the sands of its tributaries you may wash gold, diamonds, and precious stones; from its forests you may gather drugs of virtues the most rare, spices of aroma the most exquisite, gums and resins of the most useful properties, dyes of hues the most brilliant, with cabinet and building woods of finest polish and most enduring texture. Its climate is everlasting summer, and its harvests perennial.

Two crops of rice and four of maize could be grown every year, prospects for cotton were unlimited, the bounty of fruits, oils, and nuts was eternal. "The country drained by the Amazon," declared Maury, "would be capable of supporting ... the population of the whole world" if it were "reclaimed from the savage, the wild beast, and the reptile, and reduced to cultivation." Steamboats and immigrants from the United States and Europe, with the latest agricultural implements in their hands and the best mining processes at their command, could create another India at our very doors. The development of the enormous resources of the Amazon's basin would cure all the ills of the United States—unemployment, poverty, the race problem, and the threat of armed conflict between North and South.

Journalists soon took up the alluring theme. A writer in *Hunt's Merchants' Magazine* for July, 1854, for instance, declared that Nature had deposited her most lavish gifts in the great Amazon basin. Cotton was growing on trees eight or ten feet high. Rice, sugar cane, tobacco, and coffee were thriving everywhere. Rubber and drugs, fruits and melons, indigo and every kind of dye were abundant. Gold and silver lay beneath vast stretches of the earth or were drifting in a multitude of rivulets down the eastern slopes of the Andes; diamonds and all varieties of precious stones were on every hand. If no gilded king claimed the fealty of the inhabitants it was not because of any lack of gold dust or turtle oil.

The United States government responded further to the excitement by vigorous negotiations intended to persuade the nations bordering on the Amazon and its tributaries to throw open the great fluvial system to the flags of all the world. No doubt the authorities at Washington were confident that men whose flat-boats had long swarmed on the Ohio and the Mississippi would secure the major part of the shipping on the immense rivers of South America's interior as soon as free access could be obtained.

Ecuador, Peru, and Bolivia, sharing the enthusiasm of the time, gladly granted what the United States wanted; and both Ecuador and Peru welcomed North American colonists and miners into the regions east of the Andes, while Peru, at government expense, ordered two steamers from the United States with the intention of having Yankees man them. Brazilians, however, had shipping ambitions of their own and were frightened by aggressive tendencies in the Anglo-Saxon republic and by this sudden and almost overwhelming interest in the Amazon valley. Sharp encounters occurred between North American and Brazilian diplomats in half a dozen South American capitals; but the Brazilians could not be brought to terms either by a direct or a flank attack. They kept the gates of Paradise closed to foreign steamers until 1867.

What might have happened if domestic discord had not grown more violent in the United States with the passage of the Kansas-Nebraska Bill in 1854 one can only conjecture. The bitter conflict that followed between North and South concentrated attention on domestic affairs, and the flood of enthusiasm for South America subsided. North American mining and colonizing parties in the region east of the Andes suffered bitter hardships and provoked a boundary dispute between Ecuador

and Peru. Some found graves in the jungle; others barely escaped
with their lives. But, as we have seen, the first steamboats were
brought from the United States to the Amazon and turned over
to the Peruvian government early in 1853; and with the backing
of English and Portuguese capital, Brazilians established the
first line of steamers on the great river during the same year.

It was not long before enthusiasm for the center of South
America began to revive. This time it converged on Bolivia
and the jungle basins of the Madeira and the Mamoré. The
purple glow of romance surrounded the very names of these
rivers; like Cape to Cairo the alliteration had a seductive appeal;
and Bolivia badly needed a convenient means of transportation
to the sea. (Robert R. Brown, a citizen of the United States,
obtained the first of Bolivia's railway concessions in 1868. In
1872 another contract was granted, to the famous Henry Meiggs,
who was attempting to improve the finances of the country and
develop its resources.)

The man mainly responsible for creating the mirage of El
Dorado on this occasion, however, was a New England engineer,
soldier, journalist, and speculator named George Earl Church.
Like many a Southerner of the period he possessed a luxurious
beard and the title of Colonel. Later he became famous as a
writer on South American geography and explorations and presented his library to Brown University.

Church spent ten years creating his vision and imparting his
enthusiasm to investors and railway builders. With him the
story of the jungle railroad begins. A series of nineteen falls
and rapids which extended for 225 miles or more along the
Madeira and its Mamoré tributary made steam navigation impossible for this section and navigation by any sort of craft
perilous. If the civilizing influence of steam was ever to be felt
in the region tons of rock would have to be blasted out or else a
railway would have to be built around the obstructions.

Making numerous voyages to South America and England—
traveling half the distance around the earth—Church eventually obtained navigation and railway concessions from Bolivia
and Brazil and induced Bolivia to issue £1,700,000 in bonds to
finance his iron road through the dense forests surrounding
the falls and rapids. He visited the center of his El Dorado only

once, however; late in 1871. Standing by the side of a North American named Silas S. Totten and in the midst of a party of half-clad Indian boatmen who had guided his canoes through the treacherous rivers—standing in all his bearded dignity in the "heart of a vast tropical wilderness, fifteen hundred miles from civilization"—Church, declared one of the enthusiasts, "went through the rude ceremony of turning the first sod for a railway that, with the faith of a Columbus, he firmly believed and fondly

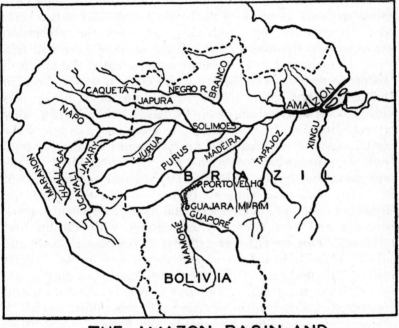

THE AMAZON BASIN AND THE JUNGLE RAILWAY

hoped would open to immigration and to the commerce of the world a country unsurpassed in latent wealth by any unoccupied territory of equal extent on the face of the globe."

Proceeding again to London, Church signed a contract with a British construction company, and engineers and other workers soon advanced to their doom. Three or four supply boats were wrecked along the Amazon; axmen made scars on the matted jungle; surveyors advanced a few miles with their instruments; myriads of mosquitoes and other insects had a feast; scores of workers died of malignant fevers; and the construction firm abandoned its contract. The English company declared it could not build the railway if all the wealth of the earth and half of its population were available for this single enterprise.

But George Earl Church was not ready to acknowledge defeat. He was sure that citizens of the United States could succeed where Englishmen had failed. The Philadelphia Centennial drew the attention of the nation to the "City of Brotherly Love" in 1876 and left hundreds jobless when the celebration was over; and the effects of the Panic of 1873 were still felt. Plenty of engineers and laborers could be had if the vision of El Dorado were dangled before them. Church settled down in Philadelphia and began to fill the columns of its newspapers with glowing descriptions of his Promised Land. Among other extravagant things he said that Bolivia was the "Garden of the Lord," and that the "wealth of Australia and California" would "sink into insignificance beside the auriferous yield of the mountains and streams of Bolivia and the teeming products of her fertile plains and valleys." It was not difficult to gain the support of construction engineers and manufacturers of railway materials and equipment. After signing with Phillip and Thomas Collins on October 25, 1877, a contract to build the railway, Church issued an appeal to national pride. "When finished," he declared, "it will be the only railroad outside the United States constructed from end to end by Americans and ironed and equipped with American rails and rolling stock."

It was not long before enthusiasm had been whipped up to such a pitch that thousands were swarming into the employment office of Collins Brothers. It is said that 80,000 in all applied in person or by letter for the privilege of going to the Brazilian frontier and working on the road. "A national interest centers in the voyage of this ship," wrote the Philadelphia reporter of the *New York Herald* as the *Mercedita* pulled into the docks and began to load its freight and passengers.

On January 2, 1878, the *Mercedita* set sail with 220 on board, many of them Irishmen. Among the passengers were also 54 civil engineers, "the ablest body ever united in a similar expedition."

Twenty-eight days later the vessel arrived at Pará; and it finally reached San Antonio, the headquarters on the Madeira River, on February 19. The *Metropolis* steamed away from Philadelphia amid loudest cheers on January 28 with 221 passengers and one stowaway, most of them Irishmen again. But the *Metropolis* never reached its destination. It was wrecked in a storm off Currituck, North Carolina, three days after setting out, and 80 of its passengers were lost. In spite of this tragedy the *City of Richmond* was able to leave Philadelphia on February 15 with 467 aboard, the bulk of them Italians and exiles from the Emerald Isle, although Mr. and Mrs. Thomas Collins were among the cabin passengers. It arrived at San Antonio on May 23, 1878.

Meantime, the assault on the jungle had been resumed. A Brazilian customs officer remarked: "When the Englishmen came here they did nothing but smoke and drink for two days, but the Americans work like the devil." Another witness declared: "Every inch of the line had to be cut through almost impenetrable vegetation. Quite frequently immense trees, after being ... [severed] at the base, would continue to stand ... held firmly in place by a network of vines.... Surveying through these forests was like surveying by the light of a lantern at midnight."

Among the engineers who worked on the road were Charles F. King, Joseph S. Ward, Paul J. White, Neville B. Craig, Joseph Byers, Charles W. Buckholz, John B. Dougherty and O. F. Nichols. Among the physicians were E. P. Townsend, Isaac T. Coats, and Edwin R. Heath. Nichols, Coats, and Heath had been with Meiggs in Peru. Dougherty and several of the others spent most of their lives building railways in Latin America's tropics.

The jungle struck back again. The humid heat was relentless; millions of stinging and biting insects made life miserable day and night; swarms of crickets and roaches ate the men's clothes and gnawed their shoes; termite ants destroyed everything except concrete and steel; rivers where bathing might have brought relief were inhabited by alligators and fierce cannibal fish. Dreadful diseases attacked the technicians, as well as the common laborers: malaria, dysentery, yellow fever, and every kind of jungle plague swept through the camps and the headquarters.

For exactly eighteen months the battle continued. Of the 719 who arrived from the United States about 140 died on the railway line. Many others perished in attempts to escape through the thick forests; perhaps the majority of those who finally got back home either died from the effects of their suffering or never fully recovered their health.

Aside from two hundred Bolivians and twice as many Brazilians who helped with the clearing and grading, the toughest of the lot were an Irishman known to this story only as "Old Mike" and a Southerner named Joseph Byers. "Old Mike" "dosed the dying and buried the dead," serving as grave-digger, priest, and nurse. Byers, who had fought the Indians in the West, fought the men in Blue during the Civil War, and dragged cypress logs out of the Louisiana swamps, was the first to plunge into the wilderness at San Antonio and the last to abandon the railroad enterprise. He bore every misfortune with a grim smile and stoic indifference, fortified by the strongest brand of whisky he could buy.

A good part of the line was surveyed, some twenty-five miles were graded, nearly four miles of rails were laid, and on July 4, 1878, an engine named for Colonel Church began to pull a few work cars over the track. The last of the victims abandoned the jungle on August 19, 1879, and left the tools and rolling stock to rust. Thirty years later some of them were found by intrepid men who returned; but most of the graves had disappeared in the rank vegetation.

"There probably never was an expedition of similar character," remarked one of the survivors, "conducted . . . with less knowledge of the peculiar but fixed conditions of the country or with less effort to obtain this knowledge." Food was improper and inadequate, and almost no sanitary precautions were taken. Even the supply of medicines gave out and "Old Mike" administered "fraudulent quinine pills" to men quaking with malaria. Few if any of the laborers ever received full pay for the work they did. In fact, the supply of money was cut off; the British bondholders embargoed the railroad funds and after a long and complicated suit in the English courts recovered most of them and bankrupted the enterprise, which the jungle probably would have destroyed in any case.

A quarter of a century afterwards Brazil, excited by the activities of Bolivia backed by rubber financiers of the United States and England, seized the Acre Territory, which had long been in dispute with Brazil's neighbor to the west. In order to appease Bolivia the Brazilian government agreed to pay the cost of building the Madeira-Mamoré Railway. A construction contract signed with a Brazilian in 1906 was transferred the next year to Percival Farquhar and the Madeira and Mamoré Railway Company which he incorporated in the State of Maine. This company then undertook to superintend the building of the iron road under another contract concluded with May, Jekyll, and Randolph of New York, an engineering firm with experience in railroad construction in Cuba and Guatemala.

Once more the newspapers and magazines were crowded with glowing news of the great undertaking. The story of the tragic efforts of the 1870's was published in 1907 more as a decoy than as a warning. Already the survivors had begun to assemble in annual banquets and take on the semblance of heroes. The account of the unfortunate episode of 1878-1879 was embellished with quotations from Church and the Bolivians. The narrative dwelt at length on Potosí and all the "treasure-houses" of the Andes, on rich soils adapted to the growth of every kind of tropical crop, and upon rubber, quinine, coca, cabinet woods, and all the products of the forests. Published by Neville B. Craig under the title of *Recollections of an Ill-fated Expedition to the Headwaters of the Madeira River in Brazil,* the book was widely reviewed. Its optimistic conclusion follows:

What the effect of making this vast and fertile region easily accessible from the Atlantic coast will be, no man can tell, but two things are certain. A greater commercial development will follow than any ever predicted by Colonel Church and the nation which controls the Madeira and Mamoré Railway is sure to exert a far-reaching influence over the trade ... of the two Americas.

Already the plantation rubber of the Orient was on the point of demolishing the hopes that were being created! But the vision of El Dorado was renewed, and once again men embarked from every quarter for the jungle. The reluctant were won over by high wages, pride in achievement, eagerness for adventure, and glowing accounts both of medical triumphs in the tropics and of the lavish facilities provided for the workers.

This time the railway was actually built. Work began in August, 1907, and the road was placed in operation section by section with as much fanfare as conditions permitted. The final section was opened to public traffic on July 15, 1912. The railroad was 227 miles (363.4 kilometers) long and of narrow gauge. The rusty old engine of 1878 vintage, the "Colonel Church," was dragged from the forests, renovated, and placed on the track for the great occasion. A tall tree had grown out of its smokestack. John Barrett of the Pan American Union sent a delegate to represent his organization at the celebration; but the president of Brazil did not appear as originally planned.

In spite of improved food, modern sanitation, and medical care, death and disease had taken a heavy toll of the builders. The total of deaths was said to have been 500 in 1909, 417 in 1910, 390 in 1911, and 222 in 1912. The fatalities for 1907 and 1908 are unknown to this writer, as are the numbers who suffered illness or returned home as invalids for the rest of their lives. The total annual average of workers and technicians employed was approximately 4000. "At times there were 25 different nationalities on the pay rolls of the company ... blacks, whites, browns, yellows, and reds"; but mostly Italians, Spanish *Gallegos,* Bolivians, and Brazilians. The turnover was large. At one period and another some 25,000 laborers must have worked on this railway. "Most of the men on this job have not been here three months," said one of them to H. M. Tomlinson in 1910. "They come and shovel a little dirt, and die. Or they get frightened, and go." "An unknown Somebody in Wall Street or Park Lane has an idea, and this is what it does. . . . It moves men . . . down to this desolation. . . . Have you seen the graveyard here? We've got a fine cemetery, and it grows well."

Among the engineers who built the road were Harvey C. Miller, P. H. Ashmead, F. C. Englesing, John Y. Bayliss, and A. E. Hess. "The admiration of the world," declared Albert Hale of the Pan American Union, "must ... be given to the plucky contractors who, against overwhelming odds, ... completed their task in this faraway wilderness." Ashmead held a different view. More than a year before the railway was completed he paid this tribute to individuals who confronted graver risks:

As the pioneer whom the construction men follow, the engineer faces the first and greatest dangers. He collects his supplies,... gathers his men together, and stoically heads up river toward the front with a knowledge of the history of the sickness, death, and hardships suffered by previous expeditions. He works during all the daylight in the field and far into the night in his camp, ... and there are few of his kind who hesitate to follow orders honestly and loyally.

Tomlinson was much impressed by a tall, lank Texan named Marion Hill, who rode the line as a sort of camp inspector, general supervisor, and guard. Hill wore muddy riding breeches, a black shirt open at the throat, boots that reached nearly to his thighs, a "ten-gallon" *sombrero,* a wicked pair of spurs, and a "waistbelt heavy with guns and ammunition." "I saw his face," said Tomlinson, "and divined instantly that this was a man." Tomlinson rode with Hill for days through the primeval forests and the work camps. He was a "leader ... who could do things, when there seemed nothing one could do."

Meantime the new vision of El Dorado had expanded enormously. The alliterative railway was but a tiny segment of the immense transportation empire that Percival Farquhar was planning. With the backing of investors in the United States, Canada, France, and a good part of Europe, this Broad Street plunger aspired to dominate the shipping business of the Amazon and all of its affluents and a railway network extending from Rio de Janeiro across southern Brazil and through Uruguay, Paraguay, Argentina, and Bolivia to the Pacific Ocean. In 1906 he had incorporated in Maine the Brazil Railway Company, which soon spawned thirty-eight subsidiaries. Through this organization he controlled not only the Madeira and Mamoré Railway but most of the steamboats on the Amazonian system, the ports of Pará and Rio Grande do Sul, thousands of miles of railroad extending across southern South America, packing houses in Brazil, and millions of acres of timber, rubber, and grazing lands in Paraguay, Brazil, and Bolivia. Twelve investment-banking houses were selling his securities in most of the markets of the world. In charge of their flotation in the United States were Speyer Brothers and Kuhn, Loeb and Company.

But if Farquhar rose like a rocket, he fell like a meteor. The first World War struck his inflated organization a mortal blow. Piece by piece his immense structure went into receivership, no doubt with tremendous losses to imprudent investors, but with plenty of commissions and fees for bankers and attorneys.

The jungle railroad, built at a cost of thousands of lives and ten million dollars, mostly Brazilian money, was a financial failure. Bolivia's minerals were indeed exploited, but they were taken out over the railways leading to the Pacific—iron roads constructed by Henry Meiggs and the British—and through the new Panama Canal. After lasting half a century, the thriving rubber trade of the great Amazon basin collapsed, practically destroyed by cheap plantation rubber of the Middle East, and little else that yielded income for a railway in the heart of the continent was developed to take its place. Depression came to the jungle before it settled on the rest of the world in the early 1930's, and left more machinery and rolling stock to rust in the rainy wilderness. Whatever profits they may have obtained from the manufacture of rubber, citizens of the United States had little share in those derived from collecting the raw product from the trees of the Amazon Basin. Here the rewards went to Brazilians and Europeans.

But realism and despair are not synonymous even in a South American jungle. In the 1940's millions of rubber trees were said to be reaching maturity on Henry Ford's Amazonian plantations, and thousands of rubber-gatherers, shielded by the Brazilian government from the worst of the cruel exploitation to which they had been subjected by the grasping local merchants of earlier years, were again roaming the forests. With synthetic rubber on the way, and with the Middle East's plantation product sure, sooner or later, to reappear in world markets, rubber might or might not become the basis of the Amazon's prosperity. Yet the material foundations of its civilization might be erected on other commodities. New men, new techniques, and new products might eventually succeed in mastering the vast basin of the Amazon, where scarcely two million people live today, the majority of them with few of the comforts and conveniences of civilization. Until they do, this El Dorado is still a myth.

AMBASSADORS OF SCIENCE AND
TECHNOLOGY IN BRAZIL

THE COMMITTEE of experts from the United States who made the tour of investigation in South America in 1941 alluded to the work of two of their countrymen in Brazil. One of its members noted that Herbert S. Polin was busy experimenting with coffee plastics and that Walter Swingle of the United States Department of Agriculture was collaborating in the development of a tung-oil industry.

These two scientists, and no doubt others then in Brazil, were but the latest of the numerous specialists who had made their contributions to the development of the resources of that country. The full list of names stretching back over a century would include almost every type of scientist and technologist from the mechanical and civil engineer, the dentist, and the physician to the explorer, the zoologist, the botanist, the geologist, the chemist, and the geographer. A history of their activities would require a volume. Among the first to arrive were dentists and physicians and the mechanics who helped to install steam engines in the rice and cotton mills. Perhaps the most important contributions were made by geologists and paleontologists. On their work this chapter will be concentrated.

Louis Agassiz, head of a group of scientists who composed the Thayer Expedition of 1865-1866, so named because it was financed by Nathaniel Thayer of Massachusetts, was surprised to discover that Brazil had neither a school of mines nor a geological survey. Largely as the result of Agassiz's influence and that of his colleagues, Brazilians would possess both within a decade. A native of Switzerland but a naturalized citizen of the United States and the most learned visitor from the north up to that time, Agassiz made his journey for the purpose of regaining his health and investigating the fresh-water fishes of Brazil. Two geologists, however, were members of his party, and one of them was a young man of twenty-five named Charles Frederick Hartt, a Canadian by birth but a citizen of the United States by adoption.

Hartt was later to organize and become the chief of Brazil's first systematic geological survey. A remarkable personality and teacher, he trained a group of students, North American and Brazilian, who were to become the leading geologists of Brazil and infuse their enthusiasm into still other generations of scientists. Hartt and his "School" discovered and examined a good part of the scientific data and mineral wealth of the country; and along with young Brazilians from the Ouro Preto School of Mines of Minas Geraes, founded in 1875 under the direction of the Frenchman Henri Gorceix, they raised Brazil to a place of distinction among the Latin-American nations in the field of geology and mineralogy. Their work came to full fruition in the 1930's and 1940's with the organization of numerous scientific services by the national government under Getulio Vargas. Most of the scientific and technological bureaus were staffed by natives, who published several treatises and surveys based upon field studies by Brazilians themselves. Starting with almost no trained scientists a little more than a half century before, the nation was rapidly achieving scientific independence.

Hartt returned to the United States from his expedition with Agassiz full of enthusiasm for the vast Empire of Brazil. In 1867 he made another tour of investigation, and in 1870 he brought out the first systematic work ever published on the geology of Brazil. A large octavo volume of more than six hundred pages, it contained an account of his own researches, a summary of previous knowledge regarding Brazilian geology, and a discussion of topography, fauna and flora, and agricultural, mining, and manufacturing enterprises. The excellent maps and sketches were drawn by Hartt himself and the appendix contained a discussion of the Botocudo Indians. A valuable contribution to the geology and physical geography of Brazil, the volume was reprinted as late as 1941.

Hartt's second expedition to Brazil had been financed by the Cooper Institute, by the New York Association for the Advancement of Science and the Arts, and by John Lockwood of Adelphi Academy in Brooklyn. Hartt also acknowledged the assistance of the principal of a "ladies' school" in Jersey City, of a Mr. Van Nostrand of Newark, and of James E. Mills and R. L. Dugdale of New York, as well as Major O. C. James, who was soon to move to Rio de Janeiro. Hartt was much in demand as a lecturer and was offered positions on the faculties of Cornell University and Vassar College. He accepted the chair of geology at Cornell in 1868. Evidently he had aroused a good deal of enthusiasm for Brazilian studies.

Shortly after the publication of his book Hartt found a new patron, E. B. Morgan of Aurora, New York, who financed two vacation expeditions to Brazil, one in 1870 and the other the next year. On the first of these Hartt took with him a Cornell professor of Botany named A. M. Prentice and eleven students, some of whom later became famous for their scientific work in Brazil and the United States. Most distinguished of all were Richard Rathbun, Orville A. Derby, and Herbert H. Smith, who later published a delightful book on the Amazon and eastern Brazil. Back in Cornell in 1872, Hartt spent two years teaching, lecturing to more or less learned audiences, and examining and classifying the results of his Brazilian investigations. He soon began to dream of a thorough geological survey of the whole of Brazil, an idea probably first suggested to him by Agassiz, who died in 1873. In the summer of 1874 he set out on his fourth trip to South America.

Hartt's reception in Brazil after an absence of many months was almost as enthusiastic as that accorded the distinguished Agassiz nine years before. He was elected to membership in most of the learned societies of the country, and requests for lectures poured in. Already a master of Portuguese, he was able to exert the full force of his personality. His plan for the geological survey embraced the organization of a large group of scientists in three divisions, each complete in itself and equipped for field work, but money was lacking for this larger enterprise. The "Geological Commission of the Brazilian Empire," finally organized under government patronage and support on May 1, 1875, was composed of only six specialists: three North Americans and three Brazilians. The former were Hartt himself, who was appointed chief of the commission, and Richard Rathbun and Orville Derby. The Brazilians were Elias Francisco de Paula Jordão, José de Freitas, and Marco Ferrez. John C. Branner, Luther Wagoner, Herbert H. Smith, and Frank Carpenter were added to the commission later; and although never officially members of the organization James A. Mills, who was interested in Brazilian gold mines, and Major O. C. James were liberal with their assistance and advice.

These scientists worked diligently and energetically, suffering the hardships of tropical climate and exposing themselves to mortal disease, for more than two years before the commission was dissolved for lack of finances. The elections which took place while Emperor Dom Pedro II was away in Europe and the United States resulted in failure to provide funds. Upon his return this magnanimous and democratic ruler urged further appropriations upon a new Brazilian parliament elected in 1878; but Hartt died of yellow fever on March 18, 1878, before funds were obtained, and the commission was not revived. Apparently Hartt and Derby worked for several weeks without financial remuneration after the survey was dissolved in July, 1877. Before his untimely death Hartt and his co-workers had made field studies in ten of the twenty provinces of Brazil and collected data which formed the basis of numerous treatises published in the course of the next quarter of a century. Hartt himself published more than twenty articles on Brazil and left in manuscript a dissertation on Brazilian antiquities, a work on the mythology of Brazilian Indians, a grammer of the Tupi language, and an annotated album illustrating life and nature along the lower Amazon. He also organized the geological department of the Brazilian National Museum.

In an address on the life and scientific work of Charles Frederick Hartt read at a meeting of the Boston Society of Natural History in 1878 Richard Rathbun, who later served for many years as head of the United States National Museum, declared that Hartt possessed in a high degree the qualities of a successful leader. Effective both in planning and in execution, he "displayed the greatest skill in utilizing ... diverse results from many sources, never, however, losing sight of the grand whole he was seeking to build up." Derby, as late as 1895, said that

Hartt was "one of the most active, profound, versatile, and disinterested investigators that ever set foot in" Brazil, and declared that his contributions to the geological and archaelogical literature of the country still outweighed "all the rest put together." Twenty years after the young pioneer's death John C. Branner expressed the conviction that "with few exceptions" all the work done in these fields in Brazil since 1875 could be traced directly or indirectly to the "impetus given it by Hartt." Discounting these claims of enthusiastic students, one may still believe that Hartt's work was of great significance. Henri Gorceix declared in 1889 that the Thayer Expedition opened a "new era of geological studies in Brazil," and Hartt constituted the major part of the Thayer Expedition so far as geology was concerned.

Brazilian writers, while not forgetting the contributions of Hartt, are more liberal in their praise of his students. Among those from the United States trained by the young Cornell professor Orville A. Derby and John C. Branner are given most attention. Both continued their Brazilian studies as long as they lived and trained other scientists to continue their work.

The achievements of Derby were truly remarkable. Born in 1851 near Auburn, New York, he enrolled as a country boy in Hartt's classes in Cornell and received his first degree in 1873 after spending two summers with his teacher in Brazil. The next year he obtained his Master's and published his thesis on the Brachiopoda of Rio Tapajós in a scientific bulletin of the University, thus winning distinction as a scientist at the age of twenty-three.

Beginning his work on the Brazilian geological survey late in 1875, Derby refused to leave the country after the commission was extinguished. In 1879 he was appointed curator in charge of geology in the Brazilian National Museum. He remained in this post, publishing a number of articles and monographs in the *Archives* of the Museum, until 1886, when he became official geologist of the Province, later the State, of São Paulo, economically the most important in all Brazil. Resigning in 1904 after years of outstanding service, he continued to reside in the country. In January, 1907, the Federal government of the recently-founded republic set up a geological survey under Miguel

Calmon, minister of public works, and Derby was made its chief, a position which he retained until his death in 1915.

As early as 1906 Branner declared that Derby had "done more than anyone else" to solve the many problems of Brazilian geology, and thirty years later a Brazilian mineralogist called Derby the "founder of Brazilian geology," the most profound scientist who had ever studied the subject, offering as the best proof of his assertions the fact that Derby's studies were still indispensable. Both of these statements may have been too generous, if for no other reason, because they ignored for the moment the fundamental achievements of Hartt. Nevertheless they emphasized the significant contributions of a man who left a lasting impression in Brazil.

Derby published a hundred and twenty-five papers on Brazilian geology, paleontology, and mineralogy and trained scores of Brazilians and North Americans in these scientific fields. Through his influence a number of other treatises, published both by natives and by citizens of the United States, drew the attention of scholars and investors to Brazil. One of Derby's assistants, the able and energetic Horace Williams from the United States, made a thorough topographical survey of the State of São Paulo. Another named Roderic Crandall, also from the United States, made hydrographic surveys in the arid states of the north and laid the foundation for subsequent conservation and irrigation policies. Derby may likewise have been partially responsible for the coal and fossil surveys of Charles Israel White and David White in southern Brazil during the years 1904 and following.

Orville Derby was a man of strong will and unflagging devotion to science. He refused to be discouraged when the Geological Commission of 1875-1877 disbanded, his chief died of yellow jack, and the rest of the North Americans left the country. He was determined to salvage the results of the work of Hartt and his colleagues, and in large measure he succeeded. Although a bachelor all his life, Derby was warmhearted and generous. His time, his sympathies, and all that he had were at the service of his colleagues and friends. "The beggars of the streets found him their easiest victim." During forty years he visited the United States only twice, and shortly before his death he became a Brazilian citizen. J. B. Woodworth of Harvard, who led the Shaler Memorial Expedition to South America in 1908, seems to have mistaken his own countryman for a native of Brazil. Woodworth mentioned Derby's aid with deep appreciation. "With true Latin-American courtesy," said the Harvard professor, Derby "paved the way for me to find what he would have been proud himself to have discovered—the actual occurrence of glaciated pebbles in the tillite beds of Paraná."

After having won the esteem of many Brazilians by his character and work and made himself the leading geologist of South America, Derby committed suicide. On the morning of November 27, 1915, a servant found him lying across his bed in Stranger's Hotel in Rio, where he had resided for several years, "with a bullet-hole in his head and a revolver still grasped in his dead hand." "He left no word of complaint" against anything or anybody. Perhaps his health and vitality were exhausted and he realized that his work was finished, or he may have been despondent because of reduced appropriations occasioned by the first World War. Brazilians of his day sometimes became impatient because of his reluctance to publish the results of investigations and his greater interest in pure than in practical science; but few ever denied the fundamental significance of his work.

The contributions of John Casper Branner, another member of the Brazilian school founded by Charles Frederick Hartt, were scarcely less important. Born of Virginia ancestry in the hills of eastern Tennessee, Branner entered Cornell University in 1870 at the age of twenty, and went to Brazil with Hartt in 1874. Soon afterwards he became a member of the Geological Commission, participating in its explorations until it was dissolved. Then he obtained a position in gold mines of Minas Geraes under the management of James E. Mills, an able North American mining engineer. Leaving this post in 1880, Branner returned to New York and was soon sent back to South America by Thomas A. Edison to search for a vegetable fiber to be used in incandescent lights. Two years later he was commissioned by the United States Department of Agriculture to make a study of cotton culture in Brazil, a task which required several months and resulted, among other things, in the discovery that the boll weevil which had been doing great damage to cotton in the United States had arrived also in the Brazilian cotton fields.

Coming back to the United States in the spring of 1883, Branner interrupted his Brazilian visits for more than a decade but never lost interest in the country. After serving on the geological surveys of Pennsylvania and Arkansas and teaching geology both at the University of Indiana and at Leland Stanford University, he returned to the field of his early activities in 1899. Although he maintained his connection with Stanford until his death in 1922 and became vice-president and then president of this institution for a time, his deep interest in Brazil continued until the last. He made a number of expeditions to the great nation of the south, collaborated with its scientists in their investigations, published a text in geology for the Brazilian schools, as well as a Portuguese grammar for students of the United States, wrote scores of papers on Brazilian geology and resources, and brought out an excellent bibliography of the writings on the geology of the country. At a time when little attention was devoted to Brazil in the academic institutions of the United States, Branner made Leland Stanford a center of Brazilian studies and invited distinguished Brazilians to lecture on the campus.

While Branner's field studies in Brazilian geology and mineralogy were less numerous and intense than those of Derby, they were nevertheless sound and significant, and his immediate contribution to cultural interchange between the two countries was much greater. Through his scientific productions and his memorial essays on Hartt, Mills, and Derby, scholars in the United States became familiar with Brazilian geology and resources; hundreds of Brazilian students used his text, which appeared first in 1906 and was reprinted in 1914, and such North American students as were induced to study the language of their big neighbor to the south depended mainly on his Portuguese grammar, which went through three editions between 1910 and 1915.

Hartt, Derby, Branner, and most of the other members of the Cornell Brazilian School were more interested in pure than in utilitarian science. In one of his reports to the Brazilian government Hartt declared: "As is the duty of every scientific man, I have carried on my investigations in a purely scientific way, hoping that later on they would not fail to be of practical importance.... My great desire has been to lay a firm foundation for Brazilian geology...." Branner asserted that Derby was much more interested in paleontology than in economic geology, far more eager to learn how minerals came into existence than to discover their location and exploit them. "To him," said Branner, "a fossil was a thing of beauty, of interest, and value, and a joy forever; but a mine or an industry was, after all, only an industry whose main object was money-getting." Branner's attitude was a little more practical. One of the last papers he published dealt with petroleum prospects in Brazil. But his primary interests were the same. He found as much delight in examining the coral reefs off the coast of Brazil as Derby did in delving into the origins of coal and diamonds. Without minimizing the scientific achievements of Brazilians themselves or of such Europeans as Wilhelm von Eschwege, Peter Wilhelm Lund, and Henri Gorceix, one may truthfully assert that these ambassadors of science and technology from the United States laid the basis for the modern development of Brazil's mineral wealth.

They were also emissaries of good will. All three possessed great charm and dignity, as well as solid intellectual virtues. The beard that each of them wore indicated neither mental lethargy nor physical debility nor lack of the social graces. Branner, in particular, was a most constructive agent in general cultural interchange, effectively continuing the movement initiated in the 1850's by D. P. Kidder and J. C. Fletcher with the publication of their excellent volume on *Brazil and the Brazilians* and stimulated by Dom Pedro II through his visit to the United States in the 1870's and by his deep interest in the literary and mechanical progress of the Anglo-Saxon republic.

THE NEW TECHNOLOGY
IN ARGENTINA

I N AN EPOCH when official relations between the United States
and Argentina are none too cordial it is pleasant to recall
happier days. Relations between the two countries were on the
whole quite friendly during the half-century or so following
the overthrow of the tyrant Manual Rosas in 1852.

The friendship grew out of mutual appreciation. Outstanding Argentines like Justo José Urquiza, Juan B. Alberdi, and
Domingo F. Sarmiento sincerely admired the institutions and
mechanical genius of the United States, and many people in
this country, gratified by the attitude of distant neighbors whom
they expected to grow more and more like themselves, were
deeply interested in Argentina. After leading the successful
revolt against Rosas, Urquiza presided over the organization of
his nation under a federal system frankly modeled on that of
the United States; Alberdi made important contributions to the
new régime; Sarmiento became the forceful educational leader
of the nation and its "schoolmaster president"; other *Argentinos*
carried on in the same spirit. Sarmiento, whose friendly contacts with the Americans of the North began in 1847 and continued for the remainder of his long life, probably contributed
more than anyone else to cordial relations between the two
peoples.

Assistance from the United States in the development of
Argentina was not confined to political and educational ideas
and practices. It extended into the realm of natural science and
technology, where a number of North Americans made valuable contributions. William Wheelwright and Thomas Jefferson
Page head the list, at least chronologically; but it contained

many other distinguished names, and the collaboration continued into the twentieth century.

Economic advance in Argentina as in other countries has been determined by its natural resources, its people, and its relations with the world beyond its borders. Among the potent foreign influences were those of capital and technology. The industrialization of Europe and the United States, which made possible the production of more goods, also made possible large accumulations of capital and a vast increase of population, provided foreign markets and adequate food could be found. Since the agricultural and pastoral commodities of the European countries were not sufficient for the growing population, those who controlled and directed European economy looked abroad for other sources of supply. Argentina seemed to be full of promise, and capital and technology promptly began to flow in that direction.

Among the new machines, devices, and processes that came to Argentina were not only the steamboat, the locomotive, and the telegraph, but also agricultural machinery, wire for fences, steel windmills, refrigeration and various means of preparing foods, scientific farming and stockbreeding, telephones, electric power, new methods of improving roads, and many more. All this technology reached the country by virtue of the emigration of ideas and technicians and the exportation of manufactured products, capital, and technical formulas; and, of course, it was an important factor in the rapid transformation of the nation into one of the world's leading exporters of meat, wheat, and other food products and an important purchaser of manufactured commodities.

It is not necessary to dwell upon the well-known fact that a good many of the new machines, methods, and processes as well as an enormous amount of money and numerous managers and experts came from the British Isles. The British, for instance, built most of the railroads, founded Argentina's packing industry, collaborated in improving farming and stock raising. The contributions of the United States to Argentine cultural and economic development are less familiar.

William Wheelwright of Massachusetts, as noted elsewhere, built the first railway of any length in Argentina, the 250 miles of track between Rosario and Córdoba. He also constructed the short line southward from Buenos Aires to the port of Ensenada. His work was so warmly appreciated that Alberdi wrote a biography to commemorate his services and praise the nation that produced him.

The annals of railroad building in Argentina contain other Yankee names besides Wheelwright's, although none whose achievements were so notable. Allan Campbell, the capable engineer brought by Wheelwright from the United States, surveyed two routes across the Andes, one of which was followed later by the famous Transandine Railway between Argentina and Chile. John G. Meiggs, brother of the remarkable Henry Meiggs, contributed to the construction of at least three Argentine iron roads. Russell R. Pealer was building a railway in the Province of Entre Ríos in 1885. Percival Farquhar's immense plans for the development of South American transportation included the improvement of the Argentine railroad system; but his efforts were frustrated, as we have seen, partly by the first World War. A Vermont Yankee named Edward Augustus Hopkins advocated numerous Argentine projects, some of which included the construction of railways; but Hopkins was mostly a visionary. He managed, however, to make a living by means of his various activities and to keep in the good graces of the Argentine government. After spending nearly forty years in the country he appeared in Washington in 1891 as secretary of Argentina's delegation to an international railway conference, and there he died on June 11 of that year. Besides introducing the first steam engines and several other machines into Paraguay, he established the first shipyard on the Río de la Plata and perhaps sent the first merchant steamers up the Paraná and the Paraguay to Asunción. These achievements, made by Hopkins in the 1850's, compensate for many of his later failures in railway and telegraph enterprises.

While Hopkins was hatching his schemes to improve his fortune and develop the Río de la Plata area, and while Wheelwright and Campbell were making their railway surveys, Thomas Jefferson Page—a Virginian, of course—was engaged in examining the rivers of the region in order to determine their navigability for steamers and ascertain the commercial potentialities of South America's Southland. Employed at first by the government at Washington and later by that at Buenos Aires, Page spent altogether nearly thirty years in Argentina.

He arrived on the scene in 1853 under the auspices of the United States Navy Department and spent three years exploring the Paraná, the Paraguay, the Uruguay, and other rivers of the Plata system. In 1859 he went back to resume his work, but returned home in 1861 to fight for Virginia and the Confederacy. Then, in 1865, he left his native land for good and settled down on a ranch in Entre Ríos. In 1871 he began further explorations of the Bermejo, and a few years later he was sent to England by the Argentine government to supervise the construction of ironclads and gunboats. He came back to Argentina for a time; but having passed threescore and ten, he decided in 1880 to move to Florence, Italy. He died in Rome in 1899, in his ninety-second year. This "unreconstructed Rebel" probably saw more of Argentina than was seen by any other man before the age of the airplane. His Río de la Plata and Argentine explorations by water and land covered more than 8000 miles.

Returning to Sarmiento, the reader may recall that this distinguished Argentinian served as minister in the United States during the bloody 1860's. Already, on his earlier visit, he had discussed educational problems with Horace Mann and developed a deep admiration for the great New England educator. Subsequently Mann had died, but Sarmiento renewed his personal relations with Mrs. Mann and later obtained through her the services of a number of schoolteachers. During his residence in Washington he also began a correspondence with Benjamin A. Gould, an able New England astronomer who was eager to scrutinize the stars of the Southern Hemisphere.

Until after the middle of the nineteenth century, Argentina had no state system of free schools for its people. The founding of free elementary schools was the joint work of the national and the provincial governments, a task in which the national government usually took the lead. The system was established during the administrations of Sarmiento, Nicolás Avellaneda, and Julio Roca, who served in turn as chief executives of the nation from 1868 to 1886. These statesmen and their administrative associates were the founders of Argentina's public elementary schools, but they were ably assisted by teachers from the United States.

Since the nation had almost no teachers with the capacity and disposition required to inaugurate a system of primary education for the children of the people, it was necessary at the very outset to establish teacher-training schools, and between 1871 and 1886 more than thirty of these were opened in almost every part of the country. Some were for men; more were for women; a few were for both sexes—"mixed" as they were described in the official documents. It was in connection with these normal schools that the Yankee teachers made their contribution to public education in Argentina.

The first of the training schools, the "mixed" normal at Paraná, was opened in 1871, with a New Englander named George Stearns as director. The fourth, the normal for men at Tucumán, was founded in 1874, with John W. Stearns, probably a relative of George Stearns, as director. Women teachers were imported in greater numbers. A total of some thirty or forty were employed during the twenty years following 1871, mainly in the women's normals and the "mixed" normals. Most of them were from Boston or other parts of Massachusetts and New England; but some were from the West, from Michigan, Wisconsin, and Missouri.

As a rule, these women went down to Argentina on three-year contracts and studied Spanish in the normal at Paraná before they began to teach. Their salaries were high for the period, for they received from 150 to 200 Argentine *pesos* a month, the equivalent of nearly as many dollars in money of the United States. Many held administrative posts of one kind or another. Twelve or fifteen were "directresses" or "vice-directresses" of normals for women or for both sexes. Others had charge of schools for practice teaching, which were connected with almost every normal, or of kindergartens, of which there were six in 1892, for instance, each attached to one of the teacher-training schools. Prominent among the women were Frances Armstrong, Edith Howe, and Mary O. Graham; practically all were noted for their character, capacity, and industry.

These normal schools were rather elementary institutions. In the majority, the course of study ran for only three years; others offered a five-year course designed to train teachers for the staffs of the other normals. But over the years the Yankee women helped to train hundreds of teachers, laying the foundations of Argentina's public-school system and advancing the nation to front rank among Latin-American countries in popular education.

During the same period, Benjamin A. Gould was promoting both pure and practical science. A native of Massachusetts, a graduate of Harvard, founder of the *Astronomical Journal,* member of the staff of the United States coastal survey, Gould first communicated with Sarmiento in 1865. At the beginning he sought merely the customary good offices of the Argentine minister in carrying out his plan to map the heavens below the equator; but under the stimulus of the enthusiastic *Argentino* his plan broadened until eventually he accepted an invitation, extended by Sarmiento as chief executive of Argentina, to found and direct an astronomical observatory. After a trip to Europe in search of equipment, Gould arrived in Buenos Aires in August of 1870. Shortly afterward he proceeded to Rosario, where he and his family spent the night at the home of William Wheelwright, and from there they traveled over Wheelwright's new railroad to Córdoba, where the observatory was soon constructed.

With the support of Argentine officials, the inspiration of his wife, who was the daughter of Josiah Quincy of Boston, and the assistance of eager young men from both the United States and Argentina, Gould won fame by his discoveries, and the rich fruits of his investigations were later published in fifteen volumes at the expense of the Argentine national government. But he suffered severe personal misfortunes while in Argentina. Two of his five children were drowned in 1874 and his wife died in 1883. Broken in health and spirit, he began to think of returning to New England and the scientific friends of his earlier years. He left Argentina in 1884 and settled in Cambridge, where he lived until his death in 1896.

Shortly after Gould departed for Cambridge, a commission sent out by the United States government to investigate the foreign trade of Latin America arrived in Buenos Aires. There its members were impressed by the intimate relationships between their countrymen and the Argentine statesmen. The venerable Sarmiento presented information on the progress of education, and several United States citizens, a few of them "old-timers" in this temperate Southland, appeared before the commission. Among the first to seek to enlighten the investigators was Edward Augustus Hopkins, who began by informing them that he was engaged in building "railroads, wharves, telegraphs, and steamboats." Russell R. Pealer presented a summary of Argentine railway history filled with enthusiasm in regard to future contributions that might be made by capitalists and engineers of the United States. Dwight W. Lowe, editor of the Buenos Aires *Herald,* a newspaper published in English, dwelt upon the recent importation of fifty ready-made houses from the United States in connection with the founding of La Plata, the new capital of the Province of Buenos Aires. Samuel B. Hale, head of an important mercantile firm which he had established in 1833, discussed commercial problems and prospects. For some reason, Benjamin D. Manton, a Rhode Island Yankee, did not come before the commission; perhaps he was too busy with his various telephone enterprises.

Always a promoter, Hopkins urged that the United States should help subsidize a line of steamers between the republics of the Far North and the Far South and transmitted a copy of a recent memorial which he had prepared on the subject. In this document he stressed the political and educational contributions made by his countrymen to Argentina. He listed more than a dozen works by citizens of the United States on political theory and constitutional law which had been translated into Spanish and published in Buenos Aires at government expense; referred to Gould and his Astronomical Observatory and the work of the schoolteachers; and offered evidence that the Argentines were willing to do their part in financing the steamship line.

Hopkins and a number of North Americans who appeared before the commission in both Buenos Aires and Montevideo expressed the conviction that a good share of the markets of the two countries could be obtained by the United States if only cheap transportation could be had and the tariff on wool reduced. Already the North Americans had the market for kerosene, and they were selling considerable barbed wire and agricultural machinery. In both Uruguay and Argentina, equipment for railways was being purchased in England, in part because the English were the owners and operators of the roads, but also in part because of discrimination in shipping rates. With reference to the cordiality of the Argentines and their appreciation for the North American schoolteachers, scientists, and technicians, all witnesses were in agreement.

After Gould left Argentina, one of his assistants, John Thome, a citizen of the United States, became head of the Córdoba observatory. Another assistant, Walter G. Davis of Vermont, took charge of the Meteorological Service, which Gould had induced the Argentine government to establish as early as 1872. This service, set up under Gould's direction and managed by him without additional compensation, became increasingly important. During the twelve years following 1872 some 52 stations were established. In several of them observations were carried on for periods of two years or more; others were discontinued after a few months for lack of appropriations. Late in 1884, however, 17 were still active. Under Gould's administration, four volumes on Argentine meteorology were published, accurate isothermal maps were constructed, and the service was established on a permanent basis. Taking over the work in 1885, Davis set up during the next thirty years more than 2000 stations in Argentina and immediately adjacent regions. He also established a weather bureau, a hydrometric section, and a magnetic section, and published a number of scientific works. He returned to Vermont in 1915 with a high reputation among meteorologists everywhere, and died four years later at the age of sixty-eight.

Davis was succeeded in the directorship of the Meteorological Service, the central office of which had been moved to Buenos Aires in 1901, by George O. Wiggins, another citizen of the United States, who retained a number of North Americans on his staff, L. G. Schults, F. H. Bigelow, and H. H. Clayton among them.

The pioneering of Page, Gould, Davis, and their associates from the United States and Argentina made the rivers and the climate of the region better known than those of any other part of South America. Their investigations and records were of immense value in navigation, flood control, electrification, and irrigation. In irrigation and electrification, Argentina forged ahead of every nation in Latin America. Theodore N. Vail, the Yankee telephone magnate, with the assistance of James W. McCrosky and an Englishman named Charles R. Thursby, built Argentina's first hydroelectric plant near Córdoba in 1897-1898 and installed the nation's first trolley lines, in Córdoba and Buenos Aires. Walter G. Davis, during one of his few vacations, had been Vail's guest at the latter's Vermont estate, Speedwell Farms! Thus one may observe the direct connection between pure science and technology and business in Argentina.

Closely related to the work of Gould, Davis, and their associates was that of Bailey Willis and his staff in northern Patagonia. Willis, still in his early fifties when he arrived in the Far South, was already a distinguished geologist. A native of New York and a graduate of the Columbia School of Mines, he had taken part in railway surveys in the Pacific Northwest, lectured on geology at Johns Hopkins and at the University of Chicago, made explorations in China, and served for a quarter of a century on the United States Geological Survey. The Patagonian survey began early in 1911 when Willis arrived with a staff composed of his own countrymen and a few citizens of Argentina. They spent four years investigating topography, climate, soils, water supply, and timber resources. The official title of the scientific organization headed by Willis was that of Commission of Hydrological Studies, but its functions were broadly interpreted.

Among the experts from the United States who served at one time or another on the commission were: C. W. Washburn and three other members of the United States Geological Survey; J. R. Pemberton, a geologist from Stanford University; Wellington D. Jones, a geographer from the University of Chicago; two civil engineers employed to make railway surveys; and two young men from the Middle West who served as general assistants. Emilio Frey of Argentina was assistant director, three Swiss-born *Argentinos* were members of the topographical corps, and two natives of the republic were employed as secretaries.

The North Americans cheerfully confronted the hardships of the Argentine frontier. Bailey and Jones worked for weeks with *machetes* in the cold rain, hewing out a trail to a pass for a railroad across the Andes after native workers had abandoned the enterprise and gone away to more civilized and less strenuous parts of the country.

Willis and his staff carefully investigated and disclosed the resources of northern Patagonia. In 1914 he published a large volume and a number of maps setting forth the work accomplished up to that time. The pampas, mountains, lakes, forests, and rivers of the region were discussed in detail and sites were suggested for towns, resorts, and industries. Jones brought back to the United States samples of various woods, which were examined by the national Forestry Service, and later published a monograph on the status and possibilities of agricultural land utilization in Patagonia.

Such, in summary, were some of the significant contributions made by citizens of the United States to the development of Argentina. Others might be mentioned, as, for instance, those in meat-packing. But sufficient illustrations have been presented to suggest that technological collaboration might become the means of improving present-day relations between the two leading nations of the Americas. At any rate, it is to be hoped that a way will soon be found to overcome commercial rivalries and political jealousies and inaugurate another era of friendly cooperation.

TECHNOLOGICAL ADVANCE IN COSTA RICA
DURING THE GUARDIA ERA

OFFICIAL RELATIONS between Costa Rica and the United States during the 1870's and 1880's were of minor importance and at times not entirely cordial; but it is not the writer's intention to discuss diplomatic history of the traditional type; his purpose is to describe an episode in the migration of technology. The twenty years following the seizure of the Costa Rican government by Tomás Guardia and his followers in 1870 were in many ways a very constructive era in that country; and foreigners, especially citizens of the United States, made important contributions to the achievements of the period.

The progress of Costa Rica during the preceding fifty years should not be ignored or minimized. These early years of the national epoch were neither an era of somnolence and stagnation nor one of grave political disorders. They were an epoch of increasing stability and prosperity. Stationary steam engines were introduced into the mining and lumbering industries; coffee trees were planted on a hundred hills; the natural resources of the country were investigated; cart roads were constructed between the leading towns of the central plateau, and from San José to the Pacific port of Puntarenas; and in the 1850's a subsidy was granted to a North American steamship company in order to induce it to furnish more frequent and speedy shipping facilities along the Pacific coast. Advances were made also in medicine and sanitation; two hospitals were founded, one in San José and the other in Puntarenas; epidemics were controlled more effectively; and plumbing was introduced into the national capital. Moreover, education received increasing support at all levels; and the latest constitution, that of 1869, proclaimed the principle of religious toleration. The achievements of this first half-century were full of promise for the future. During the two decades following 1870 much greater strides were taken.

Between 1870 and 1890 Costa Rica was almost completely "modernized" under the vigorous guidance and control of a single family. Próspero Fernández, who took charge of the national government after the death of Guardia in 1882, was Guardia's brother-in-law; and Fernández, at his death in 1885, was succeeded by Bernardo Soto, who was the son-in-law of Fernández. The epoch was signalized by rapid progress in education, sanitation, transportation, communications, and agriculture; and some advances were made in mining and stock raising. Lands and other forms of wealth were more widely distributed, wages increased, the intellectual level of the people was raised, and the dominance of the old aristocracy was broken.

Government, of course, was not conducted in an altogether democratic manner during the Guardia era. The press was not entirely free; members of the opposition were occasionally persecuted; elections were dominated by the chief executives; lawmakers were sometimes reduced to the status of puppets; and force was often used as a political instrument. But repressive policies were employed less frequently by Guardia's two successors than by Guardia himself; and in 1889 Bernardo Soto not only permitted but supported one of the few fair elections in Costa Rican history up to that time. Thus the Guardia era was not an era of democracy; but it was an epoch of preparation for democracy and one of those instances, rather rare in Latin America at that time, of dictatorship shaping the life of a nation so as to make dictatorship unnecessary and almost impossible in the future. Material progress without full individual freedom; and yet religious toleration and growing opportunities for education and enlightenment, with an inevitable trend toward greater liberty and democracy—these were the salient features of the Guardia period. Within a few decades after the end of the Guardia era, Costa Rica was to become one of the most democratic, stable, and prosperous countries in Latin America.

Costa Ricans themselves have been the first to point out the notable contributions of foreigners to this social and economic transformation. Englishmen, Germans, Frenchmen, and Spaniards, as well as citizens of the United States and of various Latin-American countries, all collaborated with Costa Ricans in introducing the latest medical practices and the latest inventions of technology. A good part of the capital was furnished by the British, and some of the civil engineers, physicians, and teachers were Englishmen, too. Several of the scientists and technologists were Germans and Frenchmen, and a number of the educators were from these two countries also, although most of the foreign educators were from Spain or Spanish America. In a surprisingly large measure the technical skills and business management which effected the modernization of Costa Rica came from the United States.

The population of Costa Rica was, of course, not large. The inhabitants of the country numbered slightly over 65,000 in 1824, less than 158,000 in 1875, and only a little more than 243,000 in 1892. Nor did foreigners bulk large in the total, for there were only 4672 aliens in the country in 1883 and 6856 in 1888. Among the foreigners, those from countries where technology was relatively advanced were far in the minority. The total for citizens of the United States was 130 in 1883 and only 250 in 1888; the Germans numbered 240 and 298 respectively, while the figures for the English were 195 and 247 and those for the French were 198 and 233. But the contributions of these foreigners to the transformation of Costa Rica during the Guardia era were far greater than their meager numbers might suggest.

Anglo-Saxon names occupy considerable space in the list of physicians who practiced their profession in Costa Rica during the nineteenth century, and the names of several citizens of the United States were among them. The first of the North American *médicos* to arrive was Stephen Curtis, who entered Costa Rica near the end of the eighteenth century and remained until he was compelled to flee in order to escape the clutches of the colonial Inquisition. He seems to have been deeply devoted to his profession, more interested in science and service than in financial gains. Of similar character was James Hogan, who arrived in San José in 1854 and was for several years in charge of the San Juan de Dios Hospital in that city. Hogan married a Costa Rican wife and practiced medicine with striking unselfishness until his death in 1864. Another prominent physician from the United States was Charles Lordly, who arrived in 1875 in connection with a railway enterprise and not only followed the medical profession but also opened a drugstore. These are only the most conspicuous; there were several others, and there were dentists as well as physicians.

Gradually, however, Costa Rica was producing a corps of physicians of its own. The first of them were trained in Scotland; others were educated in Guatemala, the United States, and elsewhere. After the middle of the century courses in medicine began to be offered at the University of San Tomás, founded in 1843. During the same period also a national board of examination and supervision, called *El Protomedicato* after the terminology of the colonial epoch, was established, efforts were made to provide "physicians of the people"—apparently a form of subsidized medical service for the poor—and more vigorous attempts were made to control epidemics.

The science of sanitation had its beginnings in Costa Rica shortly before the dawn of the Guardia era, as already observed. San José was the first Costa Rican city to install plumbing. The building of the reservoirs and laying of the water pipes were initiated in 1865 and completed in 1869. Apparently the work was supervised by a German engineer named Franz Kurtze. Plumbing was installed in Cartago in 1874, in Heredia in 1879, in Alajuela in 1880, and in Liberia and Limón in 1899. The laying of the water pipes in Heredia was supervised by an Englishman named John Brealey, probably the son of an English physician who had been living in the country since 1835. In the other towns mentioned the plumbing was installed by Costa Rican and foreign engineers, some of the latter being citizens of the United States. Even as late as 1900, however, Limón was the only town in Costa Rica equipped with underground sewers. Drainage in San José was notoriously imperfect. For several years following 1885 George Ross, a citizen of the United States, held a contract for cleaning and repairing its streets and disposing of its garbage.

In lighting, Costa Rica seems to have skipped the era of gas, making the transition from coal-oil lamps and lanterns, the first of them installed on the streets and plazas of San José in 1856, directly to electricity. Beginning in the early 1870's, ten years of vain efforts were made to introduce gas, Costa Ricans and North Americans being prominent among the promoters. Attempts to employ electricity for lights began as early as 1882. In that year Manuel V. Dengo, a Costa Rican, and Luis Batres, a Guatemalan, were granted a small subsidy by the national government to aid them in their attempts to inaugurate that system of illumination in the leading towns of the republic. Electric lights first appeared on the streets of the capital in August 1884, and they began to be used in Cartago five years later. They were not installed in Alajuela and Heredia until the middle 1890's, and they did not appear in Puntarenas and Limón until 1906 and 1927 respectively. Soon after 1884 Dengo and Batres began to receive the backing of Minor C. Keith, a prominent citizen of the United States, and his associates. Ten years later a Cuban named Francisco Mendiola Boza began to play a prominent part in the electrical enterprises of the country.

Projects for street railways with cars drawn by animals began to be advocated in Costa Rica in the 1870's; but a decade passed before the tramways began to operate. Those of San José, Heredia, and Cartago were built in 1885-1886 by a North American named Silas Wright Hastings, who also constructed and operated a Hippodrome (racetrack) in the capital and a number of markets in Heredia and Cartago. Associated with Hastings in his enterprises in the last-named towns was a naturalized Costa Rican named Thomas Calnek. Electrification of the tramways, which was mainly the work of Minor C. Keith and his British financial supporters, began in 1889. By the late 1890's trolley cars were in operation on the streets of Alajuela as well as those of San José, Cartago, and Heredia. They were among the first to operate in Latin America.

The first telegraph line in the country was built by a North American named Lyman Reynolds. Passing through San José, Heredia, and Alajuela, it connected Cartago and Puntarenas. Constructed by Reynolds in 1868, it was sold to the government the next year. The line between Limón and Cartago was completed by Minor C. Keith in 1881. By 1886 there were 389 miles of telegraph wire and thirty-four telegraph offices in the republic, and Costa Rica already had telegraphic connections with the outside world. The first manager of the government-owned telegraph system was an Englishman, Henry Twight; but Costa Ricans themselves soon took charge, and natives of the country operated the telegraph instruments almost from the outset.

Telephones were used for the first time in Costa Rica in 1886. The circuit, which was constructed under the supervision of Roberto Castro, a native son, connected the various offices of the national government in San José. Two years later Silas Wright Hastings tried to establish a system for private use, but failed. Francisco Mendiola Boza, the Cuban, organized the first telephone company in the country. This enterprise, the Costa Rica Telephone Company, installed telephones in San José, Cartago, Heredia, and Alajuela in 1894 and 1895, and in the course of the next year these new instruments of technology began to be employed in Puntarenas and Limón. Keith was a stockholder in the company.

Mining was sporadic and not very remunerative until near the end of the Guardia era. The mountain districts of the country were known to contain fairly valuable deposits of gold, silver, and copper; but efforts to work them had not been brilliantly successful, and the mineral resources of the forested lowlands stretching toward the Caribbean had not been thoroughly explored. Englishmen, among them the famous Richard Trevithick himself, had introduced steam and more modern methods in the 1820's and 1830's; but the Anglo-Costa Rican Mining Company which they organized had collapsed in 1842. In 1868 the Montealegres, the Castros, and other Costa Ricans had set up a company of their own, and soon afterwards had employed Ernest Mellis, a California mining engineer, to examine a number of mining properties. At the same time a search was made for the precious metals and other resources of the region bordering upon the Caribbean. In 1872 Minor C. Keith employed a Philadelphia geologist named William M. Gabb in this quest; and three years later a company composed of native and naturalized Costa Ricans imported some fifteen or twenty experts and laborers from the United States for the same purpose. Donald Cameron, the Meiggs family, and no doubt other North Americans made investments in Costa Rican mines during the 1870's and 1880's; but by the end of the Guardia era British capitalists were once more in control of the majority of the Costa Rican mining properties. In the course of the next twenty years or so, however, their ownership would pass largely into the hands of United States citizens.

EARLY RAILWAYS

OF CENTRAL AMERICA

The most significant contribution made to the modernization of Costa Rica by foreigners was the construction and financing of its railways. Although a part of the cost of the iron roads was paid immediately and directly by the nation, most of the capital was supplied by the British. Nearly all the building, however, was carried on under the supervision of citizens of the United States.

The first Costa Rican railway—a line only nine miles long running toward the interior from Puntarenas, with cars drawn by mules—had been completed in 1857; but it proved unprofitable and was soon abandoned. This pioneer road was mainly the result of the efforts of Richard Farrer, an English merchant. The first contracts for the construction of steam railways in the country were granted to North Americans. The pioneer concession was obtained by the distinguished John C. Frémont and four associates and was dated July 31, 1866; but nothing was accomplished. The second contract, signed in 1869 with Edward Reilly, Alexander Hay, and two other North Americans, was equally futile. The third, dated July 20, 1871, soon led to the inauguration of the era of steam railways in Costa Rica. This concession was granted to Henry Meiggs, already famous for his railway building in Chile and Peru.

The contract was signed in Lima, and neither Henry Meiggs nor his brother John G. Meiggs ever came to Costa Rica; but they were nevertheless mainly responsible for the construction of the first steam railroad in the country. Emily Meiggs, a sister of Henry and John, had married Minor Hubbell Keith and become the mother of several sons, three of whom were to sacrifice their lives in Costa Rican railway construction. A fourth, Minor Cooper Keith, was destined to become the most famous North American in all Central America. Henry Meiggs Keith, the eldest son of Minor Hubbell and Emily Keith, had acquired experience under his noted uncle in Peru; and it was this member of the remarkable family who was sent to Costa Rica to build the first steam railway in that country and the second in Central America. (The pioneer Central American railway of this type, a line running from Puerto Caballos, later Puerto Cortés, toward the interior of Honduras, was built by the British construction firm of McCandlish and Waring.) Henry Meiggs Keith urged his younger brother Minor, who was then engaged in ranching and lumbering on a small island off the coast of Texas, to come to Costa Rica and help with the railroad enterprise. The two Keiths rode into San José together toward the end of 1871 and began work at once.

The Meiggs contract provided for the construction of a narrow-gauge railroad from the port of Limón on the Caribbean through the towns of Cartago, San José, and Heredia to Alajuela. For this railway, solidly built and fully equipped with stations and rolling stock, Henry Meiggs was to receive the sum of £1,600,000. Construction was to begin simultaneously at Alajuela and Limón and the road was to be completed within three years. The Keith brothers were to have general supervision of the work; prominent among the construction engineers were Albert J. Sherzer, George K. Latham, and H. D. B. Norris; some of the common laborers were Costa Ricans, but many workers had to be imported. Minor C. Keith, it is said, looked after the Limón end of the line; Henry Meiggs Keith assumed responsibility for the entire railway, but he seems to have devoted his attention mainly to the western portion in the more densely populated highland area where the climate was agreeable and construction somewhat easier.

The first locomotive was brought from Puntarenas up to Alajuela by a train of oxcarts at a cost of 4000 *pesos*. It arrived there on February 9, 1872, amidst great rejoicing. Cars and other equipment had to be transported the same way, and the distance was more than fifty miles! The first train arrived at Heredia, eight miles from Alajuela, on August 6, 1872; on December 30 the railway reached San José; and less than a year later, November 12, 1873, it arrived at Cartago, twenty-six and a half miles from Alajuela. Banquets, oratory, poetry, music, and dancing accompanied the opening of each section.

Progress from the Caribbean terminus at Limón was not quite so rapid; but the road was completed to Matina, a little over twenty miles from Limón, by the time the first train on the other end pulled into Cartago. This part of the line was built at heavy cost in labor, suffering, and life itself. Swamps had to be filled or drained, and primeval jungle cleared away. The rains fell incessantly; lizards, snakes, and alligators were plentiful; mosquitoes, sandflies, and other insects swarmed everywhere and made constant assaults; and the heat was stifling both night and day. Malaria, dysentery, and pernicious fevers soon broke out among the workers—Irishmen, Negroes, Italians, and coolies from India and China—and they died by the hundreds.

In spite of these enormous obstacles, the Keiths and their North American collaborators, enthusiastically supported by Tomás Guardia and other Costa Ricans, would have continued their work if Costa Rica's funds had not been exhausted. In order to build this difficult railway, the Guardia government had contracted a debt of some three million pounds sterling; but the discounts and commissions taken by some of the London investment bankers were so large that less than half that sum was available for railroad building in Costa Rica. In fact, a considerable portion of the bonds had been repurchased by Guardia's agents in a vain effort to bolster a bad market, and suspicions of graft and fraud were rife. Construction had to be abandoned for lack of capital and credit late in 1873 and Guardia thereupon took over the two pieces of railway, one of which —the Limón section—was practically worthless until it could be extended to the more populous regions of the country.

Service on the bonds held by British investors was discontinued while Guardia slowly accumulated funds from the national revenues and hopefully looked forward to the day when construction could be resumed. Late in 1875 a contract was signed with John Myers and Andrew T. Douglas, citizens of the United States, for the building of the Limón division from Matina to the Reventazón River, some sixteen miles beyond. During the next two years Myers and Douglas managed to build most of this stretch; then construction ceased again. A few months later Minor C. Keith, who had settled down in the mercantile business at Limón, emerged from temporary obscurity, signing on February 14, 1879, a contract to finish the some three miles which Myers and Douglas had failed to build. Keith fulfilled his contract promptly and efficiently and received a much larger one on September 8, 1879. This contract embraced a section of over thirty miles, extending from the Reventazón to the Sucio, which he agreed to complete by May 8, 1881, for the sum of 1,750,000 *pesos,* payable in monthly installments.

At the time Minor Cooper Keith signed his second agreement he was only thirty-one years old. Henry Meiggs had died in poverty two years before and Henry Meiggs Keith was also dead. John G. Meiggs, while still living, was poor, and Minor C. Keith could expect little assistance from his parents. The young contractor had only his own resources of character and will and the backing of an English merchant, John Wilson, who signed Keith's bond in connection with both of the concessions of 1879.

To obtain labor was a great problem. Guardia, always somewhat overconfident, was employing a good many native workers on other public enterprises; and Frenchmen engaged in building the Panama Canal were bidding against the ambitious North American in the cheap labor markets of the world outside. Yet Keith managed somehow to get together a crew of a thousand workers from the four corners of the earth. Some of them were Costa Rican convicts; others were Italians, Canary Islanders, or coolies imported from China and India; still more perhaps were black men from the West Indies. For a time Guardia subjected this miscellaneous crew to military discipline, it is said. Again the laborers died by the hundreds, and two of Keith's brothers were among those carried away by tropical diseases. Nevertheless, the work went on. The railway was not being completed according to contractual schedule; but that was no cause for serious worry. Tomás Guardia was determined to finish this railroad, and he knew that Keith would complete it if anybody could. He accordingly granted Keith not only an extension of five months but also a contract to operate the Limón-Sucio division for a period of five years. Moreover, he awarded Keith a contract to build the major part of a vehicle road from Sucio to San José and still another contract to organize a system of mule and wagon transport over this new highway.

Both the railway from Limón to Sucio and the highway from Sucio to San José were finished before the middle of the year 1882. From May 7 to May 10 both events were celebrated; wines, beer, and foreign liquors flowed freely for all who liked them. Keith was now famous throughout Costa Rica. But Guardia's career was approaching the end. Already suffering from a fatal illness that confined him to his bed in Alajuela, his life ebbed away on July 6, 1882. Keith's relations with Fernández

and Soto were soon as intimate, however, as they had been with
Guardia.

Already the young North American was agent for three British
steamboat lines, each operating a steamer or two between Limón
and New Orleans or New York, and banana plantations had
begun to flourish along the route of the railway under Keith's
management. For several years he had been busy promoting
the cultivation of this new crop in order to develop freight
for the railroad. Before long he would organize a steamship
company of his own, and the production and sale of bananas
would become the most important of his business enterprises;
in 1899 he would help to organize the United Fruit Company.
Yet Keith was fundamentally a railroad man; the urge to build
railways was in his blood, inherited from the Meiggs family.
All that he lacked in 1882 was a wife and enough funds to
continue the railway through the Reventazón gorge to the plateau and Cartago. Both the wife and the capital were soon
found, one in Costa Rica and the other in England.

On October 31, 1883, at the age of thirty-four, Keith married
Cristina Castro, a daughter of José María Castro, an eminent
Costa Rican who had served on three occasions as president or
acting president of the republic and had founded the national
university. Keith and his Costa Rican wife lived happily together for more than forty years and raised a large family.

In July 1883 and in April 1884 Keith signed contracts with
the Costa Rican government which authorized him to negotiate
with the dissatisfied British bondholders, organize a railway
company, arrange for the sale of another issue of Costa Rican
bonds, and dispose of the two divisions of the railroad he had
helped to build. The scaling down of the old foreign debt, the
flotation of the new bonds, and the organization of a British
railroad company with a capital of well over a million pounds
sterling occupied a good part of Keith's time for a period of
three years. In order to induce the new company, the Costa
Rica Railway Company, Limited, to finance the construction
of fifty miles of track between Reventazón and Cartago it was
necessary to cede them a majority interest in the whole line
from Limón to Alajuela for a period of 99 years counted from

the time the Reventazón-Cartago section should be completed.
The company also obtained a land grant of 800,000 acres.

Minor C. Keith received the construction contract. Resumption of work on the railroad in August, 1886, was accompanied by a fiesta and a grand ball. The completion of the railway in December, 1890, was followed by more celebrations and a banquet. Bernardo Soto was no longer president of Costa Rica. Having permitted a free election in which the opposition won, he had magnanimously surrendered his power. The leading oration at the banquet was delivered by Cleto González Víquez, a rising politician destined soon to be chief executive of his country. Unlimited praise was bestowed upon the North American railway builder. The obstacles confronted and surmounted were fully set forth. Keith was described as a modern Hercules to whom life was synonymous with struggle and achievement. He is "a grand character even among the Yankees," said the orator; "he merits every honor." Although Keith had retained his United States citizenship, he had become a Costa Rican institution; already he had begun to sign his name as "Keith y Meiggs," after the Spanish custom.

Further discussion of the contributions of North Americans to the modernization of Costa Rica must be in the nature of an anticlimax after considering the achievements of Minor C. Keith, who not only restored the nation's finances and built its leading railway, but also added bananas to coffee as a profitable commercial crop. Nevertheless, a few more paragraphs must be devoted to the larger theme.

Early in 1879 Tomás Guardia had ordered the construction of another railway, a line from Puntarenas to Alajuela, remarking that progressive patriots had long dreamed of a railroad from sea to sea. Work was begun at the Pacific terminus at once. At first it was under the direction of French engineers employed by the Guardia government. Then a Cuban supervised the construction for a time. Finally, on April 20, 1882, John Myers, a citizen of the United States, was granted a contract to complete the short line between Puntarenas and Esparta, a distance of some fourteen miles across the tropical lowlands of the Pacific coast. The line was finished and turned over to the government in December 1883. It soon became clear that the enterprise was a dead loss unless it could be extended further into the interior; but many years passed before funds could be raised for the purpose. The railway between San José and Puntarenas was not completed until 1910. A good part of it was built by John S. Casement and Warren S. Knowlton, citizens of the United States; the rest was the work of Costa Ricans themselves. Its length is seventy-two miles. Minor C. Keith had built well over a hundred miles of track across a far more difficult terrain.

The North American contribution to Costa Rican agriculture, except for bananas, was small. In their efforts to introduce machinery, the Yankees achieved little success. The people of the United States stimulated coffee production, however, by increasing their consumption of that commodity, while Rollin P. Saxe of California and other North Americans made a small contribution to the Costa Rican livestock industry by introducing a few blooded animals either directly or through sales to Costa Ricans. It is clear that the greatest assistance given by citizens of the United States to Costa Ricans during the Guardia epoch was in the field of transportation and communications.

XIII

TECHNOLOGICAL MODERNIZATION
IN GUATEMALA

ELATIONS BETWEEN the United States and Guatemala were intimate during the fourteen years following the seizure of the Guatemalan government by Miguel García Granados and Justo Rufino Barrios in 1871. These two leaders owed the success of their thrust for power in considerable measure to Remington and Winchester rifles imported from the United States, and therefore had good reason from the outset to appreciate the technological achievements of their Anglo-Saxon neighbor. Barrios, the stronger of the two, promptly began to admire the skill, energy, and industry of the United States. His attitude toward the North Americans, as he called them, was marked by cordial esteem. He was eager for their collaboration in the modernization of Guatemala. He wished also to obtain the aid of the United States in settling a boundary dispute with Mexico and for his cherished plan to weld the five republics of Central America into a single nation.

Barrios was not a man who expected favors without compensation. He assumed that reciprocity would be required. He expected to win the support of the United States by lending assistance in the acquisition of naval bases and a canal route and by offering North Americans profitable opportunities for investing their money and talents in Guatemala.

It is unnecessary to dwell upon the strategic aspects of these relationships. Barrios offered to cede Ocos Bay on the Pacific coast of Guatemala to the United States for a naval base. He also offered to give aid in effecting the acquisition by the United States of the Bay Islands from Honduras and a canal concession from Nicaragua. That part of the story is fairly well known. So likewise are the diplomatic relations of the two countries in more recent years. The primary purpose of this essay is to deal with neglected technological phases of the subject.

When García Granados and Barrios took charge of the Guatemalan government early in 1871, Guatemala had no railways, no steamboats on its lakes and rivers, no plumbing installations, little agricultural machinery, no barbed-wire fences, no telegraphs, no tramways, and, of course, no telephones or electric lights because electric lights and telephones had not been invented. When Barrios was killed on the field of battle in April 1885, all these had been introduced into his country through his efforts and those of his Guatemalan associates with the help of foreigners and especially North Americans.

Minor activities and contributions of citizens of the United States may be dismissed with a few sentences. A physician from the United States had charge of the army hospital in Guatemala City. A police expert from New York assisted in the training and reorganization of the Guatemalan police force. Captain V. S. Storm, aided by a special tariff concession, labored energetically to introduce barbed-wire fence. He also imported machinery for the coffee, rice, and sugar-cane industries as well as other modern farming implements. Captain Robert Cleves established in Guatemala a model diversified farm, importing from the United States such recent inventions as gang-plows, planters, cultivators, reapers, mowers, and threshers and such animals as Jersey cows, Merino sheep, and Berkshire hogs. The animals were brought from California, where Rollin P. Saxe was busily engaged in persuading Guatemalan visitors to introduce into their country the best breeds of horses, cattle, sheep, hogs, and fowls. W. J. Forsyth was granted a subsidy by Barrios for the importation and cultivation of quinine trees. Doctor John Protherve of California was given land for an ostrich farm and a bonus of 250 *pesos* for each ostrich introduced. Engineers from the United States were employed in surveying the boundary between Guatemala and Mexico.

Barrios granted a number of mining concessions to North Americans. The streams and hills of northeastern Guatemala contained considerable quantities of gold. William Friedman received two concessions, one on May 31, 1881, and another in the same month of the following year. Thomas J. Potts and John

W. Knight received a similar concession on July 30, 1883. All three covered placer-mining districts in the department of Izabel.

Barrios was eager to attract immigrants in order to place under cultivation vast stretches of rich but undeveloped land. He preferred to attract them from the United States. He offered a bonus of some thirty acres to laborers on one of the railways and made at least a few colonization grants to North Americans. On September 26, 1882, Dr. Byron H. Kilbourn of Milwaukee, Wisconsin, was ceded 1800 *hectáreas* (some 4500 acres) in the department of Izabel on condition that sufficient settlers be introduced within five years to bring half of the tract under cultivation. On June 21, 1883, F. F. Millen was granted 225 *hectáreas* for every hundred adult immigrants he might introduce from abroad, each immigrant to receive from the Guatemalan government a farm of forty-five *hectáreas*. On December 7, 1882, Charles W. Luck, representing the Tropical Products Company of Boston, purchased a tract of 2000 *hectáreas* at sixty cents a *hectárea,* to which he added on December 17, 1883, another block of 3000 *hectáreas* at the same price; and it was reported in 1885 that the Andes Agricultural Company had acquired 250,000 acres. All these lands were located in the departments of Izabel, Livingston, or Alta Vera Paz. Comparatively few settlers arrived during the Barrios period; but the foundations of the future thriving banana industry in eastern Guatemala were laid at this time.

In the field of public utilities citizens of the United States made significant contributions. This was emphatically true in the case of railway construction.

The first line of telegraph was built in Guatemala in 1873. It connected Guatemala City with the Pacific port of San José, passing through a number of intervening towns on the way. By 1882, Guatemala had more than twelve hundred miles of telegraph wire and over sixty offices. Although Stanley McNider, who is said to have been a Canadian, is entitled to more credit for the system than any other foreigner, a good deal of the mileage was constructed by experts from the United States in connection with the railways. By the early 1880's Guatemala had the benefit of a cable connection with the outside world through the port of Libertad, El Salvador. This connection was provided by the Central and South American Telegraph Company, a corporation located in the United States. By virtue of an agreement signed with James A. Scrymser, the president of this company, on January 13, 1880, Barrios obtained a voice in the fixing of rates in return for the use of Guatemala's territorial waters.

Citizens of the United States played an important part in the modernization of Guatemala City. Californians installed a system of street lighting in 1879, using naphtha gas; but the system was unsatisfactory and their contract was revoked in 1881. Electric lights were installed in 1884-1885 by Guatemalans in collaboration with foreign experts. The leading spirit in this enterprise was a Polish engineer named Piatkowski, who may have been a naturalized citizen of the United States. The telephone system was established in 1885 by a company composed of Guatemalans and Californians. Barrios had granted the concession to Roderico Toledo and other Guatemalans; the manager of the company was J. D. Tracy. The street railways of the capital were constructed by J. B. Bunting and D. P. Fenner, citizens of the United States, under a contract dated August 6, 1878. The horsecars began to move in October, 1882; and by March 1, 1885, the system embraced nearly five miles of trackage. Under a contract signed on July 12, 1883, Roderico Toledo assumed responsibility for improving the waterworks of the Guatemalan capital city and installing a sewer system. It is likely that he organized a company consisting of foreigners as well as nationals and employed North American experts. Toledo had intimate contacts with California, which he visited frequently, and since he had associated Californians with himself and other Guatemalans in the telephone company, it seems logical that he should also have employed Californians in connection with this new system of water supply and sewerage.

Construction engineers from the United States had charge of all railway building in Guatemala during the whole of the Barrios epoch. Hardly more than a hundred miles of railroad were in operation at the time of the dictator's death; but railway construction in Guatemala was not an easy task, and well over four hundred additional miles were projected. Although the first contracts were signed in the early 1870's, construction did not begin until 1878.

The first Guatemalan railway opened to traffic was a short line of approximately twenty-six miles between San José and Escuintla (see map on page 121). It was built under a contract signed with William Nanne on April 7, 1877, and was completed in June 1880. The enterprise was given a governmental guaranty of a net return of 15 per cent annually on a million *pesos;* but in consideration for government advances for construction this guaranty was surrendered in 1880. The railway was owned and operated by a corporation organized by Nanne in California: the Guatemala Central Railway Company.

The ultimate objective of this railway was Guatemala City, some forty-six miles beyond Escuintla; and on July 13, 1880, William Nanne and Lewis Schlessinger signed a contract to build this line. Guatemala agreed to pay an annual subsidy of 125,000 *pesos* a year for twenty-five years and to advance half a million *pesos* at once in treasury certificates. A grant of 1500 *caballerías* (a Guatemalan *caballería* was, at that time at least, the equivalent of nearly 112 acres) of public lands was also included. The surveys already had been made by Albert J. Scherzer, a citizen of the United States, and the railway was virtually completed four years later. At any rate, the first train made the run from San José to Guatemala City in July, 1884, with Barrios on board. In the meantime, the two lines, some seventy-two miles in length, had been consolidated under a single corporation, the Central American Pacific Railway and Transportation Company. This seems to have been a New York corporation; but it was largely owned by Collis P. Huntington, Leland Stanford, and Charles Crocker, who were noted for the construction of the western portions of the Union and Southern Pacific Railways of the United States. The use of the word transportation in the company's name probably forecast steamboat aspirations. On July 7, 1884, the corporation obtained from Guatemala a contract for placing a steamboat on Lake Amatitlán and the erection of a hotel on the borders of the lake.

Before the first steam locomotive puffed into Guatemala City to the excitement and rejoicing of the residents, another short railway had been constructed by engineers of the United States in Guatemala. It was a road some twenty-seven miles long between the Pacific port of Champerico and the rich coffee region around Retalhuleu. On March 12, 1881, J. H. Lyman, D. P. Fenner, and J. B. Bunting obtained a contract to build this railway. The Barrios government agreed to pay a subsidy of 700,000 *pesos* and to grant the contractors a thousand *caballerías* of public lands to be chosen anywhere in the country. The line was finished and opened to traffic on July 4, 1883. It was built by Thomas Bell of Falkner, Bell and Company, located in San Francisco, California, and Sanford Robinson was a prominent member of the company. The railroad was owned and managed by the Champerico and Northern Transportation Company, a California corporation.

What appeared at the time to be a far more important railway enterprise than any hitherto undertaken in Guatemala was envisaged in a contract signed by Barrios with Ulysses S. Grant on October 6, 1882, while the Guatemalan chief executive was in the United States. Grant and his associates already had secured a railway concession from the Mexican government, and the purpose of this Guatemalan contract was to obtain an extension across Central America. Grant agreed to construct 250 miles of railroad in Guatemala within two and a half years from the time his Mexican line reached the Guatemalan frontier; but the severe financial reverses soon encountered by the Civil War General resulted in failure to carry out his railway enterprises.

A rail connection between Guatemala City and Guatemala's Atlantic coast was a project dear to the heart of Barrios. He initiated plans for such a railway as early as 1880 and tried to raise a loan in France, but the road was not finished until more than twenty years after his death.

The story of the Guatemala Northern Railroad, as this line was called for a time, is a long tale of human suffering, failure, success. A quarter of a century was required to build it, although the distance from Puerto Barrios on the Caribbean Sea to Guatemala City is less than two hundred miles. Its construction was another achievement of United States technology and business management in Latin America.

Along the Caribbean, for a stretch of nearly a hundred miles toward the interior, Guatemala is a "vegetable Hell," with all the torments that destroy men and hamper their works: torrential rains, oppressive heat, ravenous insects, mortal diseases. After traversing the coastal region, the line of the railway continued across rugged mountains, deep ravines, and roaring streams until it reached the plateau on which Guatemala's capital is located.

Larraonda Brothers received, on August 30, 1880, the first contract for building this railway. Although their concession included more than 400,000 acres of land, they were unable to raise the necessary funds. Barrios then tried a new plan. He required each citizen of Guatemala with an income of as much as eight pesos a month to pay four pesos a year into a railroad fund for the next ten years. On October 4, 1883, exactly two months after the plan was decreed, a group of nine engineers began the preliminary surveys. The chief of the surveying party was Sylvanus Miller, a citizen of the United States, and three other North Americans were members of the surveying corps.

On May 1, 1884, Shea, Cornick and Company of Knoxville, Tennessee, obtained a contract to build sixty-two miles of the road, the section extending from Puerto Barrios on the Caribbean to Amates. The company was to receive 30,000 *pesos* a mile; workers were paid two and a half *pesos* a day, and were offered besides a bonus of nearly thirty acres of land at the end of a year's employment on the railway.

Shea, Cornick and Company suffered tragic defeat. Money was lost, materials were lost, lives were lost. Too many laborers —mostly Irishmen and Negroes—came down from New Orleans. The contractors underestimated the climatic difficulties. Until December 1884, no doctor was employed, nor were there any hospitals except crude, open, leaf-covered sheds. Rumors of suffering and death caused James F. Sarg, consular agent of the United States, to make an investigation. On December 6, 1884, Sarg reported:

The men complain that the weather has been so bad they have not been able to work and clear themselves from debt [the company had advanced $16 for their fare from New Orleans]; that the food, salt provisions, does not agree with them...; that there is no regular pay-day; that the contractors do not pay in cash, but in checks, which are...only received at the contractor's store in exchange for goods; that the prices of the goods are exorbitant; that they cannot find an interpreter.

The contractors complain that many men come out who are ... physically unfit for the labor expected of them; that men will smuggle themselves over affected with a chronic complaint that requires immediate care; that many ... are tramps who feign sickness, and that a great number have run away owing for their passage and a considerable store bill.

Even while Sarg was in the midst of his investigation the steamer *Blanche Henderson* arrived from New Orleans with more than a hundred laborers in search of jobs. "The captain assured me," wrote Sarg on January 5, 1885, "that when his ship was brought alongside the wharf at New Orleans, there was such a press of men over and above the number engaged that they were obliged to drive them off the ship with clubs, and in spite of this twelve stowaways appeared after they got out to sea." Many workers had migrated to New Orleans in the hope of obtaining employment in connection with a grand exposition then being held in that city. Unable to find jobs, they were ready to go anywhere.

Hundreds of the victims were ill and scores were dying in Guatemala by the end of 1884. Early the next year sixty managed to find passage to the United States. Others set out for Belize, where the governor put several to work under the vagrancy law. The "frightful amount of disease and mortality" prompted the United States to send a public vessel to the scene in order to take some of the sick and destitute back to New Orleans. In all, some seventy-eight were given government transportation.

This official investigation caused the contractors to improve their labor system and give more attention to the health of the workers. A certain Captain Grant, "a southern railroad engineer of high reputation, humane principles, and a thorough understanding of the race and class of men fitted for work in this climate," was appointed general manager of construction in March 1885. In the face of discouragement and tragedy, President Barrios declared: "The line from the Atlantic to this city is being continued with indefatigable energy and a constantly increasing enthusiasm." Yet J. H. Lyman and J. B. Gordon of

New York, who had signed, May 8, 1884, a contract to complete the railway had not even begun work; and a few weeks after his optimistic statement Justo Rufino Barrios was killed in battle while vainly attempting to consolidate the five republics of Central America into a single nation.

The new Guatemalan government not only abolished the railway tax but also diverted the funds to other purposes. Thus financial difficulties were added to those of climate in bringing the Shea, Cornick effort to an end. By the beginning of August their money and credit were exhausted and the work had to be suspended. They assigned the sums due them to their creditors and abandoned the railway. The jungle was so vigorous in wiping out signs of their labor—five miles of track and a few more miles of grading—that some accounts of the building of the Guatemala Northern declare that work was not begun until 1892.

It would be almost correct to say that work was not resumed until 1892, for while many efforts were made to continue construction during the six years following 1885, practically nothing was accomplished. Among those who tried and failed were several Frenchmen and two citizens of the United States: Martin Roberts and J. T. Anderson. Work was finally renewed under government direction with Sylvanus Miller as chief construction engineer.

Once again, during the administration of José María Reina Barrios (1892-1898), a nephew of the famous Justo Rufino Barrios, money was raised through special taxes. With these revenues and the aid of two other North Americans, Charles Thornton and Walter Heston, Miller made rapid progress. Workers were brought in from the United States, from Mexico, and from the Caribbean countries. Once more they suffered and died, but mile after mile of track was laid. In 1895 railway funds were increased by a loan of 658,500 *pesos* from Hamburg bankers. The line was opened to Zacapa, slightly more than a hundred miles, on November 22, 1896, with elaborate ceremonies.

Already the trains had been running for nearly two years on the some sixty miles that Shea, Cornick and Company had failed to build. The operation contract had been granted to Miller, who received a subsidy of 22,000 *pesos* a month; and in February, 1897, he obtained a concession to operate the whole line between Puerto Barrios and El Rancho, with a monthly subsidy of 35,000 *pesos* and an allowance of 249,000 *pesos* for repairs, including two *pesos* for each tie replaced. The road was then 134 miles long; but it was all too evident that it was being operated at a large annual loss for the Guatemalan government.

After Sylvanus Miller's death late in 1897 the management of the railway was transferred to a Guatemalan named Francisco Camacho, who also died within a few months. Thereupon, April 5, 1898, Robert H. May was awarded an operation contract for a year with a subsidy of 35,000 *pesos* a month and allowances for repairs, including replacement of ties at the usual rate of two *pesos* each. May was an engineer from the United States who had lived in Guatemala since 1884 and had worked on the Northern Railroad since 1892. Associated with him in this operation contract was Arthur B. Jekyll.

May was soon in financial straits. Guatemala's public revenues were dissipated by revolution and extravagance. Government payments fell behind, and by the end of August, 1898, both the contractor's cash and his capacity to borrow were exhausted. The train crews, mainly United States citizens, went out on strike late in September because they had not received their wages. Shortly afterward Manuel Estrada Cabrera, the new Guatemalan president, took over the railway. May was deprived of his contract and two years were required to settle his accounts.

On October 28, 1898, the operation concession was transferred to Martin Roberts, who held it until his death while on a trip to California for his health in the summer of 1900. The government then took charge of the railway for a few months until an agreement was negotiated with the Central American Improvement Company, a New Jersey Corporation dominated by the famous Minor C. Keith. This company, by the terms of its contract, undertook the task of repairing the old line and finishing the railway from El Rancho to Guatemala City within three years. In compensation it was to receive the right to operate the road for ten years, large tracts of lands for timber and plantations, and the sum of four million gold *pesos* in Guatemalan bonds upon the completion of the railroad.

The Improvement Company operated the old line for nearly three years and made some repairs, but was unable to extend it to the Guatemalan capital. Washouts were frequent and the cost of repairs enormous. Concerning the state of the railway an engineer reported in July 1901:

> The track is very poor. The rails are heavy for a narrow gauge road, but the track is badly out of line. The ties are of mahogany, rosewood and ebony, but even ebony lasts only ... two years. The train runs about ten miles an hour and makes long stops. The road has nine locomotives, mostly Baldwins several years old....

The company gave up its concession on October 29, 1903.

On April 5, 1904, a contract was approved with Percival Farquhar, who was the representative of Minor C. Keith and William C. Van Horne, the last a native of the United States but a resident of Canada. Keith and Van Horne agreed to reconstruct the old road, replenish the equipment, and complete the line to Guatemala City within three and a half years. Guatemala guaranteed interest on four and a half million dollars at the rate of 5 per cent for fifteen years, granted the contractors 168,000 acres of land, and ceded them the railway for a period of 99 years after its completion. Organizing the Guatemala Railroad Company, which was incorporated in New Jersey on June 8, 1904, Keith and Van Horne took charge of the enterprise at once. Thomas H. Hubbard of the Guatemala Central Railway was a prominent stockholder in the Keith-Van Horne company and the two roads were later consolidated.

Owing to Guatemala's bad debt record and a revolution, money was difficult to raise. At one time Keith, Van Horne, and Farquhar had to dig deep into their personal reserves. Labor also was hard to assemble. Most of it had to be imported from the United States and the West Indies because Guatemalan peons were not disposed to work on the railway, particularly on the tropical sections which were badly in need of repair. The some fifty or sixty miles of new track had to be constructed through mountain barriers. Work on this section was initiated in Guatemala City on June 21, 1906, when Estrada Cabrera moved the first spade of dirt and drove a golden spike.

In spite of every obstacle the railway was completed within a few weeks of the time limit. Nevin O. Winter, who made the journey from Guatemala City to the Caribbean shortly after the line was finished, left the following record:

... The difficulties in the operation of a railroad in a tropical country are many and they are all encountered here. The ties soon decayed, and in the rainy season the streams became raging torrents which washed away bridges and the tracks along their banks. ... Hundreds of men were placed at work reconstructing the road, building new bridges, and completing the gap to the capital. This last extension ... required some remarkable engineering feats. There are many tunnels and cuts through solid rock. ... After leaving Gualan ... the road plunges into the denser tropics ... follows near the Motagua River ... where much trouble has been experienced. ... The large bridge across this stream has been torn away twice during the rainy season, and ... the track has been washed away or has slipped into the stream a number of times. Every few miles there are section houses for ... the employees built in the somber forest. ... Puerto Barrios consists of a single row of lazy, steep-roofed, palm-thatched, native huts that spring from the very water's edge. There are four large wooden buildings which shelter the customs officials, local garrison ... and officers of the transportation company.

Another writer comments upon the "remarkable feats of engineering" and the numerous tunnels and bridges. There were seventy of the latter, one of them across a ravine 244 feet deep.

The celebration of the railway's formal opening began on January 19, 1908, and lasted two weeks. After driving the last spike, President Estrada Cabrera, with his cabinet and the diplomatic corps, took a trip on the first passenger train that made the journey to Puerto Barrios. At the invitation of Estrada Cabrera, the United States sent a special representative for the festivities. The Guatemalan chief executive was voted a gold medal by his cabinet; but he sent President Roosevelt both a gold badge and a little golden spike. Roosevelt replied graciously: "I appreciate the kind sentiment which inspired your action and trust that the great work ... is but the forerunner of others . . . that will aid still further in binding the nations of the American continent more closely together in bonds of friendship and brotherly love."

Thus the twenty-five years of struggle against jungle and mountain came to an end amidst feasting, oratory, and eulogy. Too little praise was given to the humble laborers who had toiled and suffered and died in the process of construction and repair. May and Jekyll were the chief engineers under the management of Keith and Van Horne.

In order to provide freight, the United Fruit Company, of which Keith was vice-president, already had agreed to plant a million banana trees along the railway line. Within a few years Guatemala, which long had been noted for its excellent and abundant coffee, would take its place among the leading banana countries of the world. In 1908 it had in operation some 360 miles of railway—more than the rest of Central America combined. Keith soon began his efforts to consolidate practically all the lines of the entire region into a single system and expand it until railway transportation should be available to every Central American community; but death and world catastrophe intervened before his task was finished.

DAWN OF THE RAILROAD EPOCH
IN MEXICO

IN SPITE of its proximity to the United States, a great reservoir of railway technology and a growing center of finance, Mexico long lagged behind some of its sister nations in railroad building. The Railway Age arrived there later than in any of the larger countries of Latin America save Venezuela and Bolivia. Technicians and capitalists from the United States and England built important iron roads in Chile, Peru, Argentina, and Brazil before they built them in Mexico. Although the first Mexican railroad contract was signed in 1837 and many others were negotiated in succeeding years, the country had less than twenty miles of railway in 1860 and scarcely seven hundred at the beginning of 1880.

It was a case of politics retarding the migration of transport technology. Mexico was harried by revolutions until 1877, and the migratory process was further delayed by lack of official cordiality between Mexico and the United States and Great Britain. The year 1880, however, marked a turning point and the beginning of a railway boom. Within a little more than a decade Mexico would have more railroads than any other Latin-American nation. An average of thirty or forty thousand laborers worked almost constantly on them for ten years.

By the end of 1892 Mexico's mileage of steam railways exceeded 6000 and it possessed, besides, more than another thousand miles of tramways and rural lines operated by animal traction. Citizens of the United States supervised the construction of most of these railroads; the rest were built under the management of British and Mexican engineers. A good part of the capital was furnished by the Mexican government; but Mexican financiers made small investments and large sums came from England and the United States. Mexican railways, like those of other Latin-American countries, were mainly the result of an international movement of money and technology. Briefly, the story of their construction down to the early 1890's follows.

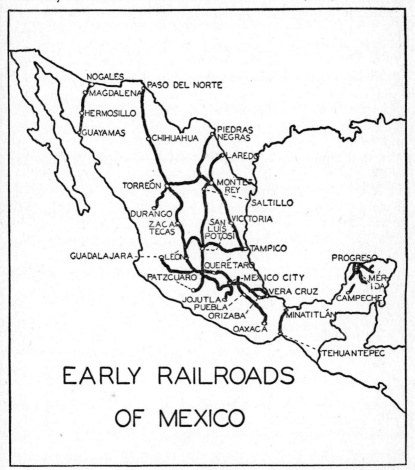

EARLY RAILROADS

OF MEXICO

1. The Mexican Railway, extending from Vera Cruz through Orizaba to Mexico City, was begun in the late 1840's, as we have seen, but was not opened to traffic until January 1873. Surveys of the whole route were made in 1857-1858 by Colonel Andrew H. Talcott, Robert B. Gorsuch, H. E. Lyons, and other citizens of the United States, some dying of pernicious fever

while engaged in the task. The first twenty-five miles or so of the road were built under Yankee technical supervision; most of the rest was the joint work of United States and British experts. Prominent among the Mexican promoters of the early period was Antonio Escandón. British construction firms in charge of the railway after 1865 were Smith, Knight and Company and Crawley and Company. William Cross Buchanan was one of the most distinguished of the English engineers. A British corporation got possession of the road in 1868 and retained ownership until long after 1900. The main line was a little over 263 miles long; branches to Puebla, Pachuca, and Jalapa added another 128 miles, but most of the 71 miles between Vera Cruz and Jalapa were operated by animal traction.

2.   The Sonora Railway, which linked the seaport of Guaymas with the northern border town of Nogales, some 264 miles away, was constructed by promoters connected with the Atchison, Topeka and Santa Fe Railroad Company. Begun at the Guaymas end in May, 1880, it was opened to Hermosillo on November 4, 1881, and to Nogales on October 25, 1882. Daniel B. Robinson was the supervisor of construction, with W. R. Morley as chief engineer. The leading promoters were Thomas Nickerson of Boston and Sebastián Camacho of Mexico City. This was the first important railway achievement of citizens of the United States in Mexico.

3.   The Mexican Central, Mexico's longest railway, was also built by the Santa Fe group of capitalists and technicians. It runs from Paso del Norte (Ciudad Juárez), near El Paso, Texas, through Chihuahua City, Torreón, Zacatecas, León, and Querétaro to Mexico City, with branches extending to Tampico on the east and Guadalajara on the west. Construction on the southern end of the trunk line was begun in the summer of 1880 and on the northern end in August of the following year, the whole being completed on March 8, 1884. The Tampico division was begun in 1881 but was not completed until 1890. Work on the Guadalajara division started in 1884 and was finished four years later. By 1892 the total length of track was 1833 miles; the distance by Mexican Central rails from El Paso to Mexico City was approximately 1225 miles. Many capable engineers took part in the construction of this important railway system.

Among them were George H. Anthony, Rudolph Fink, Daniel
B. Robinson, Charles A. Sweet, and Arthur M. Wellington, all
well known in the railroad circles of their day. Sweet had worked
with Henry Meiggs on the famous Oroya Railway in Peru.
Prominent officials of the company were Levi C. Wade, Thomas
Nickerson, the Englishman Robert R. Symon, and two Mexicans, Sebastián Camacho and Ramón B. Guzmán.

4. The Mexican National Railway, which extends from
Nuevo Laredo through Monterey, Saltillo, San Luis Potosí,
Dolores Hidalgo, San Miguel Allende, and Toluca to the Mexican capital, was constructed by promoters who had built the
famous Denver and Río Grande Railroad, William J. Palmer
and James Sullivan prominent among them. The line from
Mexico City to Toluca was opened on September 4, 1882, and
that from Laredo to Monterey on September 16; but the entire
trunk line from Laredo to Mexico City was not opened to public
traffic until November 1, 1888. By 1892 this system embraced
approximately 1060 miles of track, including branch lines from
Matamoras eastward to San Miguel, from Acambaro westward
to Patzcuaro, and from Mexico City northward to El Salto. The
distance from Nuevo Laredo to the national capital by this road
is 844 miles. The railway was built by the National Construction
Company of New York City, with G. Clinton Gardner as general
manager and W. C. Wetherill, E. Miller, S. F. Fuller, the
Englishman William Cross Buchanan, and several others as construction engineers. Considerable British and some French capital were later invested in the railway.

5. The Mexican International Railroad, intended to connect
Piedras Negras with Torreón, Durango, Mexico City, and the
Pacific coast, was begun in 1882; but it did not reach Durango
until ten years later and there it stopped. Connected with the
Southern Pacific system of the United States, its leading pro-
moters were John B. Frisbie, Collis P. Huntington, Thomas B.
Pierce, and Oliver Hoyt. The road, which consisted of two short
spurs and a trunk line of 540 miles, was built by the Inter-
national Construction Company, an organization dominated by
Charles Crocker. Among the construction engineers were W. S.
Monroe and James Converse.

6. The Mexican Southern Railway, designed originally to

link Antón Lizardo, on the Gulf coast south of Vera Cruz, with Puebla, Mexico City, Oaxaca, Tehuantepec, and Tapachula, on the Guatemalan border, was started by a New York company headed by Ulysses S. Grant; but this organization collapsed in 1884 before much work had been done. A few years later the contract passed into the hands of Read, Campbell and Company, a London construction firm, and the Mexican Southern Railroad Company, Limited, was launched by English capitalists. This company undertook merely to build a narrow-gauge line from Puebla to Oaxaca, 228 miles, which finally was opened to public traffic early in 1893.

7. The history of the Interoceanic Railroad is the story of numerous concessions to Mexicans for the construction of short lines reaching out from Mexico City toward Vera Cruz on the east and toward Acapulco on the west. The first of the numerous contracts dated back to 1878. The small companies failed, consolidated with others, and failed again; but with the support of British capital in 1888 and following, nearly 500 miles of track were finished by the end of 1892. The principal lines of the system were two: one from Mexico City southward to Jojutla, 123 miles, and the other from the capital to Vera Cruz, passing through Puebla, Perote, and Jalapa and covering a distance of more than 340 miles. This indirect route from Mexico City to Vera Cruz was surveyed by a Yankee named Arthur M. Wellington in 1881; but much of the Interoceanic was constructed by Mexican engineers themselves. Its most effective promoters were Francisco Arteaga and Delfín Sánchez.

8. Sánchez also made a large contribution to the building of the Tehuantepec Railway, which was projected as early as 1842 but was not completed until more than half a century later. Among the pioneers who tried to build this road were Simon Stevens, brother of the more famous Thaddeus Stevens, and Edward Learned. Stevens made no progress; Learned managed to build twenty miles or so before he lost his concession in 1881. Between that date and 1888 Sánchez constructed another stretch of some sixty miles and then a contract was signed with Edward McMurdo of London, who repaired the line already built and added a few more miles before his death in 1891. The railway was finally brought to completion by Chandos H. Stanhope,

Elmer L. Corthell, and J. H. Hampson, engineers from the
United States. It was finished on October 25, 1894; in spite of
all the time required to build it, the road was only 194 miles
long!

10. The various short lines of Yucatán, most of them of narrow gauge, were constructed between 1878 and 1892. Financed
and built mainly by Mexicans, their total length at the latter
date was less than 200 miles. Mérida, the center of the great
henequén region, was also the railway center of the peninsula.

11. Neither the Monterey and Mexican Gulf Railway—running from Monterey southeastward to Tampico and from Monterey westward to a junction with the Mexican International—
nor a number of minor steam railroads located mainly in the
vicinity of the national capital will be discussed in this summary. The first was built mainly by citizens of the United States
and subjects of Belgium. The others were constructed largely
by Mexicans themselves.

The Mexican railways built during this earlier period were
on the whole easier to construct than those of several other
Latin-American countries. Although scarcity of water was a
handicap for hundreds of miles in northern Mexico, no serious
topographical problems were confronted there. In the Tampico,
Vera Cruz, and Tehuantepec regions, the jungle and its diseases
made progress difficult, but the steaming lowlands were narrow.
In southern and southwestern Mexico deep gorges and mountains pitched and tumbled by volcanic disturbances interposed
barriers almost as formidable as those of Colombia, Ecuador, and
Peru. These sections, however, were not deeply penetrated during the boom era.

On its course across the center of the country from east to
west, the Mexican Railway never went beyond the national
capital. The Mexican Central, with San Blas as its ultimate
destination on the west, stopped at Guadalajara, and the International paused at Durango.

Even the narrow-gauge lines advanced very timidly toward
the south and the southwest. The Mexican National, with
Manzanillo as its final objective, got no further in the early
1890's than Patzcuaro. The Interoceanic, on its way to Acapulco,
merely reached Jojutla. The Mexican Southern, with its ambi-

tious plan to link Mexico with western Central America, barely arrived at Oaxaca.

Although financial problems as well as topographical obstacles retarded progress, it must be noted that the Southern Pacific, which began its long line down Mexico's Pacific coast in 1905 under the domination of the spectacular Edward H. Harriman, failed to close the gap between Tepic and Guadalajara during the next decade. Such railways as were built on that coast by the early 1890's ran only a few miles inland from the ports of Altata, San Blas, Manzanillo, and San Benito, the last in distant Chiapas; and some of these used mules or burros instead of locomotives.

In writing the early history of Mexico's railways due credit should be given to the humble men who moved the dirt and rocks and laid the cross-ties and rails. Most of this heavy work was done by Mexican peons at wages ranging from thirty-seven to seventy-five cents a day. In central, southern, and southwestern Mexico, hardly any other kind of labor was employed. In the north, northwest, and east, Negroes and Italians formed a part of the crews; but even there the natives were usually in the majority. In fact, the railway contracts usually required that at least two-thirds of the workers should be Mexicans.

Too little attention has been devoted to these anonymous pioneers of Mexico's Railway Age. Barefoot, clad in soiled white cotton, shielded from the sun by cheap straw *sombreros,* they worked without the customary *siesta* for ten or twelve hours a day, lived on a scanty diet of scarcely more than beans and *tortillas,* slept on the ground, and spent the silver coins that jingled into their hats at week-ends on strong drink, women, and the fiestas and ceremonies of the Church. Peons of Mexico, low-paid servants of a new technology whose full significance you never understood, we salute you! Your work was as essential as that of the engineers and bosses who ordered you to take up the pick and the shovel or that of the promoters who induced private investors to put their money into Mexico's iron roads.

The story of the financing of these railroads lies more in the economist's realm than the historian's. In most cases a third or more of the cost was paid in cash or bonds by the Mexican government itself. The rest, with the exception of small sums supplied by Mexican investors, came from the United States and Great Britain. Traffic rates were higher in Mexico than in the United States; but theoretically and sometimes actually they were regulated by Mexican officials. Remunerative heavy freight was seldom abundant. There were profits for some of the construction companies and good wages for the skilled technicians and higher officials; but the stockholders, like the section hands, received small returns. In fact, at times and in the end many of the investors obtained almost no dividends and were lucky if they recovered the principal. Mexico, while often paying too dearly for its new means of transportation, eventually profited most of all. By the 1940's the nation was fully controlling and operating a railway system built for the most part by foreign promoters and technicians.

Moreover, the story is essentially the same with respect to many other technological improvements—telegraph lines, port works, plumbing and sewers, tramways, trolley cars, gas and electric lights, oil wells, and oil refineries. The railways merely illustrate the general theme. With the exception of electric power, mining, and important telephone exchanges, the Mexicans have exercised in recent years the privilege of running their own economic affairs, at times to the detriment of foreign capitalists.

Railways were received in Mexico with less acclaim than in many other Latin-American countries. Owing to memories of the loss of Texas and further losses resulting from the war of 1846-1848 with the United States, North American emissaries of the Railroad Epoch were viewed in many quarters with suspicion. Nevertheless, upper-class Mexicans joined with the Yankee railway men in a good many celebrations, drove numerous ceremonial spikes, and took part in several excursions and banquets where oratory, music, and poetry were blended with the wine; and the humble residents of the villages often crowded around the stations to witness the arrival of the first trains or marched in processions, their banners inscribed with congratulations to the *gringo* builders and proclamations of long life for the railroad enterprises: *Viva el ferrocarril! Viva el progreso!*

Yankee railway operators of the early period in Mexico had their troubles. Sometimes they were imprisoned for weeks and months for accidents which could hardly have been avoided, and occasionally the trains were attacked by bandits or wrecked by vandals. One may recall, however, that the western part of the United States was not free from train-robbers during the 1870's and 1880's.

Mexicans sometimes expressed dissatisfaction because more of them were not employed in the upper ranks of the railway jobs. They wanted to be engineers, firemen, conductors, and brakemen as well as station masters, telegraph operators, ticket agents, and section hands; but comparatively few were permitted to occupy the highly technical and better-paid positions until after the end of the nineteenth century. The trend, however, was definitely in the direction of national ownership and native operation, a goal which was finally reached in large measure through purchase or expropriation and the deliberate dismissal of foreign labor and officials. But that is a familiar story which need not be dwelt upon here.

Mexico and its railways attracted much attention in the United States during the 1880's and 1890's. The significance of the new means of transport for Mexico and for the United States was frequently discussed. Investors were warned or coaxed; railway authorities sought to attract tourists, colonists, and capital; and North Americans who visited Mexico published their observations in articles and books. Running through much of this literature were instances of sound prediction and a strain of humanitarianism.

William H. Bishop, who was preparing a series of articles for *Harper's Magazine,* sat in the crowded hotel lobbies of Mexico City where his countrymen busily discussed their schemes for profitable ventures, but spent more time delving into social and economic conditions and observing the workers on the railway lines. He expressed the hope that a statesman would arise to educate Mexico's masses, improve their living standards, instruct them in their political rights, and see that they were given the "first essential of free government—an honest suffrage."

Alfred Conkling, grandson of a former United States minister to Mexico, spent several weeks in the country, traveled over a number of the new railroads, recalled recent railway scandals in his own country, and expressed uneasiness with reference to what these "mighty corporations and combinations" might do to Mexico. He concluded his discussion of the railways with a suggestion that Mexicans might profit by examining the experience of other countries.

Solomon B. Griffin looked upon the Mexican railroads as "messengers of enlightenment" and stimulants of economic enterprise, but doubted that they alone could effect the transformation so greatly to be desired. What Mexico most needed, he declared, was a prosperous and enlightened middle class; its creation would be a "gigantic task."

Bernard Moses, then a young instructor at the University of California and just beginning his notable career as a student of Spanish-American affairs, spent the summer of 1895 investigating the influence of the new means of transport below the border. He returned to Berkeley with the conviction that despotism and the landed aristocracy would practically nullify the influence of the railways for the vast majority of Mexicans. The rich might become richer; the poor would not receive great benefits unless some other factor came into play. They would remain approximately where they were, landless workers bound in peonage on the big estates or underpaid laborers in the mines and factories. Their condition could not be improved, he suggested, except through far-reaching reforms carried out by the Mexicans themselves.

These comments and predictions pointed unerringly, in many cases, to the future. Thirty or forty years later land would be given to the landless, the laborers would have their day, and many people in the United States would view Mexico's New Deal with tolerance and sympathy.

The main point to be emphasized here, however, is the fact that the Railway Epoch was brought to Mexico mainly through the efforts of business leaders and construction engineers from the United States. Without collaboration from this or some other quarter the modernization of Mexico's transportation would have been delayed for many years.

RAILROAD TO UTOPIA, SHORT-CUT
TO CHINA

THE MAIN STREET of the dusty, sun-baked village of San Blas, in the Mexican State of Sinaloa, has long been called *"Calle Kansas City."* Many of the inhabitants of San Blas, people whose dark skins reveal a heavy admixture of Indian blood, do not know where the street got its name, any more than they know why the words "Kansas City, Mexico y Oriente" are painted on the dilapidated boxcars and obsolete engines they see on the railroad sidings.

Forty miles to the southwest, on low hills overlooking a beautiful harbor, squat the crude stone and mud huts of the Mexican *pueblo* of Topolobampo, once envisaged as the "Metropolis of the West" and the emporium of Chinese commerce. From these hills one may observe more weather-worn locomotives and boxcars standing on sidings along the bay. Some of the villagers recall dimly that there used to be a station called Stilwell a few miles inland.

The brown inhabitants of San Blas and Topolobampo know that fields of sugar cane, tomatoes, and winter vegetables grow in the neighboring Fuerte Valley, once the property of their Indian forebears and the Jesuit Order. They also know that a Yankee company owns a good part of these fertile fields, as well as a big sugar mill at Los Mochis, about halfway between San Blas and Topolobampo. Some of them have worked for the company during the busy season. The more sophisticated know, although they could not tell you the exact distance, that the Kansas City, Mexico and Orient extends to the little town of San Pedro, seventy-eight miles from Topolobampo, at the foot of the Sierra Madre Mountains. Small trains run over at least a part of this track two or three times a week. Moreover, the natives know that the Southern Pacific Railroad of Mexico crosses the Kansas City, Mexico and Orient at San Blas, and they have heard that one may go by train from that point to Guadalajara and Mexico City or northward to Guaymas and beyond. That the builders of the *Sud-Pacifico* were North Americans they also know, and they have been told that the North Americans still own and manage the railway as well as many of the mines of Sinaloa, Tepic (Nayarit), and Sonora. They have heard, too, that it was the Yankees who began, many years ago, the excavation of big irrigation ditches and the building of immense dams in the river valleys of Mexico's West Coast.

Beyond this, all is rather blank or mysterious. They do not realize that the road which they call *Oriente* or Kansas "Ceety" had its beginning in the days of their fathers and grandfathers or that the tracks which they see are but a small part of an ambitious railroad intended to connect the center of the United States with Mexico and the Far East. They do not realize that its promoters tried to improve the lot of poor people like themselves—or, at least, attempted to raise money by Utopian appeals and attacks upon the despotic power of the rich. Of Albert K. Owen, Arthur E. Stilwell, Edward H. Harriman, and other dreamers and promoters of their kind they can tell you almost nothing. What do they know of economic discontent in the United States—of Romanticists, Utopians, railway and land booms, and agrarian protests north of the border—of Oriental trade and the stock-markets of Amsterdam, London, and New York City? For the simple inhabitants of such Mexican villages as Topolobampo, San Blas, and Los Mochis, the dynamic forces of the Machine Age are still a sealed book. They do not realize that capital and technology are likely to bring about changes in their way of living as profound, as revolutionary, as those introduced by the Spanish Conquerors and Jesuit missionaries among their ancestors.

Yankees of authentic New England breed dreamed of garnering riches from Far Eastern commerce before the end of the American Revolution and sent their first ship to China in the 1780's. Men of both the eastern and western sections of the United States employed Oriental commercial prospects, along with other arguments, to advance their continental railroad schemes. They began in the 1840's and 1850's to advocate a commercial outlet through Mexico to the Pacific Ocean, and the agitation continued for many decades. Guaymas, on the Gulf of California, was the first Mexican port to be linked by rail with the United States. But Owen's vision of Topolobampo and a railway thereto was ten years old before the iron road between Guaymas and Nogales was finished.

As early as the 1840's Ralph Waldo Emerson had written Thomas Carlyle: "We are a little wild here with numberless projects of social reform. Not a reading man but has a draft of a new community in his . . . pocket." The story of humanitarians and reformers in the United States during the next half-century and more is familiar. While capitalists were making fortunes building railroads, exploiting mines, erecting smoke-belching factories, manipulating securities, and producing slums, irate reformers turned on capitalists or sought escape by creating imaginary cities and commonwealths. Experimenting with their ideas, they established Brook Farm, New Harmony, Hopedale, and many more settlements. Industrial workers and insurgent farmers organized to demand their rights while citizens with political impulses promoted the Populist Revolt and the Progressive Movement. Meantime, Utopian books continued to appear. Among those published toward the end of the century were Edward Bellamy's *Looking Backward,* William Morris's *News from Nowhere,* and Theodor Hertzka's *Freeland.* Reformers in the United States were often in close touch with those in Europe.

Owen and Stilwell were men of their times. Owen became a Utopian Socialist. Stilwell avowed deep sympathy for the people of the West in their struggle with the capitalistic East and their determination to break the fetters which hampered their economic progress.

Not much is known regarding the early life of Albert Kimsey Owen. Born between 1840 and 1850 in Chester, Pennsylvania, he was the son of a Quaker physician named Joshua Owen, who served as a surgeon in the United States Army during the Civil War. In his youth, Albert traveled widely: in the American West, in Europe, in Mexico. His father, who had only two sons,

Albert K. and Alfred M., must have been fairly wealthy. The mother died when they were infants.

Of Albert's formal schooling, of his reading, which probably included the writings of Socialists and Utopians, of his training as a civil engineer, we have no information. After following the engineering profession for a brief period in Pennsylvania, he went to Colorado and helped to build railroads there. Later, William J. Palmer, one of the promoters of the Denver and Río Grande, sent him to western Mexico with a surveying party. While in this region, late in 1872, Owen examined the Bay of Topolobampo, bordering the Mexican main directly across from the tip of Lower California. Thrilled by its beauty and by the economic resources of the area, he is said to have exclaimed: "The day will come when these waters, now deserted and ignored, will be traveled by the great ships of the world, and this fertile ground which surrounds them will support thousands of families living a new and happy life." It is also said that, even earlier, Owen thought of founding an ideal settlement in the Mexican State of Vera Cruz, but abandoned the project because of adverse health conditions. It is likely, however, that he did not seriously consider the planting of a model colony in Mexico before the 1880's.

What he did envision in 1872 was a railway extending from Norfolk, Virginia, across the South and across Mexico to Topolobampo Bay. Returning to the United States, he laid his plan before a convention of Southern governors at Atlanta, and soon obtained from the State of Virginia a charter for a Southern Settlement Society. But the Panic of 1873 shattered his project.

This financial calamity seems to have had a profound effect on the young engineer. He promptly joined the Greenback movement, the Sovereigns of Labor, and the Knights of Labor. He also appealed to the National Congress for assistance in building his railway, requesting an appropriation for a survey, to be made by government engineers, from Austin, Texas, to Topolobampo, Sinaloa. Apparently he expected to carry the system from Austin to Norfolk by consolidating and extending lines already in existence. He described his project as "The Great Southern Trans-Oceanic and International Air Line— Asia to Europe via Mexico and the United States." The literature he submitted to Congress had nothing to say regarding model settlements. He proposed only to develop the southern part of the United States and the Mexican West Coast and build a direct line of transportation to the Pacific in order to connect with steamers engaged in Oriental traffic.

For nearly five years he made his appeals at Washington. The National Congress called upon the Army engineers for a report on the potentialities of a railroad from Austin to Topolobampo but made no appropriations for the survey. Then, in 1879 and again in 1880, Owen went to Mexico. He had devised schemes for draining the valley surrounding the Mexican capital and for building a national system of railway lines financed by paper money, as well as for the more modest railroad from Topolobampo to the Texas border and Austin. Concentrating on this smaller project, he published in *La Liberdad,* a Mexican newspaper, an article under this title: "The Occident and the Orient. A Synopsis of the Efforts Made by the Occident to Establish Commercial Communication with the Orient." Meanwhile, General Ulysses S. Grant had arrived in Mexico City in search of a railway concession; and Owen, who may have met the Civil War hero at an earlier period, attended a banquet honoring Grant and seized the opportunity to make a speech in support of the Texas-Topolobampo line.

This must have raised Owen's prestige. Encouraged by the Mexican national government, he incorporated on March 8, 1881, under the laws of Massachusetts, the Texas, Topolobampo and Pacific Railroad and Telegraph Company, with William Windom, a former senator, as president. On the board of directors, among others, were Benjamin F. Butler, Wendell Phillips, John H. Rice, two sons of General Grant, and Matías Romero, a distinguished Mexican diplomat. On June 13, 1881, through Mexican attorneys, this company obtained a ninety-nine-year concession for a railway from Piedras Negras, Coahuila, to Topolobampo, with branches to Presidio del Norte, Álamos, and Mazatlán. The terms of the grant included certain exemptions from tariffs and taxes, as well as a subsidy of 5000 *pesos* a kilometer, except for the branch to Presidio. The road was to be completed in ten years.

Owen and other engineers began immediately to make sur-

veys on the Mexican Pacific slope and through the Western
Sierra Madres; the railway company published pamphlets setting forth the immense mineral, timber, and agricultural resources of Mexico's West Coast and the advantages of the
proposed short-cut to the Orient. After the practice of the period, a construction company was also organized, the Mexican-
American Construction Company. But almost nothing was
accomplished. The Mexican government suspended subsidy
payments on railroads in 1883 and it soon was difficult to raise
money in the United States for railway building in Mexico.

The original contract was followed by a series of additions,
modifications, extensions of time limits, cancellations, and re-
newals. The plan to establish a colony in the Topolobampo
region in connection with the railway appeared for the first time
in an agreement dated December 5, 1882. In honor of Manuel
González, then president of Mexico, the new settlement was
to be called Ciudad González. Later, it is said, Porfirio Díaz
decided that the name should be Ciudad de la Paz; but in a
concession granted by the Díaz government to Owen and Rice,
dated July 22, 1886, it was called Pacific Colony, and Owen
finally settled on the name Pacific City for the Topolobampo
metropolis.

For a time the railway pushed the model-colony project into
the background; but before the end of the 1880's the relative
importance of the two was reversed. The determination to
build the railroad was not abandoned, however; it was to be
constructed by the colonists themselves, whose labor was to be
exchanged for food and other domestic supplies.

In 1886 Owen and Rice organized under the laws of Colorado
a joint-stock company which they named the Credit Foncier
Company. While their intention was to sell most of the stock
of the corporation in small installments to actual settlers, other
purchasers were solicited among those of Utopian sentiments.
A central office was soon opened in New York City under the
management of John W. Lovell, treasurer of the company;
branches were established in Kansas and elsewhere in the dis-
contented West. In 1888 Christian B. Hoffman of Kansas City
and Enterprise, Kansas, organized the Kansas-Sinaloa Investment Company and began to offer stock to non-settlers as an

investment. With funds raised in this fashion more Mexican lands were added to those already obtained by Owen and Rice.

According to the plans of Owen, the settlement at Topolobampo and in the neighboring Fuerte River Valley was to be an "integral co-operative society," a complete social fellowship

RAILROAD TO UTOPIA AND ITS RIVAL, 1912

in which no one would be exploited by another, a revolt against landlords, merchants, bankers, and captains of industry. There would be no taxes, rents, or interest; no middlemen, advertisers, salesmen, or lawyers. Ten directors elected by the colonists would have charge of public utilities, social relief, and practically all business transactions. Each settler would have a comfortable house and land for cultivation, but these would not be private property; the colonist would have only the right to use them. Rewards for labor would not be the same for all; they would vary with the skill and industry of the individual. Money, as commonly understood, would not be used; services would be exchanged instead. In brief, the colony would be a Socialist Community, a modified Communistic Society.

By the end of 1886 between three and four hundred people had arrived at Topolobampo. They pitched their tents on two town sites, one near the bay and one some thirty-five miles inland at Vegatón; began work on their houses, a road, and the railway; and cleared the fields for planting. There was an abundance of discussion and propaganda, but the Utopia did not prosper. Smallpox, measles, typhoid fever, and other diseases combined with bad management and bitter disputes, among earnest men and women drawn from the four corners of the earth, to wreck the enterprise. Within a few months families began to depart for the United States; others left later. By 1890 only 130 remained despite new arrivals. A few more settlers straggled in later, from Kansas, Colorado, Illinois, and Europe. Michael Flürscheim, a prominent German follower of Henry George, invested money in the project and became a colonist. Hoffman and Owen and Flürscheim soon quarreled. It was impossible to hold the settlers together on the basis of economic principles and theories. In 1898, after a dozen years of work, travel, and worry, and after spending $400,000 of investors' money, Owen admitted that the colony had entirely broken up. On January 2, 1899, his railway concession was finally nullified.

The settlers—from first to last, some 1000 men, women, and children—eked out no more than a scanty living while residing in the three or four colonial centers that were started. Comparatively few stayed for more than a year or two. But altogether they helped to stimulate the cultivation of sugar cane and vegetables in the Fuerte Valley and initiated an important irrigation project.

Owen, Rice, and Hoffman seem to have betrayed the interests of those who remained after the Socialist enterprise was abandoned. Owen conveyed his rights as an individual and trustee to Arthur E. Stilwell; in similar fashion Rice and Hoffman sold

out to the Sinaloa Sugar Company, which established its headquarters at Los Mochis. The remnants of the colony soon discovered that they owned nothing except their clothing, furniture, tools, and chattels. As individuals, they had no title to the
lands they had been working. As individuals, they had no title
to the immense irrigation ditch and the lateral canals they had
dug, nor even the right to use the water. For several years they
fought a losing fight with B. F. Johnston, the manager of the
sugar company. In the end, they had to accept whatever lease-
hold and water agreements they could obtain from the corporation. Meantime, Stilwell was making a mighty effort to build
the railway from Topolobampo to Texas and beyond.

Arthur E. Stilwell was a rather remarkable personality. Born
in Rochester, New York, in 1859, he was the son of a prosperous
family. Because of ill health he received comparatively little
formal schooling. At the age of fourteen, having overcome his
physical handicaps, he ran away from home. After several
months in St. Louis, he went to New York City, where he
worked for a time in a novelty store. Learning that his father
had lost the family fortune, young Arthur returned to Rochester
and established a print shop. But restlessness soon set him on
the road again, this time as a traveling salesman, a vocation in
which he was a success. At the age of nineteen he married Jennie
Wood, a brown-eyed girl from Petersburg, Virginia. A year or
two later he and his young wife went to Kansas City, but they
soon took up their residence in Chicago, where young Arthur
served for a time as agent of eastern photograving firms and
then became a salesman for the Travelers Insurance Company.
By 1886 he had originated life and accident endowment policies
and accumulated some $25,000. Then he decided to go into the
building and loan business. Opening an office in St. Louis, he
remained there only a short time before he moved to Kansas
City. Identifying himself quickly with this growing town, he
made it the center of his activities for nearly a quarter of a
century. By 1900, when he became interested in the railroad
which Albert K. Owen had hoped to build, Stilwell had already
promoted the construction of several railways and engaged in
numerous real estate ventures. The longest of the railroads he
built was the Kansas City Southern, running across Kansas,

Missouri, Arkansas, and Texas to Port Arthur, named in his honor.

Stilwell frequently denounced the railway despots and ruthless bankers of the East and often advocated cheaper rates. On the road from Kansas City to Port Arthur, of which he was president, he is said to have reduced shipping costs remarkably and to have aroused thereby the hostility of bankers and bigger railroad men—Ernest Thalmann of Ladenburg, Thalmann and Company, the financial allies of Standard Oil, John W. Gates, and Edward H. Harriman—who turned upon him, wrecked his companies, and expelled him from the presidency of the Kansas City Southern late in 1900. Anticipating events, Stilwell had already gone to Mexico during the earlier months of that year, signed an agreement with Owen to buy out his Mexican interests, obtained a railway contract by transfer from other railway promoters in northwestern Mexico, and secured a concession from the Díaz government. By these three transactions he had obtained the right to build a railroad, with several branches, from Topolobampo to Presidio del Norte, soon to be called Ojinaca; and by the terms of the various contracts a good part of the line was entitled to large subsidies from the Mexican government.

This Mexican railway, however, was merely a part of a much larger project which Stilwell had in mind. He planned to build a trunk line some 1659 miles long across Kansas, Oklahoma, Texas, and northwestern Mexico to Topolobampo, to obtain contributions from local enthusiasts along the road, to colonize the lands within its zone of influence, to build towns and cities, to exploit minerals and timber, and to furnish cheaper access to the Orient by means of this short-cut to China.

Returning to Kansas City he organized a multitude of allied corporations, with himself at their head in most cases. The following list is approximately complete:

The United States and Mexican Trust Company of Alabama
The Kansas City, Mexico and Orient Railway Company of Kansas
The Kansas City, Mexico and Orient Railway Company of Texas
The International Construction Company of Delaware
The Union Construction Company of Delaware
The Western Tie and Lumber Company of Arkansas

The Kansas City Outer Belt and Electric Railroad
The Mexican Timber Fields Company
The Rio Grande Coal Fields Company
The Sierra Madre Development Company
The Mexico and Orient Townsite Company
The Chihuahua and Sinaloa Development Company

Stilwell believed that he was an empire builder, a Cecil Rhodes, a James J. Hill, and probably imagined he was a genuine humanitarian as well. But he was mainly a promoter and a plunger. Although the terrain along most of the proposed route opposed no serious obstacles, a stretch of nearly a hundred miles in western Mexico, with dizzy precipices, and gorges deeper than the Grand Canyon of Colorado, would require the surmounting of as difficult topography as existed in North America. His projected railway would not pass through a single important town between Wichita, Kansas, and Chihuahua City; and beyond the latter urban center, there was no metropolis this side of the Hawaiian Islands. The trade of those islands, and that of Australia, China, and the rest of the Orient, was already flowing in well-beaten channels.

The greatest obstacles confronted by Stilwell, aside from sparse settlement, established commercial lanes, and the Mexican mountain section, were financial. He seems to have been opposed by both the Wall Street bankers and the railway magnates of the United States. He could not convince himself that their hostility had anything to do with the soundness of his immense undertaking. He did not ask the Eastern financiers to help him float his securities; he probably would not have solicited their aid even if he had considered them more friendly. The commissions exacted by investment bankers provoked his animosity. The fact that Edward H. Harriman, then in control of the Southern Pacific, began to extend his lines into western Mexico shortly after construction began on Stilwell's ambitious project may or may not have been proof of Stilwell's contentions, but the move was bound to affect the success of his huge enterprise. Moreover, the Panic of 1907 and Mexican revolutions of 1911-1912 should not be forgotten in this summary of Stilwell's difficulties.

The distribution of the securities of his numerous affiliated corporations was largely the work of Stilwell himself. Confident, energetic, fluent, magnetic, he was also a confirmed mystic. A member of the Christian Scientist Church, he composed sacred music, installed an organ in his luxurious official railway car, held services on Sundays, and seemed to think that the "spirits" could advise him on perplexing financial problems. Making several journeys across the Atlantic, he sold a considerable quantity of his paper in England and Holland where he had floated some of the securities of his earlier corporations. The rest he marketed in the United States, perhaps mainly in the West, and in Mexico. He took numerous parties over sections of the railway as they were completed, and conducted nine groups of prospective investors partially or wholly over other railroads to Mexico before the end of March, 1907. He also kept his activities on the front pages of Western newspapers, had them reported in railway journals, and managed to insert articles in Eastern financial magazines with the view of broadcasting them as reprints. His railway enterprise was discussed enthusiastically, for instance, by the *Financial World* in 1906 and in both *Moody's Magazine* and *Banker's Magazine* in 1910. He was usually represented as a popular hero struggling magnificently against enemies and exploiters of the people.

The net proceeds of his sales cannot be determined. Bonus was heaped upon bonus in bewildering confusion. He probably raised between thirteen and twenty million dollars in cash by 1912; but in return for this sum he had issued nearly fifty millions, valued at par, in common stock, preferred stock, and bonds. By that time he had in operation some 868 miles of railway, of which around 300, consisting of two disconnected sections, were in Mexico. One of the latter linked Topolobampo and San Pedro, at the edge of the Sierras. The other, a part of which was not built by Stilwell, extended from Miñaca to Chihuahua City and from there northeastward toward the international boundary. The longer line in the United States extended from Wichita, Kansas, to San Angelo, Texas.

Such was the Kansas City, Mexico and Orient after twelve years of busy effort by Stilwell. Before the end of 1912 his railway was forced into bankruptcy and he was ousted from its control. This ended his business career, but already he had begun to use his pen. Between 1911 and 1921 he published seven books in spite of an accident in 1914 which left him an invalid. In 1927-1928, shortly before his death, his memoirs, written in collaboration with James R. Crowell, appeared in the form of six articles in the *Saturday Evening Post*. Filled with egotism, optimism, and mild bitterness toward the financial foes of his active business days, they were entitled, "I Had a Hunch."

After years of bankruptcy and receivership, the northern part of the Kansas City, Mexico and Orient was absorbed by the Santa Fe system in 1928 and was extended shortly afterward through Alpine to the Mexican boundary. The Mexican portion of the road was purchased in 1928 by B. F. Johnston, the sugar magnate of Los Mochis, who managed to continue the line northward to Ojinaja, but failed to finish the southern mountain section. Late in 1940 he sold the railway to the Mexican national government, which, no doubt, will complete the line as soon as war-time restrictions on construction materials are lifted.

Owen's dream of a Socialist commonwealth on Mexico's West Coast may eventually become a reality also. The advance of the Southern Pacific—a far more important railway than the *Oriente* from the viewpoint of Mexico—down to Tepic, which it reached in 1912, helped to incite a land boom, in which Californians and other Westerners eagerly participated. Vast tracts were bought up in the river valleys of northwestern Mexico, huge irrigation works were begun, and Yankee and Mexican farmers began to pour in; but the movement was interrupted by Mexico's revolutions and the reform epoch that followed. The national government eventually took control of irrigation, declaring it a public utility, pared down the big estates, and distributed lands among the natives. Although the Southern Pacific of Mexico, which had been pushed across the Sierras toward Guadalajara in the late 1920's, was still in private hands in 1943, a definite trend toward State Socialism was evident. Whatever the future of the West Coast region, Yankee capital, enthusiasm, and energy, in building these hundreds of miles of railway, inaugurating irrigation systems, stimulating the growth of sugar, and working the mines, had made an important contribution to the development of that section of the country. Under Mexico's new régime, however, contributions from the United States, whether to this or to other regions of Mexico, probably will be confined more and more to technological services, government loans, and commercial interchange.

A FORGOTTEN EPISODE IN
PLANTATION RUBBER

MILLIONS OF AMERICANS, North and South, doubtless would agree that an ample supply of rubber trees in the Western Hemisphere would have been a great convenience during the acute rubber shortage of the 1940's. If plans initiated half a century before had been carried to success, such a supply might have been at hand. Many people in the United States once dreamed of large-scale rubber cultivation in the neighboring tropics.

During the twenty years or so following 1880 consumption of rubber expanded enormously, especially in connection with the electrical and vehicle industries where huge quantities were used in insulation and for bicycle, buggy, and automobile tires. With consumption rising rapidly and with the natives of Africa and Latin America destroying the wild trees by careless and ruthless methods of extracting *latex,* it was clear that the demand for crude rubber would soon far outrun the supply unless rubber could be cultivated. British scientists had been trying to domesticate the plant since the 1870's and had started a number of "rubber orchards" in Ceylon and Singapore during the two decades that followed; but at the end of the century rubber cultivation was still in the experimental stage and rubber prices were still soaring.

Late in 1890 the State Department at Washington had sent out a circular to consuls in all parts of the world calling for information on the rubber industry and sources of the raw product. The replies, published in 1892, forecast a rubber famine and aroused hopes of large and comparatively easy returns from cultivated rubber. These and subsequent consular reports, widely circulated by the Commerce Department and reinforced by propaganda of tropical real estate salesmen, determined the location of the plantation experiment. Southern Mexico and Central America, both right at our door, were the native habitat of a species of rubber trees known as *Castilloa elastica*. These were the regions and the trees selected. The British, it is true, were carrying out their experiments in the Orient and mainly with Pará, or *Hevea brasiliensis;* but no one had yet demonstrated that *Heveas* planted in the Middle East would be better producers than *Castilloas* cultivated in America.

Scores of enterprising Yankees and Southerners had for some time been engaged in growing bananas, sugar, coffee, and cacao in tropical lands to the south. They now began to cultivate rubber, proceeding rather cautiously. It was not long, however, until others with far less experience or none at all plunged wildly into the rubber-plantation business. Eager for profits and careless with other people's money they made full use of the corporation, which was at that time almost unhampered by government regulation.

Their first step was to get possession of vast stretches of jungle located in areas receiving the bountiful and evenly distributed rainfall, seventy to a hundred and twenty inches annually, required to produce rubber trees. The necessary real estate was promptly secured by a few individuals and several land and lumber companies, old and new.

The second step was the organization of plantation corporations designed to emphasize rubber culture while giving some attention to other crops and to cattle. These were rapidly created. A few were organized by the land speculators themselves, some of whom possessed experience in tropical agriculture. The majority were set up by promoters who knew almost nothing about the American tropics.

If the promoters had been interested solely or primarily in growing rubber trees, the organization of the rubber-plantation business might have stopped with the setting up of the plantation companies, whose managers, employing such experts as they could assemble, could have set to work directly, clearing away the jungle, planting the nurseries, and putting out the infant rubber trees. This would have been the most economical procedure, and it was followed by a few of the plantation companies. It involved, however, a little more risk on the part of the managerial group and the sacrifice of a further opportunity for profits at the expense of stockholders.

A third step was therefore taken. Under the same management as the plantation companies, development corporations were set up similar to the construction companies employed with such brilliant success by the "insiders" in building railways. These development corporations could be used like the railroad construction companies to siphon away the funds from plantation company treasuries. Controlling as a rule both the plantation corporations and the plantation development corporations, the managerial group could fix their own price for clearing, planting, and cultivating. They would be negotiating with themselves. They could obtain their profits, double profits, whether they produced rubber economically or not. They could obtain profits even if they produced no rubber at all. Profits, not rubber, were too often the primary objective. "Saps" would yield better returns than saplings, and the harvest would be more immediate. Sometimes the same groups controlled the plantation, the development, and the land companies, all three.

With this triple assemblage of machinery, or even merely a dual combination, the promoters and managers would be bound to succeed provided they could sell the rubber securities. And the securities were sold. They were floated by as clever propaganda as the people of the United States had ever experienced. The Wall Street bankers were not employed; they were in rather ill repute at the time among the little fellows, especially those of the West, whose confidence the rubber executives were determined to win. The managerial group and their agents approached the investors directly.

Prominent men and men whose integrity was likely to be assumed were given places on administrative staffs and boards of directors: Thomas A. Edison, former State governors, former congressmen, ex-officials of the National Treasury or State treasuries, university professors, public-school superintendents, local business men of one sort or another, prominent physicians, and preachers. Such men were trusted by the common people of the country.

Having employed this impressive personnel, the promoters

sent out overwhelming appeals in hundreds of prospectuses and pamphlets. They also published numerous advertisements and colored news items in local newspapers, in the *Mexican Herald, Modern Mexico,* the *Mexican Investor,* the *India Rubber World,* and some of the popular magazines. In learned short essays apparently filled with scientific caution, "oldtimers" of the "hot lands" assured prospective investors that they would make no mistake if they ventured their savings in rubber plantations. Sir Thomas Lipton, the tea millionaire, was quoted as declaring that tropical agriculture, from which the bulk of British wealth was said to have come, was the soundest and most profitable investment in the world. Collis P. Huntington, magnate of the Western railways, was represented as advising that rubber was a surer means of accumulating a fortune than the railroad business. William Allen White was quoted as early as 1901 to the effect that automobiles were swarming on the streets of Emporia and that fine Kansas country boys were all driving their best girls about on Sunday afternoons in rubber-tired buggies. Californians were told that Joaquin Miller, popular "poet of the Sierras," was spending his vacations on rubber *fincas* in Mexico. The tropics were a delightful region where Harvard men could read Homer after the day's work was finished.

Dividends of five, ten, and fifteen per cent on rubber investments were promised immediately from "side crops," and higher returns after six or seven years when the rubber trees should begin to pour forth their liquid gold. Annual yields of from three to twenty pounds from a single tree were forecast. Rubber securities were placed within the reach of all. Small farmers, little business men, policemen, firemen, clerks, teachers, preachers, harassed widows, all the hard-driven poor who longed for greater comforts and security in old age were offered a chance to escape from their bondage of toil and anxiety. Bonds and other securities could be bought on the installment plan for as low as two dollars a month. Attractive bonuses were offered and discounts to those with more liquid assets. Investors were insured against the calamity of death by policies providing for cancellation of the indebtedness of the deceased and transmission of the securities to their heirs.

Here was a vision of prosperity for common men and women! Did it seem too good to be true? Reverend A. J. Scott of Chicago exhorted all doubters to read their Bibles and find abundant evidence of God's love for the poor. Scott was the Chicago salesman for J. W. Ellsworth, missionary, preacher, and the first president of the Chiapas Rubber Plantation Company of California. Not to be outdone in this enterprise of serving the meek and lowly, the Zacualpa Rubber Plantation Company displayed some of its product at an Epworth League Convention held in San Francisco in July, 1901. The good Methodists may or may not have learned that the rubber came from wild *Castilloas*.

Plantation companies sprang up like mushrooms during the decade following 1898. The number devoted partly or entirely to rubber cultivation certainly exceeded two hundred; there may have been a good many more. Plantation companies were organized in half the States of the Union; in the lead were Illinois, California, Missouri, New York, Massachusetts, Ohio, Indiana, Wisconsin, and Minnesota. Most of the corporations were operating in Mexico; some twenty-five or thirty owned plantations in Central America; a few held property in Cuba or Ecuador.

Germans from St. Louis and Milwaukee, Scandinavians from Minneapolis and St. Paul, men of many races in Chicago, Anglo-Saxons in numerous towns and cities scattered from Maine to Texas and Oregon, Californians with a flavor of Spanish culture, all were soon busy pronouncing and mispronouncing Spanish names. There were rivers, towns, and other administrative units: Tuxpam, Grijalva, Usumacinta, Tulijá, Trinidad, Chamelicón; Tierra Blanca, Tonalá, Santa Lucrecia, San Juan Bautista, Escuintla, Matagalpa, and San Pedro Sula; Campeche, Oaxaca, Chiapas, Tehuantepec, Soconusco, and Zelaya. There were such *haciendas* as Dos Ríos, Tres Ríos, Rúbio, Del Corte, La Junta, Zacualpa, Colombia, Esmeralda, Esperanza, Roblito, San Silverio, El Obispo, Lolita, Doña María, Buena Ventura, Vista Hermosa, Triunfo, Aztec, Montezuma, and many more. These became familiar names to thousands who invested their savings or emerged triumphant from repeated encounters with sharp and aggressive salesmen. A few of the promoters preferred to carry Yankee names into the hot countries. On placards erected at jungle edges one might read Plantación Yale, Iowa, Tennessee, Philadelphia, Pittsburg (final *h* deliberately omitted), and Joliet, or Finca Chicago or Manhattan, or plain Daytonia. Several Mexicans and Central Americans owned small rubber plantations, but the majority of the Latins were content to sell their lands at a profit and leave the enterprise of rubber cultivation to the impetuous North Americans.

In spite of efforts made by national officials to keep the movement within bounds, in spite of warnings published in *Consular Reports* and bulletins of the Department of Agriculture, the people of the United States indulged in a rubber-plantation speculation spree. Federal agents were berated for presuming to give advice on matters concerning which they were not qualified to speak. One was said to have lost his position for reporting adversely and without adequate evidence on the rubber plantations of Mexico.

Full confidence and complete optimism were necessary if the little investors were to continue their installment payments. They were told that they could well afford to risk a few dollars a month for six or seven years even without any dividends at all if thereafter they were likely to secure in return a comfortable income of fifteen hundred or so annually for life. Reputable individuals—preachers, lawyers, physicians, dentists, school superintendents, college professors—were sent down by the managers to make annual inspections of the plantations. Many of them knew nothing about rubber. Some of their reports were phrased in moderate language; the majority were exaggerated and ardent; a few were completely deceptive. Sometimes the value of the reports could not be assessed without passing judgment on the inspector's capacity as a prophet. Charles C. Lasby, a Brooklyn preacher sent down to inspect the Mexican Plantation Company's "Philadelphia," filled his report with predictions regarding the state of the rubber trees on this tract and prices of rubber six or seven years hence. The predictions, of course, were bullish; but they might have been almost as glowing if he had made them while standing on the Brooklyn Bridge at midnight. Photography was used effectively. Photographs of luxurious tropical vegetation, a few rubber trees, probably of the wild variety, in the foreground, with barefoot men under big *som-*

breros engaged in clearing or tapping, were employed to the limit. In the meantime, some of the holders of stocks, bonds, or certificates were receiving small dividends derived from Indian corn, coffee, sugar, cacao, and cattle or drawn from more mysterious sources.

Installment payments continued to come in and new companies continued to be organized. The rubber enthusiasm was kept up in spite of bankruptcy in some cases and revelations of fraud in others. One or two instances of fraud were discovered in 1900; others were exposed in 1903, 1905, and as late as 1908. The financial panic which began in the United States in October, 1907, caused a number of liquidations and reorganizations; but thousands of rubber trees were planted as late as 1910. In short, the rubber-plantation boom lasted more than ten years.

The aggregate of stocks, bonds, and "rubber-harvest certificates" bought by the public during those years has not been precisely determined. Lands purchased or leased at from a few cents to a few dollars an acre were sold to rubber-plantation companies at a good profit and then capitalized for developmental purposes at from $250 to $300 an acre. The authorized capitalization of the various corporations probably amounted to well over $100,000,000; but the promoters and managers did not succeed in marketing all of their securities. Lands acquired in one way or another in Mexico and Central America probably totaled some two million acres; but only a hundred thousand or so were actually cleared and planted in rubber before the boom collapsed. An equal or a considerably larger area was devoted to other crops and to grazing. Jungle, some of which was exploited for timber and wild rubber, remained on the rest. First and last, between forty and fifty million *Castilloa* rubber trees and a sprinking of *Heveas* were planted at an actual cost of almost as many million dollars.

Rubber planting was an expensive business. The development corporations did not fail to charge for their services. A few collected for clearing, planting, and cultivating which they never did. Two or three rubber-plantation companies sold securities and paid dividends without ever acquiring plantations anywhere.

These and other extravagances got a number of the promoters

into trouble. The law prohibited some things even in that day of corporate liberty. Statutes forbade the payment of dividends from the proceeds of security sales, and patently false advertising was likely to cause difficulty with the Federal postal authorities. Dr. Frank B. Bittinger, an Ohio promoter, was jailed for a year and a day and fined a thousand dollars. Francisco Borges, a Spanish-American security salesman, served ten years in the Massachusetts State Penitentiary. William B. Owen, an Indiana politician associated with Borges in the launching of numerous plantation and development companies, managed to escape to Europe with half a million dollars mulcted from stockholders. Talton Embry and Hiram E. Rose of Chicago created the San Miguel Plantation Company in 1900, developed a plantation which never existed on land or sea, issued regular annual inspection reports, photographs and all, paid several annual dividends, and were not convicted of fraud until 1908.

No doubt there were other similar cases and still more instances of abuse of stockholders in ways not then forbidden by law. But it is likely that many of the companies, perhaps the majority, made honest, vigorous, and conscientious efforts to produce plantation rubber in the American tropics. In fact, some of them did produce rubber, but at costs greater than investors could afford even in a period of soaring rubber prices. Several rubber experts were discovered or trained: James C. Harvey, J. Herbert Foster, C. A. Lesher, Professors L. A. Ostien, V. O. Petterson, Pehr Olssen-Seffer, H. H. Markley, A. B. Luther, R. O. Price, and a number of others. They call forth our sympathies. They deserve to be remembered because of their industry and perseverance. The companies should have employed more men of their kind.

From the practical standpoint, however, it was of little importance who was employed. The effort was doomed. It was doomed by a fatal error at the outset in the selection of trees. The tamed *Castilloas* were not good producers. They could not compete with the *Heveas* on British and Dutch plantations across the Pacific, which began to yield considerable quantities of the raw product in 1905 and were producing by 1914 more rubber than all the rest of the world combined. *Castilloa* plantation rubber could not even compete with the wild rubber collected in South America and Africa or with *guayule* growing in northern Mexico. The pounds dreamed of from each tree turned out to be ounces or less.

Promoters and men on the ground were coming to realize their failure by 1908 or earlier. But they were reluctant to admit defeat so long as the little installments trickled in. They shifted their emphasis to other crops, cut down the rubber trees or left them to face a death struggle with tropical rivals, and quietly laid plans to sell out their properties. While jungle lands and rubber orchards were being transferred to banana and sugar corporations in Central America, private speculators and real-estate companies laid schemes to attract small farmers from the South and West into the Mexican *tierra caliente*. Land agents swarmed in Mexico and over a good part of the United States. Crowded excursion-trains crossed the border. Tens of thousands of acres changed hands briskly. Hundreds of settlers from Illinois, Kansas, Oklahoma, Texas, California, and other parts of the Union moved into southern Mexico. They might have occupied the major part of it if the climate and political conditions had been more agreeable. The migration was rudely interrupted by the long Mexican revolution which broke out in 1911.

North Americans were soon subjected to abuse—beaten, robbed, killed, forced to flee for their lives, warned to leave the country by the government back home. Lush jungle growth spread itself over the fields and continued to crowd and choke the remnants of the *Castilloas*. It was a tropical tragedy.

Yet, if the Mexican revolution with its slogan of "Mexico for the Mexicans" had not occurred, the bulk of Mexico's lands would soon have been owned by the people of the United States and the Mexicans would have been tilling them for forty or fifty cents a day. Already the peons had been toiling for several years on *haciendas* and ranches owned by the North Americans. On the rubber plantations the treatment they received, though sometimes worse, was often better than that accorded them by their Mexican employers. Practically all of the workers were *enganches,* debt slaves whose bondage was not very different from the slavery of other regions in other days. They were shipped down to the rubber lands by labor agents who collected commissions on every laborer sent. They worked, under Mexican foremen as a rule, from dawn to sunset, eked out a *peso* (about fifty cents in United States money) or less a day, received scant medical attention, bought their meager supplies from the company stores, and sometimes were compelled to sleep in rough barracks under lock and key. Piece- or task-work was the custom; a stipulated sum was paid for so much land cleared, weeded, or cultivated, or a certain number of rubber trees tapped.

Under Díaz and upper-class Mexicans and the North Americans the bondage of the Mexican masses would have continued, perhaps a little alleviated by employers accustomed to deal with free labor in the United States. Following 1910 the peons were "liberated" by the army recruiting officers of Francisco Madero, Emiliano Zapata, and other insurgent leaders.

Dynamic corporate capitalism from the United States had penetrated Mexico, gained possession of mines, oil regions, ranches, and farms in the North, bought up plantations in the South, sent managers and overseers into all parts of the country, developed some regions, failed in their efforts to produce rubber economically in the *tierra caliente,* and then pushed in the small farmers and ranchmen. But the dynamic thrust of corporate capitalism encountered Mexican nationalism and Mexican longing to possess the land, confronted tremendous resentment and widespread violence. Only military intervention by the United States and the prevention of rapid social change could have shielded the movement from across the border and made it remotely safe. Not a few would have welcomed such intervention, but it was denied. The restraint on the part of the United States government was unusual; but the policy was approved, perhaps even dictated, by majority sentiment in this country. A potent force was halted, thrown back, frustrated, at least for a time.

Would the experiment in plantation rubber have succeeded under better auspices and in more favorable circumstances, if *Heveas* had been selected instead of *Castilloas,* if there had been less defrauding of stockholders and no Mexican revolution? Granted all this and an abundant supply of docile labor, considerable rubber might have been produced on Mexican plantations located on proper soil and in areas free from seasonal droughts. It might also have been grown in some regions of Guatemala, Nicaragua, Honduras, Costa Rica, and Panama, where revolutions were less disturbing factors. If the local labor supply had proved inadequate, it could have been supplemented by Orientals and Caribbean Negroes.

Labor conditions would have tended, however, to remain as deplorable as they were in Java, Ceylon, Sumatra, and British Malaya. Otherwise American plantation rubber could not have competed with plantation rubber from the Middle East. Unless labor standards can be raised in both regions, unless sanitation, refrigeration, and air-conditioning can make workers in these torrid zones healthier and more comfortable, the synthetic product would seem preferable from the humanitarian viewpoint. Can men really be happy in the rain and in perpetual sweltering heat? Under improved management of the world's affairs will the inhabitants of these unhealthful and miserable sections be removed to better climates? Or will more and more human beings be thrust into the rainy tropical lands to cultivate more and more rubber?

ARRIVAL OF THE TELEPHONE IN
LATIN AMERICA

Y ANKEE INVENTORS and owners of the original telephones
were a farseeing and energetic group. Men like Alexander
Graham Bell, Frederic Allen Gower, Gardiner G. Hubbard and
his nephew Charles Eustis Hubbard, William H. Forbes,
Thomas A. Edison, Henry S. Russell, and Theodore Newton
Vail made vigorous efforts to send their new means of rapid
communication speedily to all parts of the civilized world.

In considerable measure they succeeded. These men and their
allies were the telephone pioneers in most of Europe and Latin
America. In the late 1870's, they introduced their telephones
into England, France, and Switzerland; and before the middle
of the next decade, they carried them to Belgium, Holland,
Denmark, Norway, Sweden, Russia, and Portugal. Their chief
agency of promotion in that region was the International Bell
Telephone Company. In Europe, however, this company and
its operating associates were soon hampered by a strong trend
toward government ownership and management. In Latin
America, where such a trend was not often encountered in the
pioneering years, progress was restricted by political revolutions and poverty of the masses. In 1913, a third of a century
after the telephone's appearance, there were hardly more than
half a million instruments under private ownership and operation
in the whole of Europe and there were less than a quarter of a
million under all types of ownership and management in Latin
America.

The parent organization for promotion in Latin America was
the Continental Telephone Company, which was incorporated
in Massachusetts on January 7, 1880, by Theodore Vail, William H. Forbes, George L. Bradley, Charles E. Hubbard, and

Charles Emerson, all connected with the growing Bell system. From this parent company stemmed a number of subsidiaries and associates organized in many cases by the same group or close allies. During the early 1880's the Continental signed contracts covering practically all Latin America, including the little countries of Central America and the West Indies.

In collaboration with these subsidiary and associated companies, the Continental began promptly to set up telephone exchanges in most of the Latin-American countries. Expansion, however, was not rapid; and, at places where the new instrument proved most popular, European capitalists, especially the British, often took control sooner or later.

The Telephone Company of Brazil, under concessions obtained from the Brazilian government by Charles P. Mackie and others, installed telephones in Rio de Janeiro early in 1881 and in other Brazilian towns shortly thereafter. Within four years it established seven exchanges, three in the capital and four in other centers, Pernambuco (Recife) and Bahía among them. Rival companies backed by British, Brazilian, and Yankee capital soon sprang up; and by 1890 most of the leading towns of the country had at least a few telephones, although the majority of the instruments were still in the national capital. Between 1897 and 1907 Germans strongly entrenched themselves in the Brazilian telephone business; afterward, a combination of Canadian and United States capital took over the principal exchanges, which were then located in the states of São Paulo and Rio Grande do Sul, as well as in Rio de Janeiro and the Federal District. At the end of 1913 Brazil had a total of only 39,183 telephone instruments, with 11,379 in Rio de Janeiro and most of the remainder in São Paulo City and Porto Alegre, the capital of Rio Grande do Sul. None of the other states had as many as 1500 telephones in 1913, and the majority of them possessed only a few hundred. Yet at that time Brazil occupied third place among the Latin-American nations in the total number of telephones in operation.

Argentina's first telephones were established by Yankee and British promoters in the city of Buenos Aires in 1881. The first concession went to Benjamin D. Manton, who was the representative of the brilliant Yankee inventor and promoter Frederic Allen Gower. Manton is said to have been a descendant of Roger Williams. Opening his first exchange with only thirty-four subscribers, he confronted rivals immediately. The competing groups got together the next year, however, forming a new company called the Union Telephone Company. But this new organization likewise encountered a rival in the River Plate Telephone and Electric Light Company, Limited, an organization formed in London in 1882 by Frederic Allen Gower, Alexander Graham Bell, Thomas A. Edison, and half a dozen Englishmen, including Sir Julius Vogel and Sir William Drake. Vigorous competition continued until 1886 when both companies were absorbed by the United River Plate Telephone Company, Limited, another corporation located in London. This latest organization, which was for a time closely associated with the Continental Telephone Company and the Tropical American Telephone Company of Boston, dominated the field for several decades. Incomplete statistics for the year 1896 indicate that the United River Plate Company was operating nearly 90 per cent of all the telephones in Argentina. The progress of the telephone in the country was not very rapid until after 1900. There were hardly more than 8000 instruments in 1896; but at the end of 1913 the total was 74,296, with 47,781 telephones in the national capital. Small as this total for 1913 was, it represented nearly a third of all the telephones in Latin America at the time. In the employment of the new means of communication Argentina was far ahead of any other country in the region.

Benjamin D. Manton was also among the telephone pioneers in Uruguay, where he installed the first telephones in Montevideo and probably in Colonia as well. In Uruguay, Manton was the representative of the Consolidated Telephone Construction and Maintenance Company, Limited, which was organized in London in 1881 by Gower, Bell, Edison, Vogel, Drake, and their associates. Uruguay's first telephone exchange was set up in Montevideo during the spring of 1882 by Manton and an Englishman named E. F. Powers. The system was immediately taken over by the River Plate Telephone and Electric Light Company, Limited, an organization then in the telephone business in Argentina, as we have seen. Although it was acquired by the United River Plate Telephone Company, Limited, in 1886, the River Plate Telephone and Electric Light Company continued to manage the service in Uruguay until 1889, when the system was taken over by the Montevideo Telephone Company, Limited, which had been incorporated in London the year before. In 1889, likewise, the Uruguayans set up an organization of their own, the National Telephone Co-operative Society, which was for several years a strong competitor of the Montevideo Telephone Company. In 1896, for instance, the co-operative group had 1510 telephones in their system while the Montevideo company had only 1287. Shortly afterward, however, the British company began to forge ahead. At the end of 1913 Uruguay had 13,599 telephones, 8049 of them in the national capital. Only five Latin-American countries had more telephones than this small country at that time. Uruguay was the only South American country that was revealing a strong tendency toward government ownership.

The pioneer promoter of the telephone on South America's Pacific Coast was Joseph D. Husbands, a citizen of the United States but long a resident of Chile. Having gone to the United States and obtained a contract for the use of the inventions of Edison, Husbands received from the Chilean government on April 26, 1880, a concession providing for the installation of telephones in the leading towns of the country. The next year he organized the Chilean Edison Telephone Company and set up an exchange in Valparaíso. Half of the shares of the company were taken by Husbands himself, an eighth by Lucius H. Foote, United States consul at Valparaíso, and the rest by Chileans and Englishmen.

Lacking sufficient funds and afraid he might be sued by the Bell group and owners of other patents, Husbands made voyages to England and the United States in search of capital and additional rights. After many months of negotiation he seems to have obtained agreements with all the telephone inventors and all the companies engaged in promoting the new invention abroad. Among the companies he dealt with were Gower's Construction and Maintenance Company, Limited, the Continental Telephone Company, and the Tropical American Telephone Company. His efforts to float a corporation in England failed;

but in the United States he succeeded in organizing the West Coast Telephone Company, which was chartered in New York on September 20, 1884. Among the stockholders were H. L. Storke, George W. Piper, Albert P. Sawyer, and O. E. Madden, who was assistant manager of the American Bell Telephone Company.

Returning to Chile, Husbands bought out the Edison Company and secured a new franchise covering the entire country. By the summer of 1889 his new organization was operating exchanges in fourteen or more Chilean towns, with nearly 2000 subscribers, although most of the telephones were in Santiago and Valparaíso. In that year the West Coast Company's Chilean properties were acquired by the Chili Telephone Company, Limited, a London corporation. The latter company was almost without a rival in Chile until the Chileans themselves set up the National Telephone Company in 1897, and even this company furnished little competition. At the end of 1913, Chile had 19,709 telephones, with 6299 in Santiago, and more than 60 per cent of them were a part of the Chili Telephone system. The National Company possessed less than 10 per cent; the rest were divided among several small organizations operating in the minor towns of the provinces. At the close of 1913, only Argentina, Mexico, and Brazil, among the Latin-American nations, ranked ahead of Chile in the number of telephone instruments in use.

Until after 1900, the telephone made very little progress in the rest of the South American nations. Telephone statistics for these countries at the close of 1913 follows: Venezuela, 5029; Peru, some 4000; Colombia, 3177; Ecuador, 2926; Bolivia, approximately 2500; Paraguay, 499, often out of commission. Political disorders and poverty among the masses, as we have noted already, were the main factors accounting for the slow advance of the new means of communication.

The story of telephone pioneering in Paraguay and Bolivia is obscure. The Continental Telephone Company and the Tropical Telephone Company may have obtained concessions in both countries in the early 1880's. At any rate, they seem to have assigned to the Argentine and Chilean companies the right to use their patents in Paraguay and Bolivia. No doubt the first exchanges were set up in Paraguay shortly before 1892, and it is likely that the telephone arrived in Bolivia about the same time. The exact dates and the names of the pioneers have not been ascertained.

The first telephone exchange in Peru was installed in Lima in 1888, by the West Coast Telephone Company; but the exchange was taken over by the British shortly afterward. Gradually, during the next twenty years, the telephone appeared in the leading towns. At the end of 1913 half of Peru's 4000 telephones were in Lima, with most of the remainder in Mollendo and Arequipa. The Lima exchange was still owned by English capitalists.

Ecuador's first telephones, as noted in another chapter, were established at Guayaquil by the West Coast Telephone Company in 1885. A decade later they began to be used in the national capital. The Guayaquil exchange was taken over by the Chili Telephone Company in 1912. At the end of the next year, approximately 2250 of the nation's 2926 telephones were in that city. Nearly all the rest were in Quito, many of them in government offices. The long-distance lines were built by William L. Russell and Claude B. Wynn, citizens of the United States.

Venezuela's first exchange was installed in Caracas in 1883 by the Inter-Continental Telephone Company, which may have installed the first telephone in Valencia shortly afterward; at any rate, it was citizens of the United States who inaugurated the pioneer system there. They may likewise have been the pioneers in Maracaibo, and they certainly constructed the first long-distance lines. By 1890, however, most of Venezuela's exchanges were acquired by the Venezuela Telephone and Electric Appliances Company, Limited, which was a British corporation. At the close of 1913 more than half of Venezuela's telephones were located in the national capital.

Although Colombia's first telephones were installed late in 1884, in Bogotá, their use seems to have been limited for some time to the offices of the national government. The first public system in the country was established in Santa Marta shortly before 1889 by the West India and Colombia Electric Company, owned by citizens of the United States. In 1889 and immediately following the first exchanges were opened in Cartagena and Barranquilla by a North American technician, probably Roger Case, in the employment of the West India Company, with J. P. Dieter of Chicago as manager. The year 1890 witnessed the arrival of the telephone in Cúcuta, and two more exchanges were installed in 1892, one in Medellín by the departmental government of Antioquia and the other in Bogotá, probably by Eugene Betts, a citizen of the United States. The exchange in Cali, opened by a local company headed by Jorge Zawadsky, was not set up until 1912. By that time Colombia's telephones, although scant in number, were rather widely distributed. Only 940 of the country's 3177 instruments at the close of 1913 were in Bogotá. In the course of the next twenty years most of the Colombian exchanges were acquired and expanded by the Associated Telephone and Telegraph Company, a corporation controlled by Chicago capitalists. The Medellín exchange, however, continued to be government-owned, and in the early 1940's the municipality of Bogotá bought out the system in the national capital.

Satisfactory information is not in hand with reference to the early telephone systems of the Latin countries of Central America and the Caribbean islands. Haiti did not have any telephones as late as 1913 and Cuba, with 16,097 at that time, possessed more than all the rest of these nations combined, although well above three-fourths of Cuba's telephones were in Havana. The following are the statistics for the rest of the countries: Panama, 2635, mostly in the Canal Zone and owned by the United States government; Guatemala, 1769; El Salvador, 1728; Costa Rica, 934; Honduras, 500 or less; Nicaragua, 466; and the Dominican Republic, 690. The systems of Nicaragua, Honduras, and El Salvador were largely government-owned and government-operated.

The first telephones in the majority of these small countries were installed in the 1880's, mainly by citizens of the United States. The patent contracts signed by the Continental Telephone Company and the Tropical Telephone Company, as we have seen, embraced Central America and the West Indies. The first telephones were set up in Guatemala City by Roderico Toledo, probably in collaboration with Californians, before 1885. The first were installed in Costa Rica in 1886, although the first public system was not opened until the early 1890's. It will be recalled that the pioneers here were Roberto Castro, Silas W. Hastings, Francisco M. Boza, and Minor C. Keith. Castro was a Costa Rican and Boza a Cuban; Hastings like Keith was a North American. The first telephones reached Cuba as early as 1882 and El Salvador in 1888. In 1908 the leading exchanges of Cuba were taken over by Hernand and Sosthenes Behn, natives of the Danish West Indies but naturalized in the United States. The company which they formed in that year was called the Cuban Telephone Company. More than three-fourths of Cuba's telephones at the end of 1913 were in Havana, nearly all of Guatemala's were in Guatemala City, and most of Costa Rica's were in San José. Elsewhere in Central America and the Hispanic West Indies they were better distributed.

The Mexican Telephone Company, owned by citizens of the United States, was the pioneer telephone organization of Mexico, although it is likely that the first telephones were installed by others in the offices of the national, state, and local governments. This company opened its first exchanges in Mexico City and several other towns in the early 1880's. Confronting few strong competitors, it owned and operated most of the telephones of Mexico for many years. At the close of 1892, for instance, 1749 of Mexico's 2487 telephones were connected with the Mexican Telephone Company's system. Its leading exchanges at that time were in Mexico City, Monterey, Guadalajara, and eleven other towns, including Puebla, Oaxaca, Vera Cruz, Progreso, Mérida, Guanajunato, San Luis Potosí, Querétaro, and Saltillo. Its name was later changed to The Mexican Telephone and Telegraph Company, but ownership remained in North American hands. Of Mexico's 41,816 telephones in operation at the close of 1913, almost half were in Mexico City, and the majority were connected with this company's system. At that time Mexico had more telephones than any other country in Latin America except Argentina and 18 per cent of the instruments of the entire region.

The use of the telephone expanded considerably in Latin America during the second decade of the twentieth century. Between 1913 and 1919, the aggregate of telephones increased from 231,176 to 350,337. During the next twenty years, advance was still more rapid, the total reaching approximately a million and a quarter by the end of 1939. These two decades also witnessed the rapid expansion of Yankee operations in the region's telephone business, with the International Telephone and Telegraph Corporation taking the lead by a wide margin.

This company, organized in 1920 by the Behn brothers and their associates, with the backing of J. P. Morgan and allied banking groups, owned at first only the leading operating companies of Cuba and Puerto Rico (not included in this essay) but it soon acquired properties in five other countries. It secured a controlling interest in the Mexican Telegraph and Telephone Company in 1925; in the Montevideo Telephone Company, Limited, and the Co-operative Telephone Society of Uruguay in 1927; in the Chili Telephone Company, Limited, in 1927; in the Rio Grande Telephone Company of Rio Grande do Sul, Brazil, and the Argentine Telephone Company during the same year; in the United River Plate Telephone Company, Limited, in 1929; and in the Peruvian Telephone Company, Limited, in 1930. Although the I. T. and T. disposed of its Uruguayan investments in 1934, this contraction was partially counterbalanced by taking over a telephone system in the important Brazilian State of Paraná a few years later.

It will be observed that this large company thus acquired within a decade the leading telephone organizations of Argentina, Chile, Peru, and Mexico, and that it held for a time the two most important companies of Uruguay. Its holdings in Brazil, while smaller than the Yankee-Canadian systems serving Rio de Janeiro and São Paulo, were located in promising frontier regions of the South Temperate Zone. At the end of 1939 the I. T. and T. was operating nearly all the telephones of Chile and Cuba, most of the instruments of Argentina and Peru, over 40 per cent of Mexico's, and nearly 10 per cent of Brazil's. And it was in these six countries that more than three-fourths of all Latin America's telephones were located. At the close of 1939 well over half of the telephones of the region were owned and operated by this company and its subsidiaries and affiliates, and it is likely that the majority of the remainder were under the control of citizens of the United States and Canada.

Here were cultural contacts of great significance for the two Americas! Here also were opportunities for expansion and service. At the beginning of the 1940's Argentina, with nearly a third of the telephones of Latin America, had less than 40 instruments for each thousand of its inhabitants, and the region as a whole had no more than ten or twelve. The ratio in the United States was 158 per thousand. In Canada and Australia the ratio was 123 and 95 respectively and in the Scandinavian countries it ranged from 85 in Norway to 136 in Sweden. Expansion in Latin America was largely a matter of rates and income. In building the Pan American front telephones may be more important than poetry.

To complete the story of progress in rapid communications summarized here and in the chapter on the coming of the telegraph, achievements in the field of wireless should be mentioned. By the end of 1941 every Latin-American nation except Bolivia and Paraguay was connected by radio-telephone or radio-telegraph, or both, with the United States and, either directly or through the United States, with most of the countries of the world. Moreover, there were over two hundred broadcasting stations and several millions of the upper and middle classes of Latin America possessing radio receiving sets which enabled them to listen, by short wave or by means of local relay, to programs sent out from the world's leading cities. In this remarkable new phase of communications citizens of the United States and nationals of Great Britain did most of the pioneering in Latin America, building the wireless stations, establishing the wireless telephone and telegraph circuits, constructing broadcasting stations, owning and operating many of the new systems, and helping to instruct the people in their use. The principal Yankee organizations engaged in the work were the United Fruit Company, the Radio Corporation of America, the American Telephone and Telegraph Company, and the International Telephone and Telegraph Corporation, all operating directly or through subsidiaries such as the Tropical Radio Telegraph Company, R. C. A. Communications, Incorporated, All America Cables and Radio, and Radio Corporation of Puerto Rico.

MINERALS FOR THE MACHINE AGE

FOR FOUR CENTURIES Latin America has been famous for its minerals. During the slightly more than a hundred years since independence, however, its mineral production has far exceeded the total for the previous three hundred. Increasing world demand and the utilization of new machinery and processes account for the expansion of the more recent period. And, as in the case of so many other modern inventions and devices, the new mining techniques were brought to the region mainly by capitalists and experts from England and the United States.

Although Spaniards had imported a few stationary steam engines into Peru before 1820, the introduction of steam generally into the Hispanic-American mines did not take place until the second and third quarters of the nineteenth century. Nearly everywhere, the British were the pioneers in introducing this new means of power. Transported into the mining areas on oxcarts or wagons drawn by mules, a task requiring enormous patience, effort, and expense, the engines performed efficient services in pumping, hoisting, and crushing ores.

Among the innovations that followed soon were industrial railways and tramways, steam shovels, electricity, and the cyanide and flotation processes in smelting. In the introduction of these, citizens of the United States often shared the honors with the British and sometimes took the lead, especially in northern Latin America. Until the 1880's, however, the British supplied the major part of the capital throughout the region, and they continued to do so in southern Latin America until around 1900. Spaniards, Germans, and other Europeans participated as technicians or capitalists in some sections, and the Latin Americans themselves also played an important part in mining developments in most countries, at least until the richer ores were depleted. But with the opening of the twentieth century, and particularly after 1915, the ownership and management of the important mines of Latin America were rapidly taken over by citizens of the United States.

It is not necessary to dwell upon the well-known magnitude of the mineral resources of the Hispanic-American nations. The mineral riches of Mexico, Peru, Bolivia, Colombia, Chile, and Brazil are proverbial, and those of Venezuela, Ecuador, and Honduras are of considerable significance. A few minerals, such as nickel, high-grade coal, and mica splittings, are scarce or totally lacking; but an amazing quantity and variety of both metals and non-metals are to be found in several of the countries of the region. Even a summary treatment of each mineral product would exceed the limits of this essay, which will be centered upon the most important, and emphasize ownership, operation, and trends of production. Petroleum is reserved for another chapter.

During the colonial period, as well as several decades of the national, gold, silver, mercury, copper, and diamonds received most attention. Guano, nitrogen, and iodine began to be exploited during the thirty years following the late 1840's; tin, manganese, chromium, antimony, tungsten, bauxite, platinum, molybdenum, lead, zinc, and mica were not much emphasized until the 1890's or later. In fact, it was only in the early part of the twentieth century that a broad and imperative demand arose for the ferro-alloys and the non-ferrous metals. Moreover, the demand for old minerals greatly expanded along with the demand for the new. Turning out an ever-increasing volume and variety of industrial products, the whirling machines of the contemporary world required enormous quantities of minerals. Latin America, under the mighty impulse of capital, technology, and management from the United States and Europe, mainly the British Isles, supplied a good part of the world's growing needs. That is the essence of the story with which this chapter is concerned.

Statistics of Latin-American and world mineral production, while not wholly accurate for earlier periods, are extremely useful. Those presented by the United States Bureau of Mines are followed in this account.

Beginning with gold, which is more important as a measure of value than in industry, we may note, perhaps with surprise, that Mexico produced far more of the yellow metal between 1801 and 1927 than during the whole of the colonial epoch. This was true also of Central America, Ecuador, and Venezuela, although not of Bolivia, Brazil, Colombia, Chile, and Peru, where the colonial era stands out, except in the case of the last two countries, for its record of production.

The comparative record of silver output is even more striking. Only Bolivia, Brazil, and Peru yielded a larger total before 1800 than during the years between 1801 and 1927. The aggregates for the later period were much greater than for the earlier in Central America, Chile, Colombia, Ecuador, Mexico, and Venezuela, in all of which, except Chile, Mexico, and Colombia, silver output was of minor importance until after the middle of the nineteenth century.

The mining of precious metals during the colonial period was, of course, dominated by individuals of Spanish and Portuguese descent who made use of Indians, mestizos, and Negro slaves as common laborers. During the wars for independence and the subsequent period of political disorder, production decreased in Spanish America and water rose in the mines. Although their drainage by means of steam power, and the use of steam in hoisting and milling, were at the outset mainly the achievement of British enterprise, participation of the Yankees was not long delayed. Furnishing more and more of the capital and the new techniques, citizens of the United States were playing a major rôle in the mining of Latin-American precious metals by the first third of the twentieth century. By the beginning of the 1930's, they were producing a third of South America's gold and seven-tenths of its silver, while their share of the production in Central America and Mexico was much larger, especially in the case of gold. In Mexico and Central America, their major advance began in the 1880's; in South America, it began after 1900, with the exception of Venezuela and Ecuador, where they participated to some extent during the last quarter of the century, and possibly with minor exceptions also in Peru and Bolivia. Of the fifty leading districts, producing more than three-fourths of the world's silver in 1929, twenty-four were located in Mexico, five in Peru, and one each in Bolivia and Honduras. Bolivians themselves were in control of the rich Bolivian mines; most of the other thirty located in Latin America were owned and operated by citizens of the United States, whose investments, in 1929, in the gold, silver, and diamond mines of the region amounted to a total of $153 million: Mexico, $105 million; Central America, $7 million; South America, mainly in Peru and Colombia, $41 million.

The bulk of the diamonds was produced in Brazil, some of them by Englishmen. Mexico and Venezuela, however, were yielding a few.

Platinum is confined to a single Latin-American country, Colombia, where production began during the colonial epoch, but was not of much significance until after 1900, when Colombia became one of the leading exporters of this rare and expensive metal. In recent years, a company composed of United States citizens has accounted for more than half of Colombia's output.

The story of Latin America's iron ore is not much more elaborate than the story of platinum, in spite of the fact that Brazil's iron reserves are unexcelled and important deposits of this base metal exist in Chile, Venezuela, Colombia, Cuba, and Mexico. The truth is that the region had produced comparatively little iron ore down to the 1940's. At that time citizens of the United States were turning out most of the limited yield. The Bethlehem Steel Corporation, directly or indirectly, was the leading producer in Cuba, Chile, and Venezuela, while Yankee companies had been operating since the 1890's in Mexico, as well as in Brazil, where the United States seemed destined to an increasing participation in the exploitation of iron mines. Hitherto, Chile and Cuba have been Latin America's chief exporters of iron ore.

Not only are Hispanic-America's coal deposits, so far discovered, of rather low grade, but its production has been comparatively of minor significance. Since the 1890's, citizens of the United States have had charge of the leading coal mines of Mexico and Cuba; shortly afterward they began to participate in the coal production of Brazil, and they have taken the lead in its production in Peru since the turn of the century. In Chile, Venezuela, and Colombia, ownership and operation remained largely in the hands of local companies.

While copper had been used for many centuries in the manufacture of bells, household utensils, and cannon, the demand for this metal was comparatively small until the dawn of the age of the telegraph, the telephone, and electric power. Between 1801 and 1810 the average annual production was only 18,200 short tons; the annual average for 1901-1910 was 763,000! Hispanic America itself produced only approximately 2,600 short tons in 1800 but some 352,000 in 1926! Practically its total yield in 1800 came from Chile and Venezuela; in 1926, Chile still retained first place, but Mexico, Peru, Cuba, and Bolivia had forged ahead of Venezuela in copper production. Between 1801 and 1900, Latin America produced nearly a fourth of the world's copper; it produced more than a fifth of the aggregate in 1926.

With reference to ownership: In Chile, domestic companies were the leading producers during most of the nineteenth century, although British participation was large; later, Yankee companies were dominant. In Venezuela, the British have been almost the sole owners and operators since Venezuelan independence; in Bolivia, the nationals appear to have begun copper production in the 1870's; but shortly after 1900 a large British company began to forge ahead and produce the major part of the Bolivian yield. In the other countries, the pioneers in copper mining were mainly from the United States, although the French developed the famous Boleo mine in Mexico. Beginning operations in Cuba and Mexico in the 1890's and in Peru on a large scale a few years later, by 1929 capitalists and technicians from the United States held a dominant position in copper mining in all the producing countries of Hispanic America except Venezuela and Bolivia. At that time, about ninety per cent of all the copper extracted from the region was coming from mines owned and operated by citizens of the United States; their total investment in these mines was more than $450 million: $305 million in Chile; $98 million in Mexico; $42 million in Peru; some $5 million in Cuba.

Nitrates require no more than brief comment. The only natural deposits in Latin America, or in the world, are in Chile. Their importance for fertilizer and in the manufacture of explosives was not fully realized until around 1850. Thereafter, Chileans, Spaniards, Englishmen, Germans, and other Europeans competed or collaborated in working the Chilean nitrate regions, which are located in the northern part of the country. Yankees had little or no participation until 1909 and later. At the outbreak of the first World War, the Germans occupied an influential position in Chilean nitrate production. Cut off from their source of supply during the conflict, they began large-scale extraction, or fixation, from the air. Other countries soon followed the German example, and Chile's monopoly of nitrates was demolished. International cartels were resorted to, but they proved rather ineffective. Gradually, in the 1920's and following, citizens of the United States, alone or in a kind of partnership with the Chilean government, gained a dominant place in Chilean production. By 1935 their investment was over $58 million.

Chile likewise had a monopoly of iodine until that mineral began to be extracted from sea-salt. The major part of the world's supply—it is used as an antiseptic, for goiter, and in photography—was still furnished by Chile as late as the 1930's. A byproduct of the manufacture of Chilean sodium nitrate, the story of iodine is the same as that of the commodity with which it has been associated; in recent years, citizens of the United States have had a big hand in its production.

Omitting mica, quartz crystal, and graphite, all of which are obtained from one or more of the Hispanic-American countries, and returning to the non-ferrous metals and the ferro-alloys, one may note that Brazil is the only Latin-American country reporting bauxite, having produced very little so far, and that Bolivia is the only important Latin-American producer of tin, although small quantities are obtained from Argentina and Mexico. Beginning production in the 1860's, since 1900 Bolivia has been producing between a fourth and a fifth of the world's supply. Most of its tin mines are owned and worked by international companies in which Bolivians, most of them residing abroad, are prominent. Englishmen, Germans, citizens of the

United States, and a few Frenchmen are among the foreign investors.

Mexico is the only important Latin-American producer of mercury. Small quantities of mercury, however, are produced in Bolivia, as well as in Peru, which yielded a comparatively large volume during the colonial period. Most of the Mexican mercury mines are in the hands of the Mexicans themselves; the Yankees and the British own and operate a few.

Antimony deposits exist in at least four of the Latin-American countries; but the main producers are Bolivia, where operations are carried on mainly by natives, and Mexico, where citizens of the United States and subjects of Great Britain control most of the production. Used like antimony as an alloy or as a purifier in the manufacture of steel, are chrome ore, beryllium, manganese, molybdenum, vanadium, zircomium, and tungsten (the last utilized also in electrical appliances). All began only recently to be employed in the steel industry, and all are produced in one or more of the Hispanic-American nations. Although data regarding ownership in some instances is difficult to obtain, it is likely that the situation here is not very different from that in respect to other minerals. Latin-American production of chrome ore, manganese, tungsten, and vanadium, for instance, was mainly in the hands of citizens of the United States by the 1920's and 1930's.

Turning to lead and zinc, which were produced in important volume in Mexico before 1900 and to some extent in South America a few years later, it will be observed that they are usually associated with copper and silver. Thus the important producers of copper and silver in Hispanic America in recent years were also the major producers of lead and zinc; they were and are citizens of the United States, who accounted for most of Mexico's output during the first half of the twentieth century, as well as a third of South America's lead and two-thirds of its zinc.

In short, by the 1930's, the bulk of the productive mineral resources of Hispanic America was owned by capitalists from the United States. This was especially true of iron, silver, zinc, copper, chromite, manganese, tungsten, vanadium, platinum, coal, and petroleum. Yankee ownership of tin, lead, gold, and a few other minerals was not quite so large. The Latin-American nations owed their enormous mineral production during the first century and a quarter of their independence in part to their own enterprise, but in still greater measure to the impact of capital, technology, and management from the Anglo-Saxon countries. Comparatively, British influence was more important during the first half of the period, while that of the United States was more potent after the 1880's and practically paramount after the turn of the nineteenth century, when its giant corporations began to apply the most advanced mechanical and chemical techniques in the extraction of minerals from low-grade ores. Moreover, back of the whole development was the tremendous expansion of contemporary industry, accentuated by global conflicts among the world powers.

With its growing demand for minerals in wartime and the granting of large loans for their extraction, participation of the United States in Latin-American mineral production is likely to increase enormously. Eleven of the twelve minerals now (1943) on our strategic list—manganese, chromium, tungsten, tin, bauxite (aluminum), antimony, platinum, mercury (quicksilver), mica, iodine, and sodium nitrate—can be secured in whole or in part from the Latin-American countries. Their production is being stressed and will probably be carried on more and more by United States financing and in considerable measure under its management. Latin America, which has long contributed to the comfort and prosperity of the Anglo-Saxons by serving as an outlet for surplus goods, skills, and capital and as a source of supply for foods, minerals, and other raw materials, was becoming an immense bulwark in their security.

Although owned and managed mainly by Anglo-Saxons in most Latin-American countries, and operated mainly for the benefit of Anglo-Saxons, Hispanic America's mining industry has been of great significance to the region itself. It has supplied large government revenues and paid a considerable aggregate of wages. But the distribution of the benefits has not been satisfactory to the Latins. Wages for common labor in foreign-owned mines, while often higher than the average in many native occupations, have been low in comparison with wages in a number of other mining areas. Sanitation and other social services, although gradually improving, continued to fall short of the best standards. Latin Americans were complaining that too large a share of the profits was going to foreigners. Nationalization was making advances in such countries as Mexico, Chile, and Brazil; government supervision was expanding almost everywhere. Many Hispanic-American leaders were eager to escape from what they described as their "colonial status." Desiring native or government ownership and operation, they were making some progress in that direction. Yet they were still deficient in both capital and technology, while the United States was able, and in all likelihood would continue to be able, to supply both.

The main problem during the second quarter of the new century was that of discovering a mutually satisfactory basis of operation. The Latin Americans were less opposed to foreign technicians than to foreign capitalists and foreign control. It might become necessary to grant them a larger participation in ownership and management.

In mining, as in many other economic activities, the prospectors and overseers are usually given too little attention by the historians. They deserve a better fate. The Greenes, the Hearsts, the Guggenheims, the Bradens, and the Schwabs occupy a large place in mining history, and they were important as organizers and managers; but the engineers, the skilled mechanics, the foremen, tough pioneers of the mining world, are almost ignored. Neglected also are the Latin-American laborers, illiterate and humble Indians and mix-bloods who have toiled underground for centuries and received scant rewards.

Mining in Hispanic lands, as elsewhere, has been a great collaborative enterprise in which capitalists, managers, prospectors, technicians, and common workers have each played their part. To reward each group, native and foreign, in accord with the merits of each is not and has never been a simple task. Moreover, under domestic ownership the problem of a fair distribution of benefits among the various participants would still persist. Mining may be conducted as a selfish and ruthless enterprise or a reasonably humanitarian occupation. In the past, neither system has prevailed, but operations have been carried on more nearly in the former spirit than in the latter.

May we look forward in the future to a better deal for the common man in the Latin-American mineral regions? The answer might be given by less than a hundred directors of corporations in the United States. Bethlehem Steel controls most of the producing iron mines; Cerro de Pasco, Anaconda, and Kennecott Copper Corporation are producing not only a major part of the copper but the bulk of the related metals. Add to these the American Smelting and Refining Company, United States Smelting, Refining, and Mining Company, the American Metal Company, the South American Gold and Platinum Company, and the New York and Honduras Rosario Mining Company, and you have the dominant groups in the Latin-American mining industry except for Bolivia's tin.

PIONEERING IN PETROLEUM

THE PETROLEUM AGE began during the decade following 1859 when the great oil wells of western Pennsylvania were opened. Within a few years John D. Rockefeller and his associates and such of his competitors as could manage to survive were selling kerosene, lubricating oils, paraffin, and other petroleum products not only in the United States, but in almost every country of the world. Petroleum exports from this country first appeared in 1864 as a separate item in the annual reports of the government on commerce and navigation; and, until shortly before 1900, nearly all of the world's crude mineral oil was produced in the United States and Russia, with the former far in the lead. Until then, Hispanic America's petroleum resources remained almost untouched. Their later development, an enterprise requiring a good deal of capital and well-trained experts, was mainly the achievement of capitalists and technologists from Great Britain and the United States, with the Canadians and the Dutch participating in some areas.

For more than thirty years oil producers and merchants from the United States completely dominated the petroleum markets of Latin America. Moreover, these markets were comparatively large, especially for kerosene, lubricating oil, and paraffin, with kerosene bulking larger than the other two products combined. Latin America bought more kerosene than China; in some years the Brazilians alone consumed more of the commodity than did all the Chinese. Yet the millions who read Alice Tisdale Hobart's *Oil for the Lamps of China* were not aware of the fact. Nor did any novelist or historian attempt to inform them. "Distance lends enchantment...."

As early as 1867 Latin Americans were using approximately

two million gallons of United States kerosene annually. By the early 1880's the annual total reached fifteen million gallons; by 1893 it exceeded thirty million. And the consumption continued to expand. In the 1880's, with the building of a refinery in Cuba and another in Mexico, crude oil in rather large quantities began to appear along with the refined product in the lists of exports from the United States to Latin America. Old means of illumination and lubrication rapidly gave place to the new.

Kerosene was a commodity which the poor could afford to buy. It sold at from twenty to thirty cents a gallon in the 1860's and 1870's; but thereafter the price declined, ranging from eight to twelve cents during the following decades. The principal limitations on its use were Latin-American tariffs and transportation costs. In some countries the duties reached fifty or sixty cents a gallon; they were rarely lower than seven cents on a gallon in any of them. Tariffs were the leading source of national revenues in Latin America. Because of difficult topography and lack of railways and highways, kerosene was usually transported on the backs of mules and oxen, or, in some instances, by human porters. It was therefore shipped from the United States, not in barrels, but in boxes or cases, each weighing approximately eighty-five pounds and containing two tin cans holding five gallons each. The tins themselves were useful; they became a part of the household equipment of millions of the poorer classes.

Petroleum products were a great boon to the inhabitants of Hispanic America. Beneficial to millions, they injured only a few who had made their living by selling tallow, beeswax, fish-oil, or vegetable oils. Yet there were always millions of Indians and mestizos who remained in darkness because they could not afford to buy kerosene. The misfortune would have been greater if they had ever learned to read.

In the files of the oil companies of the United States, if the records have not been destroyed, the historian may find the correspondence of the kerosene merchants. It probably contains the humble story of those who furnished oil for the lamps of Latin America, of busy salesmen, mule and ox trains, muddy or dusty trails, and barefoot peons; of light for huts, mansions, and streets; of better lubricants for whirling machinery; of paraffin for candle-makers, church altars, and processions. Until the correspondence between the companies and their agents has been examined, one can only fill the blank pages by imagination. It is certain that the oil men of the United States furnished their neighbors with a cheap and useful commodity, sometimes selling the article at a lower price than they sold it in their own country, and that they prospered, became wealthy and powerful, wrote their names in capital letters across the pages of recent history.

With the arrival of the internal-combustion engine, the crude-oil locomotive, and the Diesel engine, three remarkable inventions of the Machine Age and immense consumers of petroleum, markets for petroleum products expanded enormously; and rapidly developing markets led to fuller exploitation of Latin America's mineral-oil resources. Soon after the first realization of the vast and rich potentialities of the oil industry, men naturally had thought of discovering and developing petroleum in Latin America. As early as the 1860's and 1870's the search was initiated; and small quantities were extracted before 1900, but production was of minor significance until the first quarter of the twentieth century.

Among the pioneers of the earlier period were a few Spanish Americans, Italians, Germans, and Frenchmen, but mostly Yankees and British. The precursors in Peru, which produced more petroleum than the rest of Latin America combined during the years preceding 1901, were a Peruvian named Diego de Lama, an Italo-Peruvian named Faustino Piaggio, and four citizens of the United States: E. P. Larkin, a kerosene salesman, Henry Smith, Herbert Tweddle, and James Bishop. The pioneers in Mexico were Ildefonso López and other Mexicans, a French physician named Autry, and a Massachusetts company said to have been organized by the *Boston Post*. The first petroleum was extracted from Argentine subsoil by the *Argentinos* themselves, but they employed at least two Germans and two Englishmen as technicians: Stelzer, Zuber, Rickard, and Kyle. Antonio Pulido and Edward McGregor, the latter perhaps a Yankee, took the lead in Venezuela; nothing, or almost nothing, was done in the other countries until after 1900.

Although Peruvian production amounted to a hundred thousand barrels or so annually during the late 1890's, Mexico was the first Hispanic-American nation to produce the "black gold"

MEXICO

CUBA

VENEZUELA

COLOMBIA

ECUADOR

B R A Z I L

PERU

BOLIVIA

CHILE — PARAGUAY

URUGUAY

OIL- PRODUCING ARGENTINA

REGIONS OF

LATIN AMERICA

1940

on a large scale. The boom era began there—in the Tampico, Tuxpam, and Tehuantepec areas—during the decade following 1901, and by 1913 Mexican annual production had soared to nearly twenty-six million barrels. By that time Peru was producing a little more than two million barrels a year, Argentina some 131,000, and the rest of Latin America scarcely any at all. It was not until after 1920 that large-scale operations began in Colombia and Venezuela, while Ecuador, as late as the 1930's, was producing only a little over a million gallons annually.

Petroleum is known to exist in fairly large quantities in several of the Latin-American countries, but the oil resources of all except Mexico, Peru, Venezuela, Colombia, Argentina, and Ecuador were virtually untapped as late as the 1940's. The production of these six countries during two recent years follows (thousands of barrels):

Country	Production in 1928	Production in 1937
Venezuela	104,749	199,407
Mexico	50,151	46,905
Colombia	19,897	20,055
Peru	12,006	16,569
Argentina	9,070	16,354
Ecuador	1,084	1,207

Mexico's yield reached its peak in 1921 with approximately 194,-755,000 barrels, the subsequent decline being due in part to disagreements between the Mexican government and foreign petroleum companies. Peru's oil resources are likely to prove smaller than those of Argentina unless considerable quantities are discovered in lands recently acquired by a boundary agreement with Ecuador. Colombia's deposits may eventually prove to be as rich as those of Venezuela. Among the larger countries of Latin America, Brazil and Chile appear to have the poorest petroleum prospects.

The pioneers in large-scale petroleum production in Mexico were Edward L. Doheny, A. P. Maginnis, C. A. Canfield, and Herbert G. Wylie. Between 1901, when they brought in their first well in northeastern Mexico, and 1925, when they sold out to the Standard Oil interests, their various companies—the Mexican Petroleum Company and several subsidiaries—produced almost half of the oil that was drawn from Mexican wells. Doheny and Wylie, clearly the dominating figures in the group, became multimillionaires. Next in importance was an association of

English oilmen led by Sir Weetman Pearson (the Mexican Eagle Oil Company); but at one time or another the Gulf Oil Company, the Standard, and more than a score of smaller companies, North American, Anglo-Dutch, Mexican, and Spanish, took part in the exploitation of the Mexican fields, which extend along the Gulf coast from Tampico to Tehuantepec.

In Peru, as petroleum production rose to a million barrels a year and then to several millions, Englishmen and Canadians forged to the front. By 1916, however, a combination of Canadians and Yankees, the latter belonging to the Standard Oil group, was in possession of the richest field, Negritos. The old Piaggio interests, although then comparatively unimportant, remained in control of a fairly rich area. Peruvian production continued to be restricted to a narrow coastal region in the northwest.

In Venezuela, the subsidiaries of the Royal Dutch Shell, dominated by Henri Deterding and Marcus Samuel, did most of the large-scale pioneering. But the Shell soon confronted Standard Oil affiliates and the Gulf interests, as well as more than a dozen lesser organizations, Yankee, Canadian, French, and Venezuelan. By the 1930's, however, a good part of the producing areas was controlled by the Shell, the Standard, or the Gulf, the last of which was owned mainly by the Mellons. Venezuelan petroleum deposits extended from the Orinoco Delta in the east to Lake Maracaibo and beyond.

The story in Ecuador is essentially the same as in Venezuela. The British led the way as Ecuadorian production mounted toward a million barrels a year; but the Yankees and the Canadians, and the two in combination, represented respectively by the Gulf Oil Company, Standard Oil, and the International Petroleum Company, Limited, of Toronto, Canada, were soon extracting a share of Ecuador's petroleum. Developments were confined mainly to the Santa Elena Peninsula in the southwest.

In Argentina, where production expanded rapidly following the discovery of the Comodoro Rivadavia field in the south late in 1907, the oil industry was largely dominated by the national government. Previously petroleum production had been confined to the Mendoza-Neuquén region in the west and the Salta-Jujuy region in the northwest, but the southern field was soon producing more than the other two. Such private production as was being carried on was mainly in the hands of Argentines, Chileans, Germans, and Englishmen, with the British more or less predominant. Citizens of the United States had little share in the industry. The refineries were mainly under the control of the government or of Argentine companies, although both were assisted by foreign technologists and Standard Oil owned one or two refineries in 1940.

Although considerable prospecting for oil, carried on mainly by Yankees, Canadians, and Colombians, occurred in Colombia before 1910 and a small refinery had been established at Cartagena, another decade passed before oil began to be exploited in bulk in that country. The first important wells were sunk in the Roberto de Mares concession, in the Magdalena Valley near Barranca Bermeja, in 1919 and 1920 by the Tropical Oil Company, an organization owned jointly by Canadians and Standard of New Jersey. In 1926 a pipe line of some 334 miles, extending from these wells to the port of Mamonal, near Cartagena, was completed. A few years later a subsidiary of the Gulf Oil Company drilled other wells, in the Virgilio de Barco concession, located in the Catatumbo region close to the Venezuelan frontier. This area, however, soon passed into the hands of the Texas Company and Socony-Vacuum, both United States corporations. A second pipe line, extending from the Catatumbo region to the Colombian port of Coveñas, a distance of 263 miles, was completed in 1939.

This brief summary of large-scale petroleum exploitation in Latin America has taken no account of the technicians—the foreign geologists, drillers, carpenters, pipe-line engineers, chemists, and physicians—and the common laborers, usually native Indians and mestizos, of the oil fields. Space would not permit the discussion of this subject here even if the information were at hand. Their tribulations, their exposure to debilitating heat, insect pests, and disease, are not difficult to imagine. The writer has seen, as no doubt have some of the readers of this essay, the oil technologists at work. Sun-tanned, silent, and strong, most of them lovers of liquor, primitive women, and adventure, they were indispensable in the petroleum industry; and not a few are more entitled to eulogy than the swivel-chair financiers who sent them out into the jungles and mountains in search of this marvelous new source of light and power. But their story must remain unwritten until the records of the companies can be examined.

No subject in the foreign relations of the Latin-American nations has given rise to more controversy than the extraction of their petroleum by foreign organizations. The problem has been complicated by shifts in policy and to some extent by political instability, greed, graft, and political favoritism.

Under the Spanish system of the colonial period the treasures of the subsoil, including petroleum and asphalt, belonged to the monarch. With the winning of independence, they passed into the hands of the various new nations. Sooner or later, however, the situation was modified in most countries, so that the owner of the surface became also the owner of the minerals beneath the surface, and the oil men acquired rights from the surface owners by virtue of leases or purchases. They also acquired rights from nationals, often political favorites, who had managed by hook or crook to acquire immense concessions from the national domain for speculative purposes. Natives had neither the money nor the technical training to produce oil; they obtained their concessions with the view of transferring them by direct sale or by agreements which reserved a part of the eventual profits for themselves. Such privileges invariably passed into the hands of aliens, usually Englishmen, Yankees, or Canadians. As petroleum was discovered and developed and the rich potentialities of the various fields were revealed, disputes arose over the sharing of profits, over royalties, taxes, wages, sanitary conditions, titles, drilling permits, the establishment of local refineries, the restriction or expansion of production, the extent to which local labor should be employed, and many other subjects centering around the broad issue of production, sale, and distribution of the income. The fact that most of the Latin-American countries were strongly nationalistic, had almost no coal of the best grade, and were not yet in a position to utilize much petroleum for national economic enterprises also caused anxiety in some quarters. This valuable commodity might be exhausted before Hispanic Americans were in a position to use it in national development.

The result was long disputes, in most countries, between the oilmen, usually supported by their home governments, and the national governments of Latin America. Attempts were made in Colombia and Mexico to return to the earlier status of national ownership of subsoil products and inject the state into the business of producing and refining petroleum. In Mexico, where the struggle was most vigorous, the national government finally took charge of the foreign properties in 1938 and negotiated a settlement afterwards. In Colombia, after diplomatic skirmishes with the national authorities at Washington, skirmishes which lasted more than a decade, the foreign companies managed to preserve most of their rights. In 1937 the Bolivian government deprived the Standard Oil Company of New Jersey of its undeveloped concessions in that country. Argentina avoided difficulties by adopting a definite policy of government domination and a mixture of state and private operation before large-scale production was inaugurated. In Venezuela, occasional disagreements occurred with reference to taxation and the establishment of local refineries instead of exporting the crude to the refineries of the Dutch West Indies, but little trouble arose either there or in Ecuador.

More and more the finished products of petroleum are being manufactured in Latin America. Many refineries have been built in the region since the first were constructed in Cuba and Mexico during the 1880's. All of the countries where crude is being produced have them; most of the countries refine locally a good part or the whole of the national yield, while some which produce little or none follow the earlier examples of Cuba and Mexico and import oil for refinement in national establishments. Latin America's share of the benefits of the petroleum industry is on the increase, whether in the form of higher taxes, royalties, and wages or in the form of roads, technical training, and better labor conditions, including improved housing, sanitation, and schools.

But disputes are likely to continue. The extraction and manufacture of petroleum is a part of the broad and vital issue of controlling the instruments of production and distributing the profits of economic enterprise. Native or state ownership and operation of the oil industry *versus* alien ownership and operation is still an issue in Colombia, Venezuela, Ecuador, and Peru, or is almost certain to become an issue. This controversy will likewise continue to be a factor in Bolivia, where oil production is at the beginning, and it is likely also to arise in Costa Rica, Panama, and other countries where petroleum is known to exist or may be discovered.

Latin America is one of the outstanding oil regions of the world, and oil is a tremendous influence in contemporary affairs. One of the key problems of the Machine Age, it will persist as a problem in Pan Americanism. Upon the ability of American statesmen and capitalists to solve it will depend in no small measure the future of hemispheric solidarity.

BEGINNINGS OF THE ELECTRIC AGE

THE AGE of electricity arrived in the United States and the leading nations of Europe in the 1880's and 1890's. Thomas A. Edison installed the world's first important plant for generating electricity in 1882, in New York City. The world's first trolleys began to run in 1887, on the streets of Richmond, Virginia. For eight years steam engines drove the generators—dynamos; then water power began to be used. The world's first hydroelectric plants, two on rivers in Colorado and one at Niagara Falls, were put in operation in 1891-1895. The uses of this remarkable product of man's inventive genius, the cheapest of all sources of light, heat, and energy, proved almost unlimited: lights for factories, streets, public buildings, stores, homes, and every means of transportation; power to drive locomotives and all kinds of machinery and household appliances; heat for warming, cooking, melting, and sterilizing. Electricity began to be employed in Hispanic America promptly; but, like other inventions and processes of the Industrial Epoch, its advance was slow. There was a lag of approximately thirty years. Its utilization in Latin America in the 1920's was not much more extensive than it had been in the United States and many of the European countries in the 1890's. It was taken to the various countries of the region mainly by capitalists and technologists of the United States and England. The participation of investors and experts from other countries—Germany, France, Belgium, and Switzerland—in the migratory process was of minor importance.

Electricity began to be used to light the streets of some of the Latin-American cities, especially those of the capitals, in the 1880's. It was so used during this decade, for example, in

Mexico City, Guatemala City, San José, La Paz, Santiago, Buenos Aires, Montevideo, Maracaibo, Caracas, Havana, and a few other cities. Electric lights appeared on the streets and plazas of most of the other capitals, cities, and important towns of the region after 1890—in a few cases after 1900. In some countries they were used to light industrial plants before they were employed to illuminate the streets, public buildings, and plazas; and dwelling houses were usually the last to be lighted.

Of course, electricity displaced other means of illumination in Hispanic America, chiefly gas, naphtha, and kerosene, which in turn had displaced fish-oil, grease, tallow, beeswax, and vegetable oil, although these older types of lighting lingered in churches and many humble homes, and some of the poorest and most primitive people had no lights at all save those produced by burning brush and wood. Gaslights had begun to appear in Latin America in the 1850's and 1860's; naphtha and kerosene, in the 1860's and 1870's. As a rule the British pioneered in the installation of gas plants in southern Latin America, while the Yankees often took the lead in northern Latin America. In the introduction of naphtha and kerosene, as we have noted, citizens of the United States had almost no competitors anywhere in the area. They furnished the oil and the lamps of Hispanic America just as they supplied them in China and other parts of the Orient.

They also led the way in equipping northern Latin America with electric lights, installing the first plants in the capital and leading towns of Mexico, as well as those of Central America, the Caribbean island republics, and some of those of northern South America. In southern Latin America, where the British and other Europeans did the major part of the pioneering and furnished the finances, the Yankees sometimes served as technicians.

Before the end of 1900 trolley cars were running in Mexico City; Santiago, Chile; Córdoba and Buenos Aires, Argentina; São Paulo, Brazil; and on one of the streets of Rio de Janeiro, as well as in Havana, Cuba, and a few other cities. During the next decade they made their appearance in many large towns and cities: Montevideo, most of Rio de Janeiro, Santiago, Valparaiso, Lima, Caracas, Bogotá, Guayaquil, Maracaibo; Bahía,

Recife, Pará, Manáos, and nearly all the State capitals of Brazil; Santiago, Cuba; Vera Cruz, Monterey, Guadalajara, and several other cities of Mexico; Guatemala City; and so on.

As in the case of electric lights, trolleys displaced other technological inventions—streetcars pulled in some cases by dummy steam engines or gasoline motors, but drawn mainly by horses and mules. Universally called tramways in Latin America, streetcar lines began to be constructed there in the 1860's and 1870's, the first of them in Santiago, Buenos Aires, and Rio de Janeiro. By 1890 they could be seen in the capitals and nearly all the leading towns of the region. Comparatively inexpensive and easy to construct, several of the lines operated by animal traction were built by Latin Americans themselves. Citizens of the United States installed or helped to install many of the early systems of Mexico and Central America and constructed the first lines in Santiago, Rio de Janeiro, Bogotá, Guayaquil, and several other towns of South America, where the British did most of the pioneering and the Germans and other Europeans built some of the first lines. This type of transportation was most widely used in Mexico, Argentina, Chile, and Brazil, mainly because the larger settlements were more widely distributed there than elsewhere. In these and several of the other countries, the "mule-cars" continued to compete with the trolleys until the 1920's and the arrival of the vehicles propelled by gasoline ignited by electricity.

The story of electric streetcars in Latin America is essentially the same as the story of other inventions of the modern machine age. The British and the North Americans, including the Canadians, did most of the pioneering. One of the first trolley lines in South America was placed in operation in 1898, in Córdoba, Argentina, by Theodore N. Vail and James W. McCrosky, backed by British finance. Vail had been an able telephone promoter, as we have seen, and was soon to become head of the huge Bell system in the United States. These two Yankees, supported by English capital, began the electrification of the tramways of Buenos Aires at the turning of the nineteenth century. The Yankee promoter Percival Farquhar and the Yankee engineering genius Frederick Stark Pearson collaborated with Canadians and Englishmen in the installation of the trolleys of São Paulo, beginning operations in 1899-1900. A few months later a combination of British and Yankee capitalists and technologists electrified the tramway systems of Rio de Janeiro, Bahía, and Mexico City. Citizens of the United States, either alone or in collaboration with British and Canadians, constructed most of the early electric railways of Mexico, Central America, Cuba, and Ecuador, as well as the trolleys of Bogotá and Maracaibo. Farther toward the south, the British usually took the lead among foreigners, although the Germans participated to some extent in that region and also in Guatemala and Mexico.

Because of their large investments in mining and industry, citizens of the United States and subjects of Great Britain were often the first to employ electricity in these enterprises. In fact, the very first use of electricity in some of the Latin-American countries occurred in mines, smelters, textile mills, or meat-packing plants. In some cases the owners of breweries, Germans for the most part, were among the first to utilize the electric current. In industrial enterprises owned by Latin Americans themselves, the first installations were usually made by Yankees, Britons, Germans, or Canadians.

One of the earlier uses of electricity in Latin America as elsewhere was in connection with refrigeration, without which perishable products could not have been transported in good condition to distant markets. Refrigeration laid the foundation for remarkable developments during the late 1870's and afterwards in the livestock industry and in the marketing of fruits and vegetables. Moreover, it was of primary importance in the production and marketing of candies and sweets as well as of beer and various other beverages. Men in the United States and Europe had learned the value of cold storage by means of natural ice long before electricity was harnessed for practical purposes. They had invented "ice machines" even before 1800 and had begun to employ cold storage on railway cars and boats in the 1860's and 1870's. Of course, machinery required for ice plants and all types of refrigeration could be driven and was driven by steam engines; but electricity proved far less expensive and was especially adapted to utilization in automatic cooling and freezing units.

Electricity was not merely useful for refrigeration employed in the transportation of perishable commodities and in lands of summer heat only; it was especially useful for refrigeration in the perpetual heat of the tropics, and on the whole potentially more valuable in homes than in the large-scale business of producing fruits and vegetables and processing meats. It was a valuable asset in these hot lands not only in preserving foods and cooling beverages but also in reducing atmospheric heat so as to make living more comfortable. Electric fans could be used day and night, at work, during sleep, and at social functions. Electricity as motive power in ice-making, refrigeration, and air conditioning might eventually make possible the conquest of Latin America's undeveloped tropics.

Electricity as power for ice plants and refrigerators was carried to Latin America by citizens of the United States and subjects of Great Britain and Germany, with Yankees and Englishmen making, perhaps, the major contributions because of their extensive ownership of business enterprises. In the employment of electricity in connection with tropical plantations devoted to growing sugar cane and bananas, citizens of the United States led the way, while the Britons pioneered in its use in meat-packing and Germans introduced it into breweries, whether owned by themselves or partially owned, with Latin Americans participating in the investment and Germans acting as technicians and managers. In mining and oil production, Englishmen took the lead in the utilization of electric refrigeration in some regions and Yankees in others. In banks and mercantile establishments, where British investments were large, again it was the Englishmen who usually composed the vanguard. Germans, who frequently were the owners or managers of the tropical hotels, were probably the first to employ the new source of energy for cooling and refrigeration in such establishments.

Back of the introduction of electric energy for refrigeration in Latin America is a long story of ice trading and a shorter story of ice manufacturing by means of steam power. Merchants from the United States sold ice in the Latin-American tropics for decades before artificial ice was produced for export, and they had little competition. They later competed with Europeans in installing the first ice plants, which date back to the late 1870's or early 1880's. It is likely, however, that Germans did much of the pioneering, for many of the earliest ice plants of Hispanic America were established in connection with breweries and hotels. Until well after 1900 ice was not much used in Latin-American homes.

On at least two occasions, in 1899 and again in 1923, consuls of the United States were asked to investigate and report on the subject of ice plants and refrigeration. Their inquiries revealed that refrigeration did not begin to be widely used in most of the countries of the area before the second or third decade of the twentieth century.

There were, according to the statements of the consuls, only five ice plants in Guatemala, five in El Salvador, three in Costa Rica, two in Honduras, and one in Nicaragua at the end of 1899. Colombia had six or eight, Peru seven, Ecuador three, and Venezuela three. In tropical Brazil there were two plants at Pará, one at Bahía, and one at Recife (Pernambuco). Montevideo apparently had only a single ice factory, but a very good one owned by a German. In Chile artificial ice was fairly abundant, and there were several ice factories in Argentina, as well as a number in Mexico and Cuba, although the published reports of this inquiry contain no data on the last three countries. No ice plant was in operation in Bolivia, and it is likely that there were none in Haiti or the Dominican Republic, unless they were in use on the sugar plantations, some of which were already owned by citizens of the United States.

By 1923 many more were in existence. Guatemala then had eight ice plants, El Salvador thirteen, Costa Rica four, Honduras eight, Nicaragua ten, but only five running. Panama, by this time an independent country, with a large North American colony residing in the Canal Zone, had ten ice factories and two cold-storage establishments. In 1899 it had possessed only two of Colombia's quota.

Ecuador had in 1923 some fifteen ice factories, but only ten in operation, and Venezuela had fourteen or fifteen. In Colombia they were rather numerous, although small: three in Barranquilla, three in Cartagena, two in Santa Marta, one in the

banana town of Ciénaga, several scattered along in the small
Magdalena River towns, one in Cali, and so on.

In tropical Brazil, three plants were in operation in Pará,
two in Manáos, three in Recife, and three in Bahía, all except
the last also having cold-storage plants, Recife possessing two.
Farther south, in Rio de Janeiro, there were seven ice factories
and two establishments for cold storage. São Paulo had six of
the former and two of the latter, several of the smaller towns of
the State of São Paulo also possessed means of refrigeration, and
ice plants were in operation in several other towns of southern
Brazil.

In Uruguay means of refrigeration seem to have been confined in 1923 mainly to Montevideo, were there were two ice
plants and seven for cold storage. In Chile ice factories were
scattered from Arica to Punta Arenas; but refrigeration was
little used except in the hot northern region; in the center and
the south the climate is cool throughout the year. Argentina
probably possessed in 1923 as many ice and cold-storage plants
as all the rest of South America combined. There were fifty-one
cold-storage establishments in Buenos Aires Province, and the
city of Buenos Aires alone had at least fourteen ice factories,
several of them the biggest in Latin America. An ice factory
was in operation at Posadas in the northeast and at Río Grande
in the distant south.

Ice and refrigeration were still not much used in Mexico's
hot lowlands, and they were not greatly needed on its Central
Plateau. Acapulco had one plant, Manzanillo three, Guaymas
two, Vera Cruz four, and Tampico four. Mexico City, with a
population of approximately a million, consumed less than 350,-
000 pounds of ice a year and this was made in eleven factories.
There were only three cold-storage plants in the city.

In the utilization of refrigeration Cuba, taking its smaller
population into account, was practically abreast of its big sister
in the far south, and there was a similar concentration of facilities in its capital. The Dominican Republic was served by
seventeen ice factories, but Haiti had only two.

The extent to which electricity was used in operating the
machinery of the various factories has not been ascertained. It
was probably very little employed in 1899, but utilized in a

good part of the factories in existence in 1923. A bulletin published by the department of commerce as late as the spring of 1927 pointed out repeatedly, however, that small household refrigerating units were rarely used in Hispanic America except by some of the wealthy families. Its author also declared that there was no great demand for household electrical appliances of any kind except curling irons.

This bulletin of 1927, which was based upon reports of consuls and commercial agents throughout the region, revealed nevertheless that electricity had made considerable progress. Mexico, for instance, had 126 *central* electric light and power plants, Cuba 91, Brazil 68, Chile 44, and Argentina approximately 280. The number in the rest of the countries ranged from 32 in Venezuela and 27 in Colombia to 24 in Guatemala and only 2 in Haiti. The capacity of most of the plants was small; but a few were large. The one supplying Buenos Aires had a capacity of 230,000 kilowatts, while the plant supplying Havana had a capacity of 75,000, the one supplying Santiago, Chile, 66,000, and the plant furnishing Mexico City's electricity 62,000.

Water power was also being used rather extensively. Probably the first large hydroelectric plant constructed in Latin America was the one completed in 1898 at Córdoba, Argentina, by Theodore N. Vail and James W. McCrosky, with the backing of British finance. In 1899 and the years immediately following Frederick Stark Pearson, who went down with the *Lusitania* in 1915, Percival Farquhar, and a number of Canadians and Englishmen built hydroelectric plants near São Paulo, Rio de Janeiro, and Bahía, Brazil, as well as at Necaxa in the State of Vera Cruz, Mexico. At the same time a German company was installing plants in Chile, Argentina, and other South American countries. By 1913 these various installations throughout Hispanic America were capable of producing some 282,000 horsepower of electric current, and by the end of 1928 the aggregate had mounted to almost a million and a half. Even the latter total is small when contrasted with the water resources of the area, which have been estimated as having a potential of fifty-four million horsepower. But coal and steam were generating far more electricity than was being produced by the rivers, lakes, and streams. Already electrical development had made great strides. The age of electricity had arrived in Latin America.

In recent years the Hispanic Americans, like the people of other countries, have confronted the problems of expansion, ownership, and the cost of electrical services and devices. Public ownership of electric utilities has tended to expand, especially in Colombia, Ecuador, and Uruguay; but private ownership, with attempts at public control of rates, still prevails almost everywhere, and private ownership usually means foreign ownership. Investments of Englishmen, Canadians, and citizens of the United States in the electric utilities of Latin America are large. Ownership shifts continually, so that the situation at any particular time is difficult to describe; but at one period or another these groups have had control of electric light and power systems supplying practically all the main centers of population, and in the 1940's they still owned the major part of them. Their services were enormous, but in some cases their profits may have been too large. The rewards to which pioneers are entitled are largely a matter of opinion, and that subject is now mostly water under the bridge. But the problem of rates, prices of equipment and appliances, and expansion of services is current and vital. Its solution to the reasonable satisfaction of all concerned is the task of management, stockholders, diplomats, and statesmen. Here we are dealing with a fundamental factor in inter-American relations.

COLLABORATION IN SANITATION
AND MEDICINE

MANY WHO TALK freely of the backwardness of Hispanic America have not the slightest conception of the problems of health and disease confronted in the tropics or of the heroic battles which the physicians of the region, with the co-operation of technicians and scientists from the United States and Europe, have waged against contaminating filth, insect pests, and microbe assassins. Materials are at hand here for as moving an epic as any in the history of the modern world, but the sober factual narrative upon which the epic might be based has not been written. One of the few contributions made to the subject during the years of excitement regarding Latin America came from the pen of a journalist, Charles Morrow Wilson. Both the Book-of-the-Month Club and the Pulitzer Prize Committee failed to see the significance of Wilson's *Ambassadors in White*.

Inter-American co-operation in medicine and sanitation began toward the middle of the nineteenth century with the arrival in Latin America of the first physicians from the United States and with the installation of waterworks in Valparaíso and Callao by William Wheelwright. It continued with the services of our physicians on the railroads and hospital staffs and as members of the faculties of some of the Latin-American medical schools, with the aid of our technicians in the laying of plumbing and sewer systems in various towns from Mexico to Bolivia and Brazil, and with the training of Latin-American *médicos* in several of our medical schools. It expanded to significant magnitude with the work of physicians and sanitary engineers employed by the United States government in Cuba and the Panama Canal Zone—Walter Reed, James Carroll, William C. Gorgas, and their associates, aided by Carlos Finlay and other Latin Americans. While the gallant fight was in progress there, the United Fruit Company began its medical and sanitary services in the Caribbean banana fields and the diplomats of the Americas organized (1902) the Pan American Sanitary Bureau. At the same time and later, a number of Yankee oil companies sent their medical contingents into Mexico, Venezuela, and other Latin-American countries and the Rockefeller Foundation began its campaign south of the border.

The achievements of some of these organizations were notable. The Sanitary Bureau, poorly housed and scantily financed though it was, sponsored several conferences, sent out its experts to deal with specific health problems, organized standing committees of specialists, stimulated medical research and public health organization, published nearly two hundred bulletins, and stretched its meager budget over an amazing variety of activities.

The United Fruit Company, between 1914 and 1941, spent more than $24,000,000 on disease control and the operation of its hospitals and dispensaries alone. Although by no means primarily a benevolent organization, it cleared away and subdued many a jungle of tropical vegetation and disease. Employing scientists from other American countries as well as from the United States, it waged a vigorous combat against microbes and mosquitoes and helped to train an able corps of Latin-American gladiators. It also convoked conferences on tropical ailments and remedies, opened its research facilities to other institutions, and stimulated the publication of numerous research papers. The annual reports of its Medical Division were published and distributed to leading libraries of the nation. They have gathered a good deal of dust.

The medical and sanitary work of the Pan American Bureau, the United Fruit Company, and the petroleum corporations in Latin America must be dismissed with this passing reference. But the story will be written eventually, unless men lose their interest in the heroes who have combated the enemies of their race—Hugh S. Cumming, João de Barros Barreto, Arístides Moll, Pedro A. Machado, Henry Hanson, William E. Deeks, Juan A. Ariza, Eduardo Urueta, I. W. McLain, and scores of others.

The purpose of this essay is to present a summary of the Rockefeller Foundation's campaign in Latin America.

Stirred by the uneasiness that had gripped his country regarding the Fascist threat to Latin America, President Raymond B. Fosdick of the Rockefeller Foundation announced in his annual review for 1938 that this region was a field of special interest to his institution. He summarized the Foundation's expenditures and activities in the region as follows: "Toward the work in Latin America over the last twenty years the Foundation has appropriated approximately $9,500,000. Most of this money has been spent in the field of public health, the study and control of yellow fever absorbing a large proportion of it." As a matter of fact, the first contributions of the Foundation to the health of Latin America were made more than twenty years before the 1938 review was published.

The Rockefeller Foundation's medical services in lands to the south began shortly after its organization in 1913. Work was inaugurated in Panama, Costa Rica, Guatemala, and Nicaragua in 1914 and in El Salvador and Brazil in 1917. In spite of these prompt beginnings, however, the advance of the institution's medical agents was slow. Beginning dates in other Latin-American countries were: Ecuador, 1918; Colombia, 1919; Puerto Rico and the Dominican Republic, 1920; Peru, Mexico, and Argentina, 1921; Honduras, 1922; Paraguay, 1923; Haiti, 1924; Venezuela, 1928; Bolivia, 1932; Cuba, 1935. Medical services of the Foundation were not extended to Uruguay and Chile (except for an occasional fellowship) as late as 1941. The Foundation's services were inaugurated in China in 1914 with the organization of a special medical board. They were initiated in China, Egypt, Ceylon, Java, India, Siam, and the Fiji Islands before they began in half of Latin America.

The table at the end of this essay sets forth the main expenditures for medical services in Latin America up to the end of 1938. Please examine it carefully.

From this table it is clear that the main expenditures of the Rockefeller Foundation in Latin America were for the control of yellow fever, hookworm, and malaria. The scientists and technicians of the institution—William C. Gorgas, Juan Guiteras, Carlos Chagas, Hideyo Noguchi, and many more—fought a heroic and, on the whole, a successful fight against "yellow-jack" not only in Latin America but also in West Africa, whence the disease could be carried across the Atlantic to Brazil, and several of them lost their lives in the combat. The campaign against hookworm was less successful, although a great deal was accomplished, and the war against the malarial mosquito was by no means conclusive.

Little effort was made by the Foundation to exterminate or cure other diseases. Tuberculosis, a terrible scourge in a good part of Hispanic America, was left untouched and there was no attack on pneumonia, typhus, typhoid, diphtheria, smallpox, syphilis, and a dozen skin afflictions that harassed millions of the people.

Contributions to the public health services of the region during the period were extremely small when measured against its needs. A little more than seven hundred thousand dollars distributed among fourteen independent countries and Puerto Rico were clearly far from adequate. No help was given to Argentina and Uruguay, or to Chile, Bolivia, Peru, and Ecuador, where assistance was so badly needed. While Rumania received more than thirty thousand dollars for vital statistics Colombia was granted less than a thousand and the other Latin-American countries nothing. Greece received ten times more for sanitary engineering than the whole of Latin America combined. The local health department of the Fiji Islands was granted nearly eleven thousand dollars; Colombia's was granted less than three thousand. Siam's local health department was given more than twice as much as those of both Guatemala and El Salvador. The contribution to Paraguay under this head was a little over sixty dollars!

Expenditures for medical training in Latin America were scanty. The Foundation granted the schools and institutes of hygiene and public health throughout the region less than three hundred thousand dollars; those of Japan received over nine hundred thousand. The school of nursing in Bangkok, Siam, was given over the period more than half as much as the school of nursing in Brazil's capital. The Foundation's expenditures for fellowships, for study and training courses, and for travel of visiting scientists and health workers are not itemized by countries or regions. No doubt Latin America was given considerable sums under these three designations, but far less than many more remote regions. In 1922, for instance, the Far East received 73 traveling fellowships for medical study, while all Latin America received 29 and Czechoslovakia 16. In 1925 Mexico received one fellowship of this type, while four were granted to Ceylon and ten to Siam.

The Foundation's contributions to the various medical and sanitary services of the Far East up to the end of 1938 aggregated more than five times its contributions to Latin America. The total for the Far East was $49,000,000; the total for Latin America and other countries to the south, it will be recalled, was $9,500,000. And in spite of President Fosdick's announcement in 1938 the next three years witnessed no striking increases for Latin America.

In his review for 1938 the President of the Foundation expressed the resolve to stimulate cultural relations with Latin America. Little was done, however, in this field during the next three years; only small appropriations were made for books and library services, for two or three rather "windy" conferences on university campuses, and for experiments in radio broadcasting to Latin America.

The Foundation was handicapped by meager knowledge of Latin-American civilization. It did not know that all the area south of the United States was not Latin America. It did not even know the experts within the United States itself; and, judging from the committee it organized for advisory purposes, it had not located the ablest men in the field as late as 1943. For the most part the experts selected were executives with little time for sustained research or specialists in narrow phases of the subject or men chosen for supposed prestige, some of whom had not made significant contributions to knowledge about Latin America in twenty years, if at all. Composed mainly of individuals academically connected with a single eastern university, the committee did not include a single Latin American or more than one or two scholars with a broad grasp of the civilization of the region. No vital program of research in the field was formulated.

These remarks are not intended to be ungracious. The

Rockefeller Foundation has many interests. It is under no peculiar obligation to emphasize Latin America, and its members are not alone in the comparative neglect of the field. Until recently, at least, they were more or less typical of the nation. All who are devoted to Latin America must appreciate what they have done, although some may regret the relative lack of attention to neighbors next door on the part of men evidently under the spell of the phrase "throughout the world" contained in the Foundation's charter. A little more emphasis on the "well-being of mankind" nearer home, where it is said that charity ought to begin, and a wider selection from the talent of the nation for its committee to promote and direct Latin-American studies, will no doubt seem wiser to not a few outside observers.

MAJOR EXPENDITURES OF THE ROCKEFELLER FOUNDATION, INTERNA-
TIONAL HEALTH DIVISION, IN LATIN AMERICA TO THE
END OF THE YEAR 1938

A. Control and Investigation of Specific Diseases

1. INTESTINAL PARASITES (mainly hookworm)

Central America	*$642,220.67*
Costa Rica	122,104.32
Guatemala	129,153.25
Honduras	14,644.87
Nicaragua	109,780.90
Panama	219,553.07
El Salvador	45,336.89
Administration	1,617.37
Mexico and the Islands	*$186,667.90*
Mexico	60,539.37
Dominican Republic	388.09
Haiti	10,095.96
Puerto Rico	115,644.53
South America	*$1,031,232.29*
Brazil	782,283.43
Colombia	178,928.87
Paraguay	66,156.82
Venezuela	3,863.37
Total	$1,860,280.86

2. MALARIA

Central America	*$43,955.65*
Costa Rica	11,478.95
Guatemala	539.20
Nicaragua	9,975.37
Panama	20,266.58
El Salvador	1,695.54
Mexico and the Islands	*$193,531.57*
Mexico	17,310.57
Cuba	45,468.28
Puerto Rico	130,752.72
South America	*$205,409.14*
Argentina	61,459.03
Brazil	112,690.58
Colombia	19,353.77
Ecuador	3,251.52
Venezuela	8,654.24
Total	*$442,896.36*

3. YELLOW FEVER

Mexico and Central America	*$432,482.48*
Cuba	*$1,123.36*
South America	*$4,715,321.10*
Bolivia	17,876.99
Brazil	4,227,872.25
Colombia	107,565.95
Colombia and Venezuela	73,730.37
Ecuador	92,646.65
Paraguay	13,514.95
Other South America and Administration	65,272.37
Total	*$5,148,926.94*

Total for Intestinal Parasites, Malaria, and Yellow Fever, $7,452,104.18

B. State and Local Health Services

1. PUBLIC HEALTH ADMINISTRATION

Central America	*$23,718.36*
Costa Rica	10,746.24
Guatemala	6,510.77
Panama	6,461.35
Mexico	*22,021.34*
Puerto Rico	*33,977.57*
Total	*$79,717.27*

2. PUBLIC HEALTH LABORATORIES

Central America	*$75,536.87*
Costa Rica	11,589.74
Guatemala	13,844.10
Honduras	2,698.37
Nicaragua	37,233.97
Panama	5,000.00
El Salvador	5,170.69
Puerto Rico	*6,498.23*
Colombia	*38,224.11*
Total	*$120,259.21*

3. PUBLIC HEALTH NURSING

Brazil	*$132,980.18*

4. OTHER STATE HEALTH SERVICES

South America	*$27,161.87*
Colombia	24,601.20
Venezuela	2,560.67

5. LOCAL HEALTH DEPARTMENTS

Central America	*$19,077.84*
Costa Rica	5,895.47
Guatemala	510.00
Nicaragua	5,193.65
Panama	7,367.92
El Salvador	110.80
Mexico and the Islands	*$166,048.31*
Mexico	81,553.13
Cuba	20,254.47
Puerto Rico	64,240.71
South America	*$167,604.24*
Brazil	164,832.56
Colombia	2,711.46
Paraguay	60.22
Total of Main Expenditures for State and Local Health Services	*$712,848.92*

C. Public Health Education

1. TRAINING STATIONS

Central America	*$1,394.53*
Colombia	*940.06*
Puerto Rico	*24,616.96*

2. SCHOOLS AND INSTITUTES OF HYGIENE AND
    PUBLIC HEALTH

Maintenance: Brazil, Sao Paulo $91,952.55
Buildings, Equipment, Endowment
    Brazil, Bahía and Sao Paulo   191,747.28

3. SCHOOLS OF NURSING

Maintenance
    Panama, Santo Tomás Hospital $7,835.77
Buildings, Equipment, Endowment
    Brazil, Rio de Janeiro   129,694.36

4. FIELD SERVICE
    Brazil, Central Office   85,754.96

Total, Public Health Education   *$533,936.47*
    (Fellowships not included)

GRAND TOTAL OF MAJOR EXPENDITURES   *$8,698,889.57*

RISE OF THE FACTORY

OURS IS AN epoch of enormous admiration for industrial skill and industrial power. Probably in no other era have so many people displayed so much enthusiasm for the mechanical and technological means of production. The amazing achievements of Russia, supported by the remarkable productive capacity of the United States, have created a deep conviction of the significance of industry in the struggle for national survival. The belief that industrialization can banish poverty from the earth seems to be widespread. Nations with advanced technology are clamoring for full production. Backward nations are more eager than ever before for the machines, devices, and formulas of the Industrial Age—and even if they were not, they might be compelled to accept them because of the overwhelming pressures of their environment,

The trend of the times requires a revision of our history, giving more attention to the international migration of capital and technology. Economic and technological relationships of nations now appear to be extremely important—more dynamic and more constant than relations of any other kind, and therefore more likely than any other to determine the destiny of our planet. We are aware as never before of the overwhelming tendency of capital and technology to flow out from the more highly developed centers into the backward areas. We are beginning to observe more clearly what we could have seen long ago if we had been more alert. We are becoming fully conscious of a mighty movement toward world uniformity propelled by organized industry and its techniques. The speed of the movement has been increasing for over a century, and during the years ahead further acceleration will surely occur. In all the material aspects of civilization our planet is rapidly approaching uniformity, and material uniformity is bound to exert an immense influence upon the mind and the spirit.

The full effects of this trend we cannot foresee. We only feel that material uniformity is inevitable. Our main concern is with immediate problems. The most urgent of these is the curbing of avarice and irrational discontent—the problem of preventing those who feel they are not getting their share of the good things of the earth from "reaching for their guns." One of the remedies advocated is full production, which seems to require the abolition of monopolies and cartels and many other restrictions on economic activities. Another remedy suggested is a moral regeneration by which moderation will be substituted for greed. Beyond this is the problem of preserving personal liberty and cultural variety in face of the growing uniformity and complexity of the Industrial Age.

In nations with highly developed industries and accumulations of capital, disagreements may arise with reference to policy toward undeveloped regions. But disagreements probably will not prevent the spread of industry. Rapid industrialization of the backward areas will be favored by banking and investment groups, and by producers of capital goods—industrial machinery and equipment—unless manufacturers of capital goods begin to fear a shortage of raw materials that cannot be overcome by the inventive genius of chemists and other shock troops of the Industrial Era. Whether a third group, composed of manufacturers of consumers' goods, will fall in line will depend upon acceptance by its members of the view that their markets will eventually be expanded rather than contracted by the spread of industry. There are indications that such producers will accept this view, at least for a time; and, in any case, manufacturers of consumers' goods—even manufacturers belonging to cartels—will be disposed to set up foreign plants wherever they think conditions are favorable or refusal would result in favoring competitors. Because of this alignment of forces in the highly developed countries and because of growing eagerness in backward regions, the spread of industry is certain to continue with increased tempo.

The nations of Latin America share the current enthusiasm

for industrialization. They are protesting against their lowly state as producers of raw materials—lamenting their "colonial status"—and longing for the security and prosperity they expect home industries to bring. They have made considerable progress in manufacturing already, but they are eager to advance more rapidly.

Comparatively few factories were in existence in the Spanish and Portuguese colonies of America at the end of the colonial period, but artisans and workshops were fairly numerous. In spite of restrictions imposed by mother countries, many products were manufactured or processed, on the mission frontiers as well as in the older settlements. Starting before the middle of the sixteenth century, the printing industry slowly spread until presses were in operation in all the colonies by 1800 or shortly thereafter. Maize, wheat, manioc, sugar, cacao, vanilla, meats, tobacco, indigo, cochineal, and coffee were processed. Molasses, rum, pulque, *chicha,* and other alcoholic beverages were made, and plenty of soap and candles. Precious metals and copper were extracted from their ores and various metalworkers plied their trades, turning out ornaments, tableware, perhaps horseshoes and bridle bits, and bells and cannon. Cotton, woolen, and occasionally silk textiles were manufactured by hand spindles and hand looms and made into clothing. Harness, saddles, sandals, and shoes were made from colonial tanned leather. Oxcarts, furniture, wooden plows, a few tools, and various musical instruments were manufactured, as well as pottery, tile, brick, and crude lumber. Canoes, boats, and even a few ships were built; and the concoction of medicines from such native plants as quinine and sarsaparilla forecast the beginning of the pharmaceutical industry.

These activities were carried on with the simplest tools, and most of the product was consumed at the point where it was made—carried on in or near household and mission buildings, on farm and ranch or in the mining districts, where weaving and sewing rooms turned out cloth and clothing, where small mills ground sugar cane and grains, where little kilns made brick, tile, and lime, and where small plants fabricated soap, dyes, tanning materials, sandals, saddles, carts, and various foods and liquors. In addition, there were a few small forges and foundries, numerous fairly large plants for extracting metals, and some factories turning out cigars, cigarettes, cotton and woolen goods, and salted and dried beef.

Although human and animal power continued to be widely utilized long after independence, machines and mechanical devices usually reached Latin America within a short time after their perfection elsewhere. Machines operated by water power were employed in milling grain and sugar cane before the end of the first century of the colonial period, not only in Mexico, Peru, and Chile, but wherever streams flowed near the principal settlements. Steam engines reached the mines of Peru and the sugar mills of Cuba before 1820 and arrived in many of the other countries during the next two decades, to be employed in the mines and mints or in the sugar, lumber, and cotton industries. Power looms and cotton gins began to appear between 1830 and the 1850's, along with railroads and telegraphs and a few breweries, paper mills, and railway shops.

For nearly four centuries the largest aggregations of workers in Latin America not engaged in agriculture were occupied in the mining and metallurgical industries. Although attention was concentrated during the colonial epoch almost entirely on the precious metals, some copper was mined in Cuba, Peru, Venezuela, and Chile, where charcoal furnaces were utilized to smelt high-grade ores. Production of copper did not attain importance, however, until several decades after independence, when Chile took the lead because of its rich deposits and two important innovations introduced there by Charles Lambert— the reverberatory furnace in 1842 and the blast furnace in 1857. The mining industry entered a new phase in the last quarter of the century with the introduction of modern techniques and the working of low-grade ores. Compressed air was used for the first time in drilling in Mexico in the 1870's; the Shanks process began to be employed in the Chilean nitrate fields in the 1880's, and was soon followed in Chile and elsewhere by a wider use of machinery and electricity in mining, and then by various flotation processes for the extraction of metals.

In spite of its long mining history, however, Latin America's consumption of industrial metals continued to be very small until toward the end of the nineteenth century. Several mints had been turning out coins for hundreds of years, but such forges and foundries as operated in the region during the colonial period were small and primitive, and no remarkable advances were made during the first half century of the national period. Nevertheless, some progress was registered during this period and significant advances began shortly afterward. During the last quarter of the nineteenth century metalworking establishments, slowly expanding their use of mechanical power in several of the countries, turned out an increasing variety of products from imported tin plate and sheet and bar iron; and railroads, mines, and public utilities established repair shops, which developed in some instances into fairly large manufacturing establishments that occasionally produced even rolling stock for railways and tramways.

The first modern iron and steel works in Latin America, the first to produce pig iron, steel, and mill products, were inaugurated in Monterrey, Mexico, around 1902. Intermittent attempts to manufacture pig iron began in Chile as early as 1905, but production amounted to only a few thousand tons annually as late as the 1930's. Brazil's immense iron resources were known before 1600 and some attempts were made to develop them during the colonial and early national periods; but nothing very significant was done until after 1912, when the national government began to confer special favors upon manufacturers. With the completion of the Volta Redonda plant and the utilization of coke instead of charcoal, Brazil is likely to forge far ahead of the other countries in the production of pig iron and steel. Only these three Latin-American nations have fair prospects for this type of industry, but Peru, Colombia, and Venezuela may eventually succeed in supplying a part of the domestic needs for these basic products.

Cotton mills were the earliest true factories established in Latin America. Progress was most rapid in Mexico and Brazil, both favored by native growths of cotton, the size of the domestic market, and convenient water power. But spinning and weaving by hand had been practiced for centuries in what are now Colombia, Ecuador, Peru, and Bolivia as well as in Mexico, Guatemala, and Brazil.

A cotton textile industry based upon power-driven machinery

had its beginnings in Mexico during the 1830's, and ten years later over 100,000 spindles were in operation. Progress was fairly steady in spite of economic depressions and serious political disorders. By 1909 there were 139 active cotton mills with some 726,000 spindles and more than 25,000 looms.

Mechanization of cotton manufacturing was delayed in Brazil until after 1844, when a preferential tariff favoring British imports was repealed. Only 9 mills with less than 15,000 spindles were running in 1866. By 1881 the number had reached 44 with over 62,000 spindles, and by 1909 there were 137 mills with 35,000 looms and approximately a million spindles. Brazil's cotton textile industry had forged ahead of Mexico's, and Brazil's lead would be maintained.

Machines for spinning and weaving cotton were also introduced early into Peru, Ecuador, and Venezuela; but success was delayed mainly because of prolonged political disturbances and limited domestic markets. The first power looms were brought into these countries in the 1840's and 1850's; but in all three they were a failure, some of the early mills in Ecuador being destroyed by an earthquake. It was not until after 1890 that the textile industries of these nations began to operate with reasonable success.

Guatemala's first cotton mill was established in 1882, and between that date and 1910 a few mills appeared in Chile, Argentine, Uruguay, and Colombia. By the early 1940's they had arrived in all the countries except Panama, Haiti, and the Dominican Republics, and Latin America had close to five million spindles in operation.

Since much of Latin America is tropical, woolen goods were less in demand than cotton goods, but woolen mills appeared fairly early in the nations where the climate created a market. Between the 1840's and the 1860's they made their appearance in Mexico, Ecuador, Peru, Chile, and Argentina, and during the next half century they arrived in all the Temperate Zone and mountainous countries.

Knitting mills and hosiery machines, particularly the latter, usually arrived after textile mills were successfully established. Cotton and wool were utilized at first, of course, with a little silk occasionally. It was not long after artificial silk came into gen-

eral use in Europe and the United States, however, before it
began to be used in Latin America for both weaving and knitting. The first rayon factories were inaugurated in the 1920's or
shortly before; but the manufacture of rayon yarn was delayed
for a decade or more, and only a few of the countries had such
plants as late as the middle 1940's.

Improvement of ginning facilities and expansion of domestic
cotton crops in countries with proper soils and climates followed
the growth of the cotton textile industry. The leading cotton
producers are Brazil, Peru, and Mexico; but since 1920 the
acreage has greatly increased in Argentina, and small quantities
of cotton have long been grown in nearly all of the countries
except Chile and Uruguay. The first cotton gins were introduced into Mexico in the 1830's and into Brazil and Peru
during the next two decades; but these countries were rather
slow to adopt new types of gins, and in most of the other republics efficient ginning facilities were not installed until the 1890's
and afterward.

In the chief food-processing industries significant technological "revolutions" occurred during the course of the nineteenth
century. This was particularly true in the milling of flour and
sugar and the preparation of coffee and meat.

In the milling of flour, steam engines and iron were gradually
substituted for animals or water power and stone. Flour mills
motored by steam began to operate in Mexico, Argentina, and
Chile in the 1840's. In Brazil, Peru, and the few other wheat-
producing countries they arrived three or four decades later.
In the leading wheat-growing nations cylinders began to replace
grinding stones in the 1880's; and already macaroni and spa-
ghetti factories had commenced to spring up around the flour
mills. By the 1940's steam-driven mills with the latest equipment were operating in nearly all the nations of the region.
Even countries that could produce little or no wheat levied
tariffs on flour and tried to establish a milling industry based
on imported grain.

Production of sugar was revolutionized in Latin America by
the rise of the beet-sugar industry in Europe and elsewhere.
Competition of beet sugar stimulated the invention of new
machinery and processes and their introduction into the

American cane-growing regions. Steam power began to be used in the Cuban mills around 1820 and in those of other Latin-American countries a few decades later; but steam engines could not rescue the old planters from bankruptcy. Liquidation, reorganization, and consolidation began on a large scale in Cuba and Peru in the 1880's and to some extent in Argentina and Mexico also. In Mexico, however, and in Brazil, Colombia, Ecuador, the Central American countries, and Haiti, production was comparatively unimportant until after the technological revolution had occurred elsewhere. First appearing in the 1870's and 1880's in Cuba, the Dominican Republic, Peru, and Argentina, and in some sections of Brazil and Mexico, the big *centrales,* with their tall smokestacks, centrifugals, and railways, gradually spread to most of the sugar areas, and growing and milling became separate and distinct enterprises.

Mechanized plants for hulling, pulping, drying, and polishing coffee began to spring up in Brazil in the first half of the nineteenth century and in the various other coffee states shortly afterward. By the opening decades of the twentieth century they had become standard equipment; and, as in the case of sugar, processing was gradually separated from cultivation.

The meat industry in the river Plata region was slowly transformed by the invention of refrigeration and rising demand in Europe. The meat-curing establishments (*saladeros*) of the colonial era, made more profitable by enlargement and by utilization of by-products, managed to survive until after 1900; but a factory for the preparation of meat extract by the Liebig system was erected at Fray Bentos, Uruguay, in the 1860's, and a decade later, after the invention of the Tellier machine for refrigeration, the first shipment of frozen meat was sent across to Europe. During the next quarter of a century several freezing plants (*frigoríficos*) started operation in Argentina. The production of these was larger than that of the old *saladeros* by 1904, and output was further increased during the First World War by adding chilled beef to the frozen article. The freezing plants of Paraguay and Brazil and most of those of Uruguay and Chile date from this war, but this type of plant was only beginning to be used successfully in other countries as late as the 1940's.

Other food industries, such as those making chocolate, candies, biscuits, and vegetable oils, either appeared for the first time or progressed from the shop to the factory during the latter half of the nineteenth century; and it was during the same period that the beverage industries began to be modernized. Although the first breweries appeared in some countries in the 1850's and 1860's, they did not attain efficiency and significance until the 1880's, even in the larger nations. By the end of the century, however, they were operating in most of the leading towns of the entire region; and by that time cottonseed-oil mills had sprung up in Peru, Mexico, and Brazil, wineries were turning out a fairly good product in Chile, Peru, Argentina, and Brazil, and well-equipped distilleries were in operation in nearly every country, although production of industrial alcohol was delayed until the 1930's, and even later in some of the republics.

The manufacture of such articles of popular consumption as soap and candles, tobacco, pottery, felt hats, matches, and wearing apparel remained in the household or workshop stage in most countries until the last quarter of the nineteenth century, and still longer in several of the smaller nations. Cigarette machines began to be utilized in Cuba, Mexico, Argentina, and Chile shortly before 1900. Clothing and footwear continued to be made to order. The first real factories producing these and various other articles in the group were established in the 1880's and 1890's in Argentina, Brazil, Chile, Uruguay, Peru, and Mexico and a decade or so later in the other republics. Shoe machinery was introduced into the six countries mentioned during the last decade of the century, but rapid expansion in the manufacture of shoes came after 1900. In fact, shoe factories had not by any means displaced the household and the workshop as late as the 1940's. The manufacture of ready-made clothing in factories began around the turn of the century and followed the same course as shoes. The manufacture of felt hats reached the factory stage in the 1880's and 1890's; but certain types of straw hats continued to be made in the home or the small shop.

Although a few paper factories made their appearance as early as the 1840's, the paper industry did not achieve success until the 1890's, even in the most advanced countries, which continued to import a good deal of pulp and cellulose, as well as newsprint and the better grades of paper, until the 1930's or later. Several of the smaller or more backward nations had not inaugurated basic paper mills as late as the 1940's; but by that time nearly all of them had little plants turning out wrapping paper, bags, and cardboard boxes.

Blown glass was made early in some parts of Latin America, even during the colonial period; but machines—semiautomatic and then automatic—did not begin to be utilized until the end of the nineteenth century. Bottles and household glassware were the first to be manufactured. Production of window glass did not start until the 1930's, and even then only in the most advanced countries. Half of the nations of the region were still making little or no glass in the 1940's, and only three or four had factories turning out flat glass.

A few cement plants were erected in Latin America during the last three decades of the nineteenth century, but they operated intermittently and on a small scale. More substantial enterprises were started in Chile in 1906, in Argentina in 1908, in Venezuela and Colombia in 1909, in Mexico in 1912, and in Guatemala in 1914. Large modern plants were erected in Argentina and Cuba during the First World War, in Peru in 1922, and in Brazil in 1926. Ecuador's first cement works attained success in the 1930's, and the next few years witnessed the arrival of new plants in most of the nations mentioned as well as in several others. By the middle 1940's cement works had appeared in three-fourths of the countries and production of cement had expanded until comparatively little was imported.

The first gas plant in Latin America was built in Havana, Cuba, in the late 1840's. Plants for the manufacture of gas from coal were established in Argentina, Brazil, Chile, and Ecuador in the 1850's and in Uruguay during the next decade. Gas was little used in the other countries, although a few scattered establishments made their appearance in Mexico and Venezuela before 1900. The manufacture of coal-tar by-products was not initiated until the 1920's and 1930's, and even then only in two or three of the larger countries.

Excepting nitrates in Chile and the manufacture of soap, candles, matches, fireworks, a few explosives, and some simple home remedies in all the countries, production of chemicals and pharmaceuticals did not get well under way until after 1900, and no marked progress was made until after 1920. By the middle 1940's, however, several of the larger nations were approaching self-sufficiency in drugs, paints, and cosmetics, and turning out a good many industrial chemicals besides, and some of the countries had begun the manufacture of plastics from imported materials.

Petroleum refineries were built in Latin America before large-scale production of crude oil began, the first refineries being erected in Cuba and Mexico in the 1880's. Shortly after 1900 they appeared in Peru, Argentina, and Colombia, and by the 1940's they were operating in all of the countries that possessed oil wells and in several where no crude oil was produced.

Commercial exploitation of Latin America's forests started, of course, with the cutting of cabinet and dye woods during the early colonial period. Sawmills began to be employed shortly after independence, but were not widely used until much later. Plywoods began to be manufactured in Brazil, Paraguay, and Chile in the late 1930's. Plants for the manufacture of *quebracho* first appeared in the Chaco region of Argentina and Paraguay in the 1880's and 1890's; and it was during the same decades that large establishments were inaugurated for the production of brick, tile, and pottery, and that lumber mills and furniture factories began to equip themselves with full outfits of machinery. The same period also witnessed the manufacture of rolling stock for railroads and tramways and some light farm and industrial machinery; but neither the building and construction industries nor those manufacturing machinery could reach maturity until basic iron and steel industries had been developed.

Relative lack of industrial initiative in Latin America is illustrated not only by the slow advance in the manufacture of light metal goods and machinery, but also by the long delay in initiating rubber-goods industries in a region noted for abundance of crude rubber. The manufacture of rubber products did not attain much significance in any of the countries until after 1920, nor was it of great importance in the majority of them as late as the 1940's.

This rapid summary indicates, however, that manufacturing industries began earlier and advanced more rapidly in Latin America than is commonly supposed. Initiated in the 1880's, and earlier in certain lines in some countries, they expanded with increasing speed until manufacturing became a significant part of the economy in nations like Uruguay, Colombia, Peru, and Cuba, until the gross value of manufactured products exceeded the combined value of agricultural and pastoral commodities in Argentina, Brazil, Chile, and Mexico, and until from a fifth to more than a third of the active population in these eight nations was employed in manufacturing. If processing and refining of products of mines, forests, pastures, farms, and oil wells are included, one may correctly assert that important manufacturing plants were in operation in all of the countries by the 1940's, that the total investment amounted to around $6 billion, and that the combined gross output was not less than $8 billion. A surprising amount of manufacturing can be developed without blast furnaces and heavy industry!

But in manufacturing, as in most other fields of economic enterprise, the dynamics came mainly from the outside. Progress was largely the result of the impact of foreign capital and skills migrating in response to world demands for foods, raw materials, and opportunities for investment of money and talent. Most of the genuine manufacturing industries of Latin America were founded by immigrants and foreign promoters and financiers; and in spite of nationalization by means of naturalization, government intervention, and government participation, the major part of the industrial system of the region was still dominated by alien capitalists and technicians until the 1920's, and later in several countries.

Contributions from the United States usually followed those from Europe and were small in most countries until after 1900, when branch plants of its large corporations projected manufacturing into a new phase. The United Shoe Machinery Company, the Singer Sewing Machine Company, and several firms manufacturing drugs and cosmetics aided in the establishment of new industries around the turn of the century; and beginning in 1907 the large Chicago packing houses built or bought *frigoríficos* in Argentina, Uruguay, Brazil, and Paraguay. An American cement firm took over a plant in Argentina during the First World War and entered Cuba in 1918, Uruguay in 1919, and Brazil in 1924. Ford assembly plants were established in the 1920's in Argentina, Brazil, Uruguay, Chile, and Mexico, although operations were soon discontinued in Chile. General Motors entered Argentina and Brazil in 1925 and Mexico in 1937. Manufacture of heavy paper bags for cement was undertaken by the Bates Valve Bag Company in Brazil in 1928 and in several other countries shortly thereafter. Other branches opened in the 1920's and 1930's included plants for the manufacture of elevators, agricultural and industrial machinery, explosives, equipment for railways and tramways, electric-light bulbs, electrical appliances, radio receivers, phonograph records, telephone equipment, textiles, toilet goods, pharmaceuticals, rubber tires and tubes, rayon yarns and various chemicals, corn products, canned milk, knit goods, bandages and absorbent cotton, yeast, and fountain pens. These are merely illustrations; there were many more—some 238 branch plants of such corporations were operating in Latin America at the end of 1940.

Taken together, European firms probably controlled as many or more branch plants at that time. Those of British companies were manufacturing sewing thread, textiles, tobacco, soap and other chemicals, and rubber goods. Branches of French companies were turning out drugs, cosmetics, and rubber articles, and branches of German corporations were manufacturing electrical appliances, metals, chemicals, and pharmaceuticals. Branch plants of Italian firms were making rubber articles and electrical goods, those of Swiss and Belgian firms were manufacturing electrical equipment or milk products, and branches of a Czechoslovakian company were turning out cheap shoes.

When the numerous foreign enterprises not of the branch-plant variety are added to all these, and manufacturing organizations of all kinds are included—those engaged in processing and assembling as well as plants turning out finished products— the total will rise to considerable significance even as late as the 1940's. The aggregate of foreign-owned establishments probably amounted to a third or a fourth of the manufacturing facilities operating in Latin America as a whole at that time, and to well over a half in some countries.

Nearly everywhere in the region, however, the trend was definitely toward national ownership and control. This was the goal aimed at by the economic nationalists, and in all probability it would eventually be reached in most fields and in most countries even if some form of state capitalism or socialism had to be adopted in the process. Here, indeed, is a fundamental factor in the foreign relations of the Latin-American nations, and one that diplomats and capitalists will have to take into account. Latin-American leaders are convinced that political independence has little meaning without a larger measure of economic independence, and foreign investors will continue to feel the pressure of this conviction. In the use of new processes and techniques to produce new commodities or improve the quality of old ones, however, opportunities for foreign pioneers will always be found, and no serious grievances need arise provided the pioneers can reconcile themselves to the transitory nature of their operations. The future seems to promise no abatement of economic nationalism in the retarded countries.

AIRWAYS AND THE END
OF ISOLATION

I N COMMERCIAL AVIATION Latin America's customary technological lag practically vanished. Its mountains, jungles, and
difficult rivers were no handicap to air traffic. In contrast with
the late appearance of steamboats, locomotives, telegraphs, telephones, electric lights, trolley cars, light industry, modern
metallurgy, oil refineries, scientific agriculture, and improved
sanitation, commercial air lines arrived almost as promptly as
they did anywhere else. The first commercial airlines were
inaugurated in the United States and several European countries shortly before 1920. Latin America's first commercial line
was opened that year, and within a little more than a decade
every nation of the region had its commercial air routes.

The new means of transportation were the realization of an
age-old dream in which the Latin Americans themselves had
participated. No doubt men thought of flying not long after
they began to observe the birds, but they made small progress
in aviation before 1909. Leonardo da Vinci was perhaps the first
of the "moderns" to study the problem, and Roger Bacon, the
noted English philosopher, advocated lighter-than-air flying in
the thirteenth century. Four hundred years later Emanuel
Swedenborg, the Swedish scientist and mystic, is said to have
sketched a "flying machine." The first balloon flights were made
in Europe in the 1780's and the first balloon was sent up in the
United States, at Philadelphia, in 1793. It was not until December 17, 1903, however, that the world's first mechanically
propelled plane carrying a man rose into the air and landed
safely. This event, which took place at Kitty Hawk, North Carolina, was, of course, staged by Wilbur and Orville Wright.

By the end of 1908 Wilbur Wright had managed to keep his plane above the ground for more than two hours.

Mastery of the air followed rapidly. Flying over the English Channel in 1909, the Frenchman Louis Blériot was the first to cross any part of the ocean in an airplane. Two years later Calbraith P. Rogers completed the pioneer ocean-to-ocean flight across the United States, although it was interrupted by several landings for repairs. The first crossing of the Atlantic was achieved in May, 1919, by Albert C. Read in a Curtiss seaplane; but Read landed in the Azores and in Portugal on his way from Newfoundland to England. The first nonstop flight over the Atlantic was made by John Alcock and Arthur W. Brown of the British Navy, who crossed from Newfoundland to Ireland on June 14-15, 1919. Less than eight years later, May 20-21, 1927, Charles A. Lindbergh accomplished his thrilling nonstop flight from New York to Paris. In the following June, Lester Maitland and Albert F. Hegenberger of the United States Army Air Corps flew from San Francisco to Honolulu, and in October, 1927, the Frenchmen Dieudonné Costes and Joseph Le Brix made the first nonstop flight from Africa to Brazil. The pioneer flight across the Pacific was made the next year by Edward F. Schlee and William S. Brock.

Latin America itself had a number of pioneers in aviation. Peru's *Volador*, Santiago de Cárdenas, who died in poverty in 1766, spent most of his life trying to fly; Brazil's Father Laurent invented a machine as early as 1709 which ascended "as high as a palace" in Lisbon before it crashed; and the first man to fly an airplane in Europe was the Brazilian Alberto Santos-Dumont, whose achievement occurred in 1906. Ten years later Eduardo Bradley of Argentina made the first crossing of the Andes in a balloon, and in 1918 Lieutenant Dagoberto Godoy, a Chilean army officer, flew the first plane eastward over the Andes.

Commercial airways in Latin America as elsewhere were preceded by air-mail lines, which were usually flown by army pilots. Mail began to be delivered by air in nearly all of the countries of Latin America in the early 1920's. As a rule, however, the army pilots of the region were trained by aviation missions from France, Germany, Italy, and the United States. Moreover, foreigners were influential in the establishment of Latin America's commercial routes. Advance in aviation, although rapid,

PRINCIPAL AIRWAYS
OF LATIN AMERICA
1939

——— U.S. LINES
– – – GERMAN LINES
············· ITALIAN LINE
–·–·–·– DUTCH LINE
——— LOCAL LINES

was largely promoted from the outside as in the case of other phases of technology. The people of the area possessed neither the finances nor the raw materials nor the skills to manufacture aircraft and set them flying on regular schedules for passengers and express.

Most of the foreign pioneering for commercial lines in South America was the work of Germans, Frenchmen, and citizens of the United States. The Germans led off, establishing lines in Colombia in 1920 and in Bolivia in 1925 and later extending their operations into Brazil, Uruguay, Argentina, Ecuador, and Peru. Capitalists and technicians from the United States followed in Chile and Peru in the early 1920's and in Ecuador in 1929. The French inaugurated commercial air lines in Brazil and Argentina in 1927 and in Venezuela in 1930. The local aviation companies in South America were mainly collaborative enterprises composed of foreigners and natives; the trunk lines extending across international boundaries were owned and operated by foreigners.

The story is the same in northern Latin America except that the major part of the pioneering was done by citizens of the United States. In most cases the first commercial lines were inaugurated in the late 1920's, but within a decade a web of airways was spun over Mexico and all the nations of the Caribbean.

The speed with which airways were opened in all the technologically retarded regions of the earth was due mainly to strategy, the profit motive, and the spirit of adventure. The British, the Dutch, and the Belgians were kept rather busy setting up air lines in their far-flung colonies. Germany, France, Italy, and the United States supported operations in foreign fields by diplomatic influence and heavy subsidies. The promotion of commercial aviation in distant lands and colonies was usually concentrated in a single company: the German *Lufthansa* and its Condor subsidiary, for instance, and the British Imperial Airways, Air France, and Pan American Airways of the United States. In this consolidated drive the small operators had little chance to survive in competition with Leviathans of the Air backed by national governments. The observer had the feeling that he was witnessing a mighty contest which could bring immeasurable benefits to mankind or lead to the destruction of civilization. Some day the historian will record the names, character, and achievements of the pioneers of aviation in Latin America. Only a few will be mentioned here.

Probably the first aviator to fly over the Colombian Andes from the Magdalena River to Bogotá was a North American named Knox Martin. Ernesto Samper, Camilo Daza, and other Colombian pilots also made a number of spectacular flights across Colombia's mountains; but the pioneers of commercial aviation in Colombia were Paul von Bauer, Fritz Hammer, and their German and Austrian associates who had seen service in the first World War.

In December, 1919 a few German residents of Barranquilla joined Colombian citizens in the organization of the *Sociedad Colombo-Alemana de Transportes Aéreos,* which became popularly known as *Scadta.* Its president was the Colombian Carlos D. Roca; Bauer was vice-president, and both Germans and Colombians served on the board of directors. In spite of French and Yankee efforts at competition *Scadta* soon dominated most of the country's commercial traffic. Bauer then reached out toward Central America, Ecuador, Peru, Venezuela, and the United States; but his attempts to widen his field of operations failed. In 1925 he made a pioneering flight over the jungles of northwestern Colombia and Central America to Cuba and Key West; but his requests for regular landing privileges in the United States were denied. Lindbergh's aerial visit to Venezuela early in 1928 seems to have checkmated German negotiations there; and while Bauer obtained permission to make landings in Panama for a time, he was soon crowded out of the traffic between Panama and Colombia by Pan American Airways, which also succeeded in excluding him from the lines connecting Colombia with Peru and Ecuador.

Paul von Bauer and his pilots are uniformly described as bold, energetic, and polite. Bauer, an Austrian World War "ace," was dynamic, magnetic, and astute. Fritz Hammer had courage, imagination, and the head of a "wind-tossed hawk." Karl Hermann was lithe and lean, with auburn hair and mustache and dark hazel eyes that gazed with pensive alertness through horn-rimmed glasses. Like a number of other Germans, he married a Spanish-American wife.

In Bolivia, where efforts were made to open commercial air

lines as early as 1920, almost no progress was achieved until a company composed of Germans and Bolivians and known as the *Lloyd Aéreo Boliviano* was organized in August, 1925. Its leading promoters were Wilhelm Kyllmann and Herman Schroth; and the Bolivian government, to which the German residents of La Paz had given an airplane in connection with the centennial celebrations of 1925, soon became a stockholder. Beginning with a line connecting Cochabamba and Santa Cruz, the company gradually extended its services throughout the country, including trips to the southern terminus of the Madeira and Mamoré Railway and to the borders of Chile, Paraguay, and Argentina. Without an adequate railway system and with few good highways, Bolivians welcomed the new means of transport and the company prospered from the start.

Nearly all the pioneers in Peruvian commercial aviation were citizens of the United States. Elmer J. Faucett seems to have been the first in the field, and the first commercial flight in Peru, from Lima to Pisco, was piloted on January 24, 1920, by Walter Pack, apparently with one of Faucett's planes. "Taxi" and sight-seeing flights to suit the convenience of passengers followed, and regular Faucett lines between a number of the Peruvian towns were opened in 1928 and 1929. Meantime, in 1926, the Huff-Daland Dusters Company of Monroe, Louisiana, a subsidiary of the Keystone Aircraft Company of New York, had sent down planes with insecticides to exterminate the boll weevil in Peruvian cotton fields. The first of these planes are said to have been flown to Peru by a Californian named Harold Harris, a former army pilot and a veteran of World War I who had made a flight from Milan across the Alps to Paris. A stocky, dark man with black, curly hair, he seemed more like a Latin than a Yankee. By 1928 the Huff-Daland Company had begun to carry passengers and freight, and during the same year Commander Arnold B. Grow, head of the United States Naval Commission to Peru, opened a line between Lima and Iquitos on the Amazon. With the coming of Pan American Airways in alliance with W. R. Grace and Company in 1929, Peruvian services were soon expanded until practically every settlement of importance could be reached by air. The German *Lufthansa* arrived in 1938.

In Chile most of the pioneering in commercial flying was done by native pilots with the strong support of their government. As early as 1921 the civilian flyer Clodimiro Figueroa carried the first air mail between Chile and Argentina. Later, army and navy pilots navigated most of the commercial planes. For a few years following 1924 the Testart Safety Airways operated a line between Iquique, Concepción, and other points and it appeared that citizens of the United States might play an important part in Chilean aerial development; but the government revealed a decided tendency to manage the air routes itself, and in the early 1930's all the domestic service within the country was concentrated in a National Air Line (*Línea Aérea Nacional*).

Commercial flying began late in Ecuador in spite of an aviation commission sent out from France and Italy in 1922 to train Ecuadorian pilots. It was the last of the Latin-American countries to be served regularly by commercial airways. Neither the *Scadta*, which began operations there in 1928, nor Pan American-Grace Airways, *Panagra*, which started a line between Guayaquil and Quito the next year, made much progress. The nation was disorderly, people living in sections distant from the sea were poor, and air transport apparently was not profitable. The *Sociedad Ecuadoriana de Transportes Aéreos*, or *Sedta*, failed to achieve marked success notwithstanding the excitement it raised in certain journalistic circles of the United States. Founded by Fritz Hammer and Ecuadorians in 1937, its fleet consisted of only two tri-motored Junkers flying along 900 miles of line as late as 1940. Its first plane was fatally damaged before the concession was signed. Another was wrecked in March, 1938, when Hammer flew into a mountain near Quito and killed himself and all on board. A third was destroyed the following December when it spun into a Quito airdrome. A fourth met a similar fate at Cuenca late the next year. In 1940 *Panagra* returned to the contest, and by 1942 its network of air lines covered most of the country, while *Sedta* had ceased to exist.

On the Atlantic coast of South America the most important developments in commercial aviation naturally occurred in Brazil and Argentina. In small Uruguay, which possessed good systems of railroads and highways, transportation by air was not a prime necessity, and commercial aviation arrived rather late in Paraguay and Venezuela.

Pilots trained by experts from France and the United States played an important part in the development of mail and commercial routes in Brazil, but the major pioneer commercial enterprises were promoted by Germans and Frenchmen. Germans, in collaboration with Brazilians, founded the *Viação Aerea Rio Grandense,* or *Varig,* in Rio Grande do Sul in June, 1927 and the Syndicate Condor in Rio de Janeiro in the following December. In the previous November the French *Aéropostale* entered Brazil. A third Germano-Brazilian company, *Aerolloyd Iguassú,* was established in the State of Paraná in 1933 and a fourth, *Viação Aerea São Paulo,* or *Vasp,* was founded in São Paulo in 1934. Citizens of the United States entered the field in 1930, joining Brazilians in the founding of *Nyrba do Brasil* which soon became *Panair do Brasil,* and a seventh commercial company, *Aerobrasil,* perhaps purely Brazilian, was organized in 1936. In that year these various enterprises operated over routes aggregating about thirty-five thousand miles and furnished air transportation to all the leading settlements of the country.

In Argentina, pilots trained by a French aviation commission began to fly mail and passenger routes in the early 1920's, and in 1926 Major Eduardo Olivero flew with an Argentine sportsman named Bernardo Duggan from New York to Buenos Aires; but commercial airways were not well established until 1928 and 1929 when the French *Aéropostale* and the German Condor Syndicate entered the field. The services of these two companies also extended to Uruguay and Paraguay as well as to Chile. In 1929 the New York, Rio, and Buenos Aires Line, called *Nyrba* and operated by citizens of the United States, entered Argentina, but the next year it was taken over by Pan American Airways, which soon became an important factor in the air services of the country. Before the end of the 1930's many parts of the nation were provided with the new means of transportation.

Venezuelan commercial air lines were furnished by citizens of the United States and France. Pan American Airways ex-

tended its services in June, 1929, along the northern coast of
South America from Panama to Curaçao, including the leading
Venezuelan towns on and adjacent to the coast. A year later
the French *Aéropostale* began to operate between these towns
and those of the Orinoco valley and other interior regions. The
Dutch also were flying passengers and mail along the coast
(1937—).

In Mexico, Central America, Cuba, the Dominican Republic,
and Haiti, citizens of the United States, with one possible exception, did most of the pioneering. The exception referred to
is Lowell Yerex, said to be a New Zealander educated in
Indiana, whose achievements in Central America were almost
sensational. Commercial air lines were opened in all ten of the
countries of northern Latin America in 1928 and 1929 and
mail was delivered regularly by airplane in some of them a
year or two earlier. In Mexico, two or three lines were inaugurated by the government or by native companies, but Yankee
capital and technicians were soon taking the lead. In the three
republics of the West Indies, citizens of the United States were
the major promoters and aviators from the outset. In Central
America, Yerex and his *Transportes Aéreos Centro-Americanos,*
or *Taca,* began to compete with the Yankee pioneers in 1931.
Prominent among the early companies in Mexico were Pickwick's Latin-American Lines, which extended from Los Angeles
as far south as San Salvador by 1929, and Pan American Airways, which began operations in Mexico in that year and
bought out Pickwick in 1931. Charles A. Lindbergh made a
number of pioneer flights for Pan American in Mexico, Central
America, the West Indies, and northern South America. By
the end of 1929 planes of this company were in operation on
Commercial lines extending from Miami to Cuba, the Dominican Republic, and Haiti; from Brownsville, Texas, to Panama;
from Miami through eastern Mexico and Central America to
the Canal Zone; and from Panama along the northern coast
of South America to Dutch Curaçao. In fact, Pan American Airways soon absorbed or extinguished nearly all the little operators of this vast region except *Taca,* which, from its headquarters
in Tegucigalpa, Honduras, was furnishing remarkably cheap
and efficient services in most of Central America; and *Taca*

itself probably was backed by United States capital. In the 1940's it appears to have been allied with American Export Airlines of New York.

The first of the Latin-American countries to obtain aerial connection with the world outside was Cuba. Near the end of 1920 the West Indies Airways Company (apparently later called Aereomarine Airways), organized by Inglis M. Uppercu and Major Geoffrey H. Bonnell, began to fly mail from Key West to Cuba under a contract with the Postmaster General of the United States; but the route lapsed in 1923. It was reopened late in 1927 by Pan American Airways with another mail contract, and a passenger service was inaugurated the next year.

The next Latin-American nation to be linked by air transport with the outside world was Brazil, which began to receive air mail from France early in 1928 *via* the French colonies in Africa. French destroyers were employed for several years on this route, however, between Dakar and Natal; for in spite of Jean Mermoz's experimental flight across the south Atlantic on May 12, 1930, a regular schedule of mail delivery by air between Dakar and Natal was not established until 1934. This pioneering was the work of the French *Aéropostale,* which, as we have seen, began local operations in Brazil in 1927 and soon extended its services to Uruguay, Argentina, Paraguay, and Chile. At the same time, the Germans, with the companies partly owned by them in these countries, were engaged in opening mail and commercial air lines between South America and the German Empire. The German *Graf Zeppelin* completed its maiden flight from Friedrichshafen to Pernambuco a few days after Mermoz arrived at Natal, and regular dirigible service was established between Germany and Brazil in the summer of 1931. Three years later, with greater speed than the French, *Lufthansa* planes began to fly the mail regularly *via* Seville or Lisbon, the Canary Islands, and Bathurst, Africa, to the Brazilian eastern coast and from there to the leading cities of southern South America. And it was not long before these two German lines began to carry passengers as well as mail. The first German pilot to fly a plane across the Atlantic from

Bathurst to Brazil was the husky, dark Helmuth Grautoff, who soon married a Spanish American.

In the meantime, two companies from the United States, *Nyrba* and Pan American Airways, with its close ally *Panagra,* were rapidly opening trunk lines connecting the Latin-American countries with one another and with their large neighbor to the north. The spectacular advance began in 1929 and 1930, when Pan American established its mail and passenger lines through the West Indies, through Mexico and Central America, and along the southern rim of the Caribbean; when *Nyrba* inaugurated its long flights through the West Indies to Brazil, Uruguay, Argentina, Chile, Bolivia, and Paraguay; and when *Panagra* opened its line down the South American west coast to Chile and over the Andes to Argentina and Uruguay. Late in 1930 *Nyrba* was purchased and dissolved by Pan American, which soon completed its South American circle, with one vast trunk line running through the West Indies and down the eastern coast and another passing over Mexico and Central America, along the Pacific border, and across the southern Andes. After 1936, when Pan American Airways began to send giant clippers across the Pacific, Latin Americans who could afford it might travel by air to the Far East.

Three years later they were furnished more direct connection with Rome, the center of the Latin religious world. In December, 1939, after noisy advertising and many experimental flights, the *Linee Aeree Transcontinentali Italiani,* more conveniently dealt with under the title *Lati,* inaugurated its services through Africa to Rio de Janeiro. Its managing director was Bruno Mussolini, the Duce's son.

Latin America's connections with foreign lands were complete; but the second World War made travel to Europe and the Orient dangerous, and passage over trunk lines everywhere difficult to obtain. One of the results of Fascist aggression was the elimination of all German, French and Italian lines in Latin America and between Latin America and Europe. Commercial aviation in the region was left mainly in the hands of Pan American Airways and local companies composed in many cases of natives and citizens of the United States. With its immense trunk lines and its numerous local subsidiaries Pan American was clearly the dominant organization.

Latin America's isolation is practically ended. Restrictions occasioned by the war which began in 1939 are bound to be temporary and the war is sure to result in immense strides in aviation. The total length of the commercial routes of the region approached 100,000 miles in 1943. Practically every important city and town in Latin America has an adjacent airdrome, and while travel by plane is still expensive it is little more so than other available means of transportation. Residents of the most remote settlements, if they can pay the fare, may speed through the air in large luxurious liners to the United States and Europe in four or five days and to the most distant parts of the earth in a fortnight. The new means of locomotion can either help oppress and destroy the race or lift it to new levels of achievement and culture. That depends on the disposition of those who control it.

XXIV

CONCLUSIONS

WITHOUT BECOMING a confirmed economic determinist, one may yet hold the view that economic factors are important in the relationships of the Latin-American nations and especially in their relations with the Anglo-Saxon countries. Capital and technology began to emigrate from the United States to Latin America before the middle of the nineteenth century, slowly increased during the next fifty years or so, and expanded rapidly after 1900. Their emigration from Great Britain started earlier and was larger in respect to most countries of the region until the outbreak of the first World War, but thereafter it was less significant in comparison with the influx from the United States. Beginning around 1900, the migration from Canada, usually in combination with British or Yankee capital and technology, became increasingly important. The migration from France, Germany, and other European countries, always smaller than the stream from the Anglo-Saxon nations, was rarely of more than minor significance at any time. This, very briefly, is the story of the international movement of money and technologists into the Latin nations of the New World and the historical background for an analysis of the present situation.

The Latin Americans, of course, have acquired a good many of the skills and habits of the Industrial Age. Naturally, they have desired to control their own resources and manage their own mechanical devices.

In respect to railways, the trend in most countries of the region has been emphatically in the direction of state ownership of common carriers. At the close of 1941, governments owned the majority of such railways in ten of the countries:

Argentina, Brazil, Chile, Ecuador, Colombia, Mexico, Honduras, Nicaragua, Panama, and the Dominican Republic. In four other nations—Bolivia, Peru, Uruguay, and Venezuela—they owned from twenty to forty per cent of the common carriers. Only six of the Latin-American governments owned no railways, or none of much importance, at the end of 1941. These six were those of Costa Rica, El Salvador, Guatemala, Cuba, Haiti, and Paraguay.

While the most extensive state-owned lines were located in Argentina, Brazil, Chile, and Mexico, the highest ratio of state-owned common-carrier lines to total national mileage prevailed in other countries. The Dominican government owned all the common-carrier railroads of the nation, the national government of Ecuador owned practically all the Ecuadorian railways, and national or local governments in Colombia owned nearly all of the Colombian lines.

Although from one to half a dozen or more railways in several of the countries belonged at the end of 1941 to companies composed of nationals, privately-owned railways in Latin America usually meant foreign-owned, and foreign-owned usually signified ownership by the British, including Canadians, or by citizens of the United States. The British owned and managed railways in thirteen of the twenty countries; Yankee ownership of common carriers (excluding Panama, where the most important road belonged to the United States government) was confined to eight, or possibly nine.

The British were in possession of some 30 per cent of the Argentine railways, about half of the Bolivian, a fifth or more of the Brazilian, 15 per cent of the Chilean, nearly all of the Costa Rican common carriers, half of the Cuban, an eighth of the Mexican, all of the Paraguayan, 60 per cent of the Peruvian, three-fourths of the Uruguayan, and 30 per cent of the Venezuelan, but only one short line in Colombia and one in El Salvador. This was the situation at the end of 1941; perhaps British capitalists have sold a few railway properties to Latin-American governments since that date.

Citizens of the United States, at the end of 1941, owned slightly less of the common-carrier mileage than the British in Chile and Cuba, somewhat more than the British in Mexico, and practically all of the common carriers in Haiti and Guatemala. They also possessed railway interests in Peru and perhaps some interests in Brazil, owned an important line in El Salvador, and were participating in the management of the main railroad of Ecuador, although they owned only a minority of its stock.

In the electrical field, smaller municipalities in several of the Latin-American nations owned and operated numerous systems at the end of 1941; public ownership of electric power had made less notable progress in the big cities. Only Uruguay, among the twenty nations, had definitely adopted the policy of ownership by the national government.

Among private owners, the nationals of the various countries usually occupied a comparatively minor position. As in the case of the privately-owned railways, and to a greater extent in some instances, private ownership signified possession by the English and the Canadians or by citizens of the United States. Only a few of the important electric plants of the region belonged to Continental Europeans. Everywhere save in Colombia, Uruguay, Ecuador, and a few other smaller nations the light and power facilities were mostly foreign-owned. At the end of 1941, 30 or 35 per cent belonged to the British, including the Canadians; corporations of the United States owned from 40 to 45 per cent.

Note, for instance, the situation in the twenty capital cities. Subsidiaries of the American and Foreign Power Company, controlled by Electric Bond and Share, a holding company owned by citizens of the United States, were furnishing light and power to six Latin-American capitals: Havana, Guatemala City, San José, Panama City, Caracas, and Santiago. Smaller organizations owned by citizens of the United States controlled the electric systems of Ciudad Trujillo, Port-au-Prince, and Tegucigalpa. The International Power Company, Limited, controlled by Canadians and Yankees, owned and operated those of San Salvador and La Paz. Corporations controlled by the British and the Canadians owned the electric utilities of Mexico City, Quito, and Rio de Janeiro. Those of Buenos Aires, Lima, and Bogotá were controlled by combinations of native and European capital—Swiss, Italian, Spanish, German, perhaps a little French, and, in the case of Lima, a small amount of

English capital. Those of Asunción belonged to a similar combination of European capitalists, with the British omitted. Those of Montevideo and Managua were owned and operated by the national governments of Uruguay and Nicaragua respectively.

With respect to the ownership of telephones, the situation at the end of 1941 was roughly analogous. Smaller municipalities in some countries owned several exchanges; ownership by the large cities was less prevalent. National ownership was the rule only in Uruguay, Guatemala, Honduras, and Nicaragua. As in the case of the railways and electric utilities, private ownership was likely to mean British, Canadian, and Yankee ownership, with companies from the United States, in this instance, owning the greater part of the telephones. In Latin America as a whole, approximately seventy per cent of the telephones were owned by the International Telephone and Telegraph Corporation, the Associated Telephone and Telegraph Company (partly English and Canadian), and other organizations in the United States. Capitalists of Great Britain, Canada, and Continental Europe owned some fifteen or twenty per cent. The remainder were owned, privately or publicly, by Latin Americans.

Note again the situation in the twenty capitals. The American Telephone and Telegraph Corporation owned the exchanges in Havana, Lima, and Santiago, most of the telephones of Buenos Aires, a share of those in Mexico City, where the L. M. Ericsson Company (Swedish), in which citizens of the United States held small investments, was a strong competitor. Companies owned in the United States were also in control of the telephone systems of Panama City, San José, and Cuidad Trujillo. The International Power Company, controlled, as already observed, by Canadians and citizens of the United States, owned the telephone exchanges of San Salvador and La Paz. The telephone systems of Bogotá and Quito belonged respectively to the governments of these cities, the former having been purchased from a Yankee company early in 1941; those of Montevideo, Guatemala City, Managua, Tegucigalpa, and Port-au-Prince were the property of the national governments of Uruguay, Guatemala, Nicaragua, Honduras, and Haiti respectively.

The state of ownership was similar at the end of 1941 in most other enterprises engaged in communications or transportation. Although Latin-American telegraph lines, except those operated in connection with privately-owned railroads, were mainly government-owned, all the cable, radio-telegraph, and radio-telephone systems providing communication with foreign countries belonged to capitalists of the United States or the British Empire, who not only owned them at the end of 1941 but had possessed most of them from the beginning. Nearly all of the transoceanic steamship lines were likewise owned by foreign companies and had been foreign-owned since the first lines were established. All of the trunk-line airways and some of the local systems were controlled by companies of the United States.

Most of the mineral areas in active production belonged to the Anglo-Saxons, with citizens of the United States owning the major part except in the case of petroleum. Outside of Mexico, Argentina, and Bolivia, most of the oil wells of Latin America belonged to capitalists of the United States, the British Isles, Canada, and the Dutch Netherlands.

To complete the picture, other important items need to be added. At the close of 1941 a very considerable portion of the banana and sugar lands of the Caribbean countries belonged to United States companies, which owned a still larger share of the sugar mills and refineries. In meat-packing, Anglo-Saxon ownership was dominant; and various mining, petroleum, agricultural, lumbering, and dyewood enterprises under Anglo-Saxon control owned the major part of Latin-American pipelines and industrial railways, which, in several countries, totaled a mileage exceeding the aggregate for common carriers. Anglo-Saxons also owned numerous manufacturing plants of one kind or another.

The contributions of the people of the United States and of the British Empire to the development of Latin-American resources have been immense. If British contributions were larger during the first half of the period surveyed, those from the United States were of greater significance during the second half; and if technicians are separated from investors, the relative contributions from the United States will assume greater importance, to say nothing of the work of Germans, Frenchmen, and other Western Europeans.

Although this point has not been especially emphasized, many foreigners who have engaged in the development of Latin-American resources have suffered hardships, including financial losses. The losses, however, probably have been confined mainly to small operators and little investors. The corporation is an instrument that can be used by managerial groups to shift financial risks to uninformed stockholders, usually persons of small means. This is illustrated by the Peruvian railways, the rubber-plantation companies, the Farquhar enterprises, and the railroads promoted by George Earl Church and Arthur E. Stilwell, neither of whom spent his last days in poverty.

Capital and technology, particularly under corporate management, press out continuously from the wealthier and more highly developed regions into the relatively undeveloped areas and modify the culture of their inhabitants. The overwhelming tendency of these forces is to possess and develop and, if not watched and regulated, to exploit, siphoning away more than they leave behind.

That foreign corporations, including some from the United States, have done a good deal of exploiting in Latin America has been widely assumed. The assumption has been expressed by William Jennings Bryan, Woodrow Wilson, Franklin D. Roosevelt, and many others both in the United States and in the Latin-American countries. But the concrete details have not been disclosed or thoroughly investigated, nor has the general cultural influence of capitalism and technology in the region been carefully examined, although it is obvious that they have shifted the people into new occupations, modified their consuming habits, and changed their way of life for better or for worse.

In an address made during his visit to Mexico in the spring of 1943, President Roosevelt declared: "We know that the day of the exploitation of the resources and the people of one country for the benefit of any group in another country is definitely over." But how can we be sure that the day of exploitation is over unless we can be certain that these financial and technological forces will never be controlled and directed except by men who are actuated by a democratic and humanitarian spirit?

Foreign business enterprises—and native also, for that matter—may raise Latin-American living standards slightly, considerably, or not at all; they may improve wages and working conditions decidedly, improve them a little, or make them worse. A banana plantation, a rubber plantation, a mine, or an oil industry may operate under a sort of jungle régime or as a reasonably humanitarian enterprise. Steamboat lines, railways, cables, telephone exchanges, electric power systems, and airlines may furnish efficient services at moderate rates or they may furnish services, good or bad, at high rates. All will depend upon control, management, and objectives.

It is safe to assert that financial-technological relationships between the United States and its neighbors to the south have, in general, been neither perfectly good nor absolutely bad, neither white nor black, but a kind of gray, the shade depending upon time and circumstances. It is likely that the services of the technicians have been more satisfactory to Latin Americans than those of the capitalists, but they have erected monuments to both. The work of the physicians and other scientists of the Rockefeller Foundation, the United Fruit Company, and the oil companies seems to deserve high praise.

The main contention of this volume, stated bluntly, is this: Capital and technology under corporate control have been and will continue to be a very fundamental factor in Pan American relationships. Whoever fails to recognize this fact convicts himself of superficiality; whoever seeks to divert attention from it must be viewed as prejudiced or uninformed. Capital and technology affect the daily lives of millions of people. At a time when attention is being shifted in some quarters to the purely cultural, to literature, art, folklore, folk-costume, and folkways, these economic forces should be emphasized. They are the constant, dynamic, and relentless forces in Latin America and all the world. They will not be conjured away by the magic of poetry and song.

Around them many problems in Pan Americanism have arisen and may continue to arise. Those of the past have not been stressed in this volume, but they were numerous. One of the key problems of the future in inter-American relations and human relations in general will be the problem of fairly distributing the benefits of technological achievements. Fairness and justice will not be easy to determine in all circumstances even with an abundance of good will; but, to paraphrase Justice Holmes, it should not be difficult to identify crass injustice when it appears.

We cannot win or keep the friendship of our neighbors by joining them in reciting their poetry if at the same time some of our compatriots are oppressing their workers and charging exorbitant rates for services. We cannot drown their resentment by praising their music and art while we exploit their people and resources. If we are to gain and hold their friendship we must treat them as friends in these matters which so profoundly touch their everyday lives. To some extent these principles apply in reverse: the good-neighbor attitude should be reciprocal; but we are the active agents, the rôle of the Latin Americans is largely passive.

The problem of distributing the benefits of technological advance will spin itself out through the years in a continuous series of problems. Exponents of the "higher" culture can help to solve them by gaining an understanding of their nature and origin and making them the theme of their art. They can serve the cause of humanity by filling the atmosphere of the Americas and the world with democratic and humanitarian ideals.

In the future development of these countries the people of the United States may be destined to play a larger part than they have played in the past. The Industrial Age is hardly more than in its infancy in many of them. The quality of our achievement will depend upon our wisdom, our ideals, and our skills. It ought to be improved by the right sort of history and by awareness of the great epic in which we are participating: the Epic of the Two Americas.

BIBLIOGRAPHICAL NOTES

GENERAL

There is no satisfactory guide to information on the large subject with which this volume deals. *The Economic Literature of Latin America* (Cambridge, Harvard University Press, 1935-1936. 2 vols.) is incomplete and sometimes inaccurate. It gives little attention to manuscripts, technical journals, or even official documents. The *Handbook of Latin-American Studies,* compiled annually since 1936 and also published by Harvard University Press, deals mostly with current materials and is rather uncritical because of the conditions under which it is prepared. Within the limitations set by the author, James B. Childs's *Bibliography of Publications and the Administrative Systems of Latin-American Countries* (Washington, Government Printing Office, 1938) is excellent. A crying need exists for a guide to the writings on Latin America contained in scientific and technical journals.

Since goverments of highly developed countries seek outlets for national capital and technology, they collect an immense quantity of data on the subject. Government publications are therefore a very valuable source of information. A surprising amount of the correspondence and reports of the diplomats, consuls, and commercial agents of the United States and Great Britain has been published. The most important British series is the *Diplomatic and Consular Reports* (regular and special) issued annually by the Foreign Office. Valuable also are the publications of the Department of Overseas Trade, as well as the British *Parliamentary Papers.* Even more important, perhaps, are the publications of the United States government: *Commercial Relations; Diplomatic Correspondence; Consular Reports; Monthly Consular and Trade Reports;* various bulletins and monographs issued by the Department of Commerce, Bureau of Foreign and Domestic Commerce; and the huge collection usually described as *Congressional Documents* or *Public Documents.* Likewise of great value, of course, are the materials deposited in the archives of the two governments, particularly those of the State Department and the Foreign Office.

On the Latin-American side, the most valuable published sources are the official *Diarios* and the annual reports—*Informes* and *Memorias*—of the various cabinet officers and heads of bureaus, which are satisfactorily described by Childs in the work mentioned above. The congressional documents of the various Latin-American nations, including laws (*leyes*) and decrees (*decretos*), are also most useful. Complete collections of such publications are rare. Those in Washington, D. C., in the Library of Congress and the Columbus Memorial Library of the Pan American Union, are as satisfactory as can be found in the United States.

Business records of firms and corporations with Latin-American interests are, of course, very useful; but many of them are not accessible. Among such corporations in the United States are the United Fruit Company, All America Cables, various oil, mining, and electric power companies, the International Telephone and Telegraph Corporation, and a number of earlier telephone companies, many of which have published annual reports to their stockholders. Useful also are Moody's manuals.

CHAPTER I

The committee of experts sent on the official mission to South America in 1941 submitted a number of confidential reports, excerpts and summaries of which were printed under the title of *Tour of Industrial Exploration: South America* (Washington, D. C., National Research Council, 1941). The papers read at the 1940 session of the American Historical Association were edited and published by Arthur P. Whitaker, who added a suggestive essay of his own: *Latin America and the Enlightenment* (New York, D. Appleton-Century Company, 1942). The quotations in the last paragraphs of my narrative are from this little volume.

CHAPTER II

An important manuscript source of information on the arrival of the river steamers in Latin America is the Consular Letters written from Barranquilla, Pará, Buenos Aires, Guayaquil, and other port towns. John Bassett Moore's *History and Digest of International Arbitrations* (Washington, 1906, 8 vols.), II and III, contains useful material on the first two companies organized for the navigation of the Orinoco. For the beginnings of steamboat traffic on the Amazon, see D. P. Kidder and J. C. Fletcher, *Brazil and the Brazilians* (Philadelphia, 1857); F. J. de Santa Anna Nery, *The Land of the Amazons* (New York and London, 1901); and *Commercial Relations of the United States*. For the early steamers on the Río de la Plata system, consult Michael G. Mulhall, *The English in South*

America (Buenos Aires, 1878), and Harold Peterson, "Edward A. Hopkins: A Pioneer Promoter in Paraguay," in *The Hispanic American Historical Review*, XXII (1942). On Ecuador's Guayas River and Colombia's Magdalena, see the bibliographical notes on Chaps. VI and VIII below. For the early ocean lines and Vanderbilt's isthmian route, consult Wheaton J. Lane, *Commodore Vanderbilt* (New York, 1942); William Hadfield, *Brazil, the River Plate, and the Falkland Islands* (London, 1854); Franklin Lawrence Babcock, *Spanning the Atlantic* (New York, 1931); Arthur C. Wardle, *Steam Conquers the Pacific* (London, 1940); Thomas A. Bushell, *Royal Mail* (London, 1939); John Haskell, "The Genesis of the Pacific Mail Steamship Company," in *California Historical Society Quarterly*, XIII (1934); and F. N. Otis, *History of the Panama Railroad; and of the Pacific Mail Steamship Company* (New York, 1867). For a friendly Latin-American view of Wheelwright's work, see Juan B. Alberdi's *Vida y los trabajos industriales de William Wheelwright en la América del Sud* (Paris, 1876). An English edition of this work was published in Boston in 1877.

CHAPTER III

The early Cuban railroads are described by José María de Torre, *Guía de los ferrocarriles en la isla de Cuba* (Habana, 1858), and by Jacobo de la Pezuela y Lobo, *Diccionario . . . de la isla de Cuba* (Madrid, 1863-1866. 4 *tomos*). David Turnbull, who was present during the celebration of the opening of the Havana-Güines Railway, comments briefly on the road and its builders in his *Travels in the West* (London, 1840). The story of Brazil's early railways is told briefly by Francisco Pereira Passos, *As estradas de ferro do Brasil em 1879* (Rio de Janeiro, 1880), and by Cyro D. Ribeiro Pessoa, *Estudo descriptivo das estradas de ferro do Brasil* (Rio de Janeiro, 1886). Hadfield, mentioned above, was present at the running of the first locomotive over a short section of Mauá's railroad in 1853. On railway beginnings in Argentina, see Ramón J. Cárcaño, *Historia de los medios de comunicación y transportes en la República de Argentina* (Buenos Aires, 1893. 2 *tomos*); George S. Brady, *Railways of South America. Part I: Argentina* (*Trade Promotion Series,* No. 32, Washington, 1926); and Peterson's article on Hopkins referred to in the previous section. On the first railways built in Chile, consult Samuel Núñez Olaechea, *Los ferrocarriles del estado* (Santiago, 1910); Santiago Marín Vicuña, *Los ferrocarriles de Chile* (Santiago, 3rd ed., 1912); Rodney W. Long, *Railways of South America. Part III: Chile* (*Trade Promotion Series,* No. 93, Washington, 1926); and Alberdi's biography of Wheelwright. On those of other countries, see the works of Long, Powell, Ortega, Costa y Laurent, and Fernández Montúfar mentioned below.

CHAPTER IV

On the spread of telegraphy in Europe, see George Sauer, *The Telegraph in Europe* (Paris, 1869) and Sir James Anderson, *Statistics of Telegraphy* (London, 1872). Good secondary accounts of its progress in several of the South American countries are contained in the following monographs by Victor M. Berthold: *History of the Telephone and Telegraph in the Argentine Republic* (New York, 1921) and subsequent monographs with similar titles on Colombia (New York, 1921), Brazil (New York, 1922), Chile (New York, 1924), and Uruguay (New York, 1925). A good historical summary of the Brazilian telegraphic lines, with some attention to cables, was published by the national government under the title *Memoria histórica* (Rio de Janeiro, 1909). Useful information on Mexico is given by Antonio García Cubas in his *Mexico, its Trade, Industry, and Resources* (Mexico City, 1893). On the introduction of the telegraph into Cuba, see the *Diccionario* of Pezuela y Lobo listed above in these *notes,* Chapter III. For data on mileage and number of offices, consult the various folders published by the American Telephone and Telegraph Company under the title of *Telephone and Telegraph Statistics of the World* or *Telephone and Telegraph Statistics of American Republics.* Much information is also included in the government documents of the United States and the Latin-American countries mentioned at the beginning of these bibliographical notes. The national directors of telegraphs of Latin America usually function as members of the staffs of one or another of the national cabinet officers. In Argentina and Chile, for instance, they are subordinate to the ministers of *Gobierno* (Interior); in Colombia the director was now under *Gobierno* and now under *Obras Públicas* (Public Works); and in Bolivia he was subordinate also to the minister of Public Works. On cables, see F. J. Brown, *The Cable and Wireless Communications of the World* (London, 1927); *A Half Century of Cable Service to the Three Americas* (New York, 1928); George A. Schreiner, *Cables and Wireless* (New York, 1924) and *Hearings* of the U. S. Congress cited therein; James A. Scrymser, *Personal Reminiscences* (New York, 1915).

CHAPTER V

In the preparation of this essay I received the generous aid of my friend and colleague Watt Stewart, who kindly sent me his manuscript volume on Henry Meiggs. The quotations in my work are taken mainly from this manuscript. Federico Costa y Laurent, *Reseña histórica de los ferrocarriles del Perú* (Lima, 1908), presents brief accounts of each of the Peruvian railways, including those built or started by Meiggs. James Orton's *The Andes and the Ama-*

zon (New York, 3rd ed., 1875), pp. 443-453, contains one of the best descriptions of the Meiggs lines in English. Other good descriptions will be found in *The Geographical Magazine*, I (London, 1874), 36-41, 90-92 (written by Sir Clements Markham), and in *Scribner's Monthly*, XIV (New York, 1877), 449-464 (J. Eglinton Montgomery). Contracts and other documents for the period before 1877 were published at the order of Meiggs himself: *Los Ferrocarriles del Perú. Colección de leyes, decretos, contratos y demás documentos relativos á los ferrocarriles del Perú* (Lima, 1876. 2 tomos). Rodney W. Long's, *Railways of South America, Part II: Bolivia, Colombia, Ecuador, Guianas, Paraguay, Peru, Uruguay, and Venezuela* (*Trade Promotion Series*, No. 39, Washington, 1927) is helpful but inaccurate at many points. Among the newspapers published in Peru during the epoch, *El Comercio, El Nacional,* and *The Callao and Lima Gazette* are especially valuable for the attention they gave to Meiggs and his railways.

CHAPTER VI

The best secondary account of the history of steamboats and steamboat traffic on the Magdalena is Enrique Naranjo Martínez's *Monografía del Río Magdalena* (Bogotá, 1917). Useful data are presented by Salvador Camacho Roldán in his *Notas de viaje* (Bogotá, 1890) and by Consul Thomas C. Dawson in his letters from Barranquilla, many of which are still in manuscript (see Consular Letters, Barranquilla, deposited in the National Archives, Washington, D. C.). A good description of navigation on the Magdalena is given by Dawson in a letter of November 10, 1884, *United States Consular Reports*, Vol. 14 (1884), pp. 334-347. Other information may be found in *Leyes de Colombia* (Bogotá, 1823–) and various annual reports of the Colombian Comptroller General published under the title of *Anuario general de estadística* (Bogotá, 1931–). The best sources for an exhaustive study of the subject are the Consular Letters of Dawson and his predecessors and successors at Barranquilla, the correspondence and reports of the Colombian *Intendente de la navegación del Río Magdalena,* and the archives and publications of the various steamboat companies. Very useful also are the accounts of travelers. The reader will have no difficulty locating those printed in English. Among those in Spanish, in addition to the one by Camacho Roldán already mentioned, Miguel Cané's *Notas de viaje* (Bogotá, 1907) and José Antonio García's *Un viaje* (Bogotá, 1863) deserve commendation. The author of the present volume has made the journey over this difficult route, going up the Magdalena by freight boat.

CHAPTER VII

The standard work on Colombia's railways is Alfredo Ortega, *Ferrocarriles colombianos* (Bogotá, 1920-1932, 3 *tomos*). Useful also are Carlos Tanco's *Ferrocarril de la Sabana* (Bogotá, 1886) and Consul-General Victor Huckin's "Report on the Railways of Colombia," in Great Britain, *Diplomatic and Consular Reports* (No. 678, *Miscellaneous Series,* London, 1910). Gabriel Lattore's "Francisco Javier Cisneros y el Ferrocarril de Antioquia," in *El Ferrocarril de Antioquia,* October 12, 1924, is a good summary of Cisneros's career in Colombia. Useful information is also contained in "Reports of the Central and South American Commission," printed in *House Executive Documents,* No. 226, 48 Congress, 2 Session, Serial No. 2304 and No. 50, 49 Congress, 1 Session, Serial No. 2392. The Consular Letters in the National Archives, Washington, D. C., and the various railroad laws and contracts, of which those of the national government of Colombia are the only ones easily accessible, are the best sources. See also Long's work mentioned in the notes on Chap. V; and, for full citations, consult my article in *The Hispanic American Historical Review,* XXIII (November 1943).

CHAPTER VIII

For assistance in the preparation of this essay I am indebted to Professor E. Taylor Parks, who has thoroughly investigated relations between the United States and Ecuador. Much of the essay is based upon manuscript sources—Consular Letters and Diplomatic Despatches—preserved in the National Archives of the United States. Some of these have been published in *Commercial Relations, Diplomatic Correspondence,* and *Consular Reports.* Satisfactory descriptions of the Guayaquil and Quito Railway and its construction may be found in *Engineering News,* Vol. 52 (1904), and in the *Bulletin* of the Pan American Union, Vols. 7 (November, 1899), 11 (September, 1901), 27 (August, 1908), 33 (October, 1911), and 35 (November, 1912). For mining and petroleum, see Moody's *Manual of Investments* (New York, 1920-1942) and various reports of the Ecuadorian Director General de Minería y el Petróleo. For the eradication of yellow fever, consult Lois F. Parks and G. A. Nuermberger, "The Sanitation of Guayaquil," in *The Hispanic American Historical Review,* XXIII (1943). Summaries of electrical development have been published by the United States Department of Commerce, Bureau of Foreign and Domestic Commerce, *Trade Information Bulletin,* Nos. 178 and 469. See also Long's volume mentioned above in the notes on Chapter V, Albert B. Franklin, *Ecuador* (New York, 1943), and Roberto Crespo Ordóñez, *Historia del Ferrocarril del Sur* (Quito, 1933).

CHAPTER IX

Materials on the enthusiasm of the United States for the Amazon Valley, and particularly on the Madeira and Mamoré Railway, are abundant. Matthew F. Maury's articles will be found in the *National Intelligencer,* files for 1849-1850, and in *De Bow's Review* for 1850-1851. His *Memorial* submitted to the Memphis Convention of 1853 was published in *House Miscellaneous Documents,* No. 22, 33 Congress, 1 Session, Serial No. 741. William R. Manning's *Diplomatic Documents, Inter-American Affairs,* contain a wealth of information on the opening of the Amazon to the vessels of foreign nations. Neville B. Craig's *Recollections* mentioned in the text are a fascinating account of the first effort of United States engineers to build the railroad. The later effort is described in part by Frank W. Kravigny in his *The Jungle Route* (New York, 1940), which contains a short bibliography. *The Railroad Gazette,* Vol. 36 (1904), contains an article by O. F. Nichols; *Engineering News,* Vols. 58-62 (1907-1909) and 68 (1912), prints a number of news items and articles written by participants. Information can be obtained also from the *Bulletin* of the Pan American Union, especially Vols. 30 (1910), 32 (1911), 33 (1911), and 35 (1912). *World's Work,* XX (May, 1910), published a propaganda article by Herbert M. Lome. Church's numerous publications on his efforts of 1869-1878 are listed by the Harvard Bureau of Economic Research in its work on the economic literature of Latin America. They may be discovered likewise by consulting the catalogues of the Brown University Libraries. The Brazilian Ministry of Transportation and Public Works published a useful collection of documents—*Actos officaes referentes a Estrada de ferro Madeira-Memoré*—in 1917. H. M. Tomlinson's classic volume, *The Sea and the Jungle* (New York, 1920), deals largely with the railway project and is based on personal observations. A hint of the Farquhar's vast transportation plan may be obtained from *Monthly Consular and Trade Reports,* November, 1907, pp. 103-106. See also, in this connection, Simon G. Hanson, in *Hispanic American Historical Review,* XVII (August, 1937) and *Bulletin* of the Pan American Union, Vol. 36 (January and May, 1913).

CHAPTER X

I am indebted to Dr. John McKian of Loyola University for assistance in locating references for this essay. John C. Branner's publications have been most helpful: "Bibliography of the Geology, Mineralogy, and Paleontology of Brazil," in *Bulletin of the Geological Society of America,* Vol. 20 (1910); "Memorial of Orville Derby," in *ibid.,* Vol. 27 (1916); "Memoir of James E. Mills," in *ibid.,* Vol. 14 (1902). The brief account of Hartt's work in Brazil is based mainly on the following: Richard Rathbun, *Sketch of the*

Life and Scientific Work of Prof. Charles Fred. Hartt (Boston, 1878), and his briefer account in *Popular Science Monthly*, Vol. 13 (1878); *Cornell Magazine*, II (1890); Royal Society of Canada, *Proceedings and Transactions*, V (1899). On the third member of this able group, two items have been most useful, namely, R. A. F. Penrose's "Memorial to John Casper Branner," in *Bulletin of the Geological Society of America*, Vol. 36 (1925), and George P. Merrill's sketch in *The Dictionary of American Biography*. Good background is presented by S. Fróes Abreu, *A riquesa mineral do Brasil* (Rio de Janeiro, 1937), by Josias Leao, *Mines and Minerals of Brazil* (Rio de Janeiro, 1939), and by José Jobim, *The Mineral Wealth of Brazil* (Rio de Janeiro, 1941). The last two works contain brief bibliographies which reveal the scientific progress that is being made by Brazilians.

CHAPTER XI

An account of the major part of Page's explorations is contained in his *La Plata, the Argentine Confederation, and Paraguay* (London, 1859). Later editions of this work, one of them in Spanish, are difficult to locate. See also the sketch of Page in the *Dictionary of American Biography*, which also contains a sketch of Gould. For a fuller account of Gould's career, see the *Memoirs* of the National Academy of Sciences, XV (1924). For a good summary of the activities of Hopkins, consult Harold F. Peterson's article in *The Hispanic American Historical Review*, XX (1942). On Wheelwright, see Alberdi's biography mentioned above. *Science*, Vol. 50 (July 4, 1919), contains a brief account of the work of Walter G. Davis; see also his two books: *Climate of the Argentine Republic* (Buenos Aires, 1910) and *The Argentine Meteorological Service* (Buenos Aires, 1914). On the Willis Commission, consult Willis's *Northern Patagonia* (Buenos Aires and New York, 1914) and Wellington D. Jones, "Present Status and Future Possibilities of Agricultural Land Utilization in Patagonia," in *Pioneer Settlement*, Special Publications of the American Geographical Society, No. 14 (New York, 1932). I have utilized also a series of letters in possession of Professor Jones. Further data on Willis is given in *Who's Who in America, 1942-1943*. See also the standard biographies of Sarmiento, the annual reports of the Argentine minister of public instruction, 1870-1895, and the reports of the Central and South American Commission referred to in previous sections of these notes.

CHAPTER XII

This essay is based upon diplomatic dispatches and consular letters, some in manuscript in the National Archives and others published in *Diplomatic Correspondence* and *Consular Reports;*

upon a thorough examination of the *Leyes* of Costa Rica from 1850 to 1895; and upon a number of secondary works. The most useful of the last are: Chester Lloyd Jones, *Costa Rica and Civilization in the Caribbean* (Madison, 1935); Francisco Iglesias and various collaborators, *Revista de Costa Rica en el Siglo XIX* (San José, 1902); Joaquín B. Calvo, *The Republic of Costa Rica* (Chicago, 1890); Joaquín Fernández Montúfar, *Historia ferrovial de Costa Rica* [San José, 1934]; Luis F. González, *Historia de la influencia extranjera en el desenvolvimiento científico de Costa Rica* (San José, 1921); Francisco María Núñez, *Iniciación y desarollo de las vias de comunicación ... en Costa Rica* (San José, 1923); and Alberto Quijana Quesada, *Costa Rica ayer y hoy* (San José, 1939). W. Rodney Long's *Railways of Central America and the West Indies* includes a discussion of Costa Rican railways, but this work is often inaccurate. The reports of the Central and South American Commission mentioned in the notes on Chapter VII also contain considerable information.

CHAPTER XIII

Sources of information on technological progress in Guatemala are similar to those for Costa Rica. The *Leyes* of Guatemala for the years 1870-1904 contain a wealth of information, as likewise the diplomatic and consular letters, published and unpublished. Among secondary works the following have been found most useful: Chester Lloyd Jones, *Guatemala, Past and Present* (Minneapolis, 1941); Paul Burgess, *Justo Rufino Barrios* (Philadelphia, 1926); Víctor Miguel Díaz, *Barrios ante la posteridad* (Guatemala City, 1935); and Casimiro D. Rubio, *Biografía del General Justo Rufino Barrios* (Guatemala City, 1935). See also the last two items mentioned in the notes on Chapter XII; and, for more detailed citations, consult my article dealing with the Barrios epoch in *The Hispanic American Historical Review*, XXII (November, 1942).

CHAPTER XIV

The standard summaries of railway development in Mexico, Fred Wilbur Powell's *Railroads of Mexico* (Boston, 1921) and W. Rodney Long's *Railways of Mexico* (Bureau of Foreign and Domestic Commerce, *Trade Promotion Series*, No. 16, Washington, 1925), devote little attention to the technician and the laborer. Information on this important phase of the subject is available in *U. S. Consular Reports*, in the manuscript files of consular and diplomatic correspondence in the National Archives, in *The Railroad Gazette* and *Engineering News*, and in the newspapers both of the United States and Mexico. The best descriptions of the Mexican railways in the 1880's and 1890's are: Thomas Janvier, *The Mexican Guide* (New

York, various editions); *U. S. Special Consular Reports,* XII ("Highways of Commerce"); Great Britain, Foreign Office, *Report on the Railways of Mexico (Miscellaneous Series,* No. 309, London, 1893); Antonio García Cubas, *Mexico, Its Trade, Industries, and Resources* (Mexico, 1893). The most useful of the newspapers is *The Mexican Financier,* published in both Spanish and English in Mexico City; but *La Nacional* and *El Correo de las Doce* contain significant news and comment on the railway boom. The numerous contracts of the period were assembled and published by the Mexican Secretary of Fomento, Colonization, and Industry under the title of *Legislación sobre ferrocarriles* (Mexico, 1882-1875. 5 *tomos*). Bishop's articles appeared in *Harper's Magazine* for January, February, and March, 1882, Vol. 64. John Bigelow published in the same journal, Vol. 65, October, 1882, a warning to investors which attracted a good deal of attention. The title of the volume by Bernard Moses is *The Railway Revolution in Mexico* (Berkeley, 1895); Conkling's volume was called *Mexico and the Mexicans* (New York, 1883); Griffin's, *Mexico of Today* (New York, 1886). See also the reports and other publications of the various railway companies.

CHAPTER XV

The correspondence of United States consuls at Guaymas and Mazatlán, published and in manuscript, describes economic activities on Mexico's West Coast. Albert K. Owen, a prolific writer, discussed his Utopian theories and plans in numerous pamphlets, many of which may be found in the Library of Congress. Incomplete but useful accounts of his work in Mexico are contained in two articles which include citations to sources of information: Leopold Katscher, "Owen's Topolobampo Colony, Mexico," in *The American Journal of Sociology,* XII (September, 1906); and Sanford A. Mosk, "A Railroad to Utopia," in *The Southwestern Social Science Quarterly,* XX (December, 1939). Clarence O. Senior's *The Kansas City, Mexico and Orient Railroad* (MS., M. A. Thesis, University of Kansas City) is an intelligent preliminary survey of that subject, with useful citations to both manuscript and published sources. Shortly before completing his thesis in 1942, Senior visited San Blas, Topolobampo, and Mochis, observed the condition of the railway, and talked with the natives. Good descriptions of the building of both the Kansas City, Mexico and Orient and the Southern Pacific of Mexico are contained in *The Railway Age,* 1901 and following. The various concessions made to these two Mexican lines are published in Dublán y Lozano, *Legislación Mexicana* and in *Diario Oficial,* volumes for 1881 and following years. For rather enthusiastic accounts of Stilwell's work on the Kansas City-Topolobampo line, see *Financial World* for 1906 and

Moody's Magazine and *Banker's Magazine* for 1910. For similar accounts of the completion of the Southern Pacific of Mexico, consult *World's Work* and the *Bulletin* of the Pan American Union for 1928. P. L. Bell and H. Bentley Mackenzie, in their *Mexican West Coast and Lower California (Special Agents Series,* No. 220, Washington, 1923), present a useful survey of the development of that region and the contributions of Yankees until their activities were interrupted. The hearings of the Senate Committee on Mexico (Fall Committee), published under the title of *Investigation of Mexican Affairs (Senate Documents,* No. 285, 66 Congress, 2 session, Serial Nos. 7665 and 7666), although highly prejudiced against Mexico, throw a flood of light on the activities and troubles of citizens and corporations of the United States engaged in developing and exploiting the Mexican West Coast and all parts of the country. Stilwell's memoirs appeared in *The Saturday Evening Post,* December 3 and 31, 1927, January 14 and 28, and February 4, 1928.

CHAPTER XVI

Letters of the consuls of the United States from southern Mexico and Central America, many of which have been published in *Consular Reports, Special Consular Reports,* and *Commercial Relations,* are the best source of information on the rubber-plantation boom. Volume 6 of *Special Consular Reports* contains the replies to the "rubber circular" of 1890. State Department circulars of September 26, 1905, and July 6, 1906, regarding citizens of the United States residing in Latin America and corporations of the United States with investments in Latin America, resulted in the compilation of lists which have not been published; but they may be consulted, under certain limitations, in the National Archives. Another list, including rubber and other plantations, is contained in Percy G. Holms, *A Directory of Agencies, Mines, and Haciendas of Mexico* (Mexico, 1906); and still another, including later data, is on file in the Library of the U. S. Department of Commerce. The most convenient index to the character of the advertisements and other literature circulated by the rubber plantation and development companies is contained in the *India Rubber World* and *Modern Mexico,* 1895-1912. In 1923 and following the Department of Commerce published a number of bulletins and monographs on rubber. Among these, *Trade Promotion Series,* No. 40 (Washington, 1926) deals with rubber in "Northern Tropical America," with allusions to the rubber-plantation boom of 1898-1910. Useful data regarding the unhappy fate of citizens of the United States in southern Mexico during the revolutionary period is contained in the hearings of the Fall Committee referred to in the previous section of these notes. Individuals appearing before this committee unwittingly made some disclosures regarding labor conditions on the plantations. Accounts equally if not more biased in the opposite direction were written by Herman Whitaker in a novel entitled *The Planter* (New York, 1909) and in an article in *The American Magazine* (1910). *Modern Mexico*, XX (February, 1906), 13-14, gives a brief and surprisingly impartial description of the labor system. For the history of the rubber industry, consult Howard and Ralph Wolf, *Rubber, A Story of Glory and Greed* (New York, 1936).

CHAPTER XVII

Most of the materials described in the bibliographical notes (Chapter IV) on the arrival of the telegraph also contain information on the migration of the telephone. See especially the works of Berthold and García Cubas and the statistical folders published by the American Telephone and Telegraph Company. Through the kindness of Arthur H. Cole of the Baker Library, Harvard University, I have obtained the pertinent contents of three pamphlets which throw light upon the Latin-American operations and contracts of the Tropical Telephone Company, which sponsored a good deal of the telephone pioneering in the region. The annual reports of the national directors of telegraphs in the various countries contain useful data. These functionaries, who in recent years have had the title of minister or secretary of communications, have had charge of the state telephone as well as the state telegraph systems, and have given some attention to private telephone systems in their reports. Further information is contained in the letters of United States consuls, published or in manuscript in the National Archives. See also the annual reports of the various companies mentioned in the text and files of the *Bulletin* of the Pan American Union.

CHAPTER XVIII

The most satisfactory accounts of the trends of mineral production in Latin America and the world are contained in the *Economic Papers* (Washington, 1928–) published by the United States Bureau of Mines. Valuable for recent developments is the report of the United States Tariff Commission, entitled *Latin America as a Source of Strategic and other Essential Materials* (Washington, 1941). For data on ownership and recent operations see: G. A. Roush, *Strategic Mineral Supplies* (New York, 1939); William P. Rawles, *The Nationality of Commercial Control of World Minerals* (New York, 1933); William Y. Elliott, Alexander Skelton, and others, *International Control of Non-Ferrous Metals* (New York, 1937); and Cleona Lewis, *America's Stake in International Investments* (Washington, 1938). The best source for the history of Anglo-Saxon participation in Latin-American mining is the immense bulk of diplomatic and consular correspondence of these two nations so frequently referred to in these notes, a good deal of which has been published in the various series already mentioned. The major part of it, however, is still in manuscript in the National Archives of the United States and in the British Public Records Office. Much information may also be gleaned from such newspapers as the *South Pacific Mail* (Valparaíso) and the *West Coast Leader* (Lima) and such technical journals as *Mining and Engineering World* (Chicago), *Mining Magazine* (New York), and *Engineering and Mining Journal* (New York). There are a number of histories of mining in individual countries, written for the most part by Latin Americans, such as Vicente Restrepo's *Estudio sobre las minas de oro y plata de Colombia* (Bogotá, 2nd ed., 1888); but it is not necessary to list them here. The bulletins, reports, and monographs of the mining departments or bureaus of such important mineral countries as Mexico, Honduras, Colombia, Peru, Bolivia, Chile, and Brazil will likewise be found useful, and the various books of travel, especially those of the first half of the nineteenth century, contain many illuminating details: H. G. Ward on Mexico, John Miers on Chile and Peru; and many others. See also Benjamin L. Miller and Joseph T. Singewald, *The Mineral Deposits of South America* (New York, 1919) and H. Foster Bain and Thomas T. Read, *Ores and Industries in South America* (New York, 1934). For an intimate view of activities and conditions in foreign-owned mines, such books as Grant Shepherd's *The Silver Magnet* (New York, 1938) may be read with profit. The Shepherd family had charge of the Batopilas mines of Mexico for forty years. See also *Foreign Minerals Quarterly*, Vols. 2-4 (Washington, Bureau of Mines, 1939-41).

CHAPTER XIX

Data on petroleum exports from the United States, listed separately under "Oil, Mineral," as a rule, are presented by an annual publication of the United States entitled *Foreign Commerce and Navigation of the United States*. As in most other phases of the subject dealt with in this volume, the most useful published sources of information are the *United States Consular Reports* and the *British Diplomatic and Consular Reports*, neither of which, however, contains more than a small fraction of the letters from the consuls and commercial agents of the two countries in Latin America, letters which may be found in manuscript in the Public Records Office and the National Archives. Published reports of the appropriate Latin-American cabinet officers and government bureaus are likewise valuable, as well as various bulletins and monographs of the United States Department of Commerce, particularly the following:

Trade Information Bulletin, Nos. 81, 178, 494 and 784; commercial and industrial handbooks of the various Latin-American countries; and *Trade Promotion Series,* Nos. 20 and 126. Valuable also are the publications of the United States Department of the Interior, Bureau of Mines, which include petroleum bibliography and compilations of the oil laws of Latin America. Of these, bulletins Nos. 149, 165, 180, 189, and 216 are especially useful. The petroleum laws of the Americas will be found in the session laws (*Leyes*) of the several Latin-American countries, as well as in a number of compilations, such as J. W. Thompson's *Petroleum Laws of All America* (Washington, 1921) and others published by the Latin-American governments. "Reports of the Central and South American Commission," referred to under Chapter VII of these *Notes,* contain useful information on the kerosene trade of the 1880's. Secondary works on petroleum development in the Latin-American countries are too numerous to list here. An article by Fritz L. Hoffmann in *Mid-America,* Vol. 24 (1942), deals with Doheny's pioneering in Mexico. Two works by the present author, namely, J. Fred Rippy, *The United States and Mexico* (New York, 2d ed., 1931) and *The Capitalists and Colombia* (New York, 1931), contain accounts of diplomatic controversies arising between the United States and these countries over the oil issue. Rivalry between the United States and Great Britain is dealt with by Ludwell Denny, *We Fight for Oil* (New York, 1928); E. H. Davenport, and S. R. Cooke, *The Oil Trusts and Anglo-American Relations* (New York, 1924); and many others. Numerous controversial publications, issued by the oil companies and the Latin-American governments, are useful. See also various scientific and technical magazines, especially *Economic Geology, Oil and Gas Journal, Foreign Minerals Quarterly,* and *The Lamp.*

CHAPTER XX

The best printed sources for the study of the migration of electrical utilities and appliances to Latin America are *Consular Reports* of the United States, the *Diplomatic and Consular Reports* of Great Britain, and various bulletins and monographs of the United States Department of Commerce, Bureau of Foreign and Domestic Commerce. Of the last, see especially *Trade Promotion Series,* Nos. 154, 167, and 169; *Trade Information Bulletin,* Nos. 209, 229, 362, 382, 426, 466, 469, 496, 508, 511, 515, 519, and 536; and numerous bulletins of the Electrical Division. On F. S. Pearson, consult the *Dictionary of American Biography* and *Transactions* of the American Society of Civil Engineers, Vols. 58 (1907) and 87 (1924). See also Albert B. Paine, *Theodore Vail* (New York, 1929); J. P. Wileman, *Brazilian Year Book, 1909* (London, 1910); Frederic M. Halsey,

Investments in Latin America and the British West Indies (Washington, 1918); and *Memorias* of the various Latin-American ministers of *fomento* to whom the directors of electrical services are usually subordinated.

Historians of Latin America have given comparatively little attention to electrical developments in the region. Among the few works published on the subject is the monograph by Ernesto Galarza, entitled *La Industria Eléctrica en Mexico* (Mexico City, 1941). Galarza's volume discloses an attitude more or less typical of Latin Americans, dissatisfaction with foreign ownership and policies. For further indication of the sentiments of Latin Americans, a summary of which may be gleaned from Moody's manuals on public utilities, consult their newspapers and magazines and their many projects of laws on file in the Columbus Memorial Library and the Library of Congress.

CHAPTER XXI

The sources upon which this essay is based are alluded to in the text. They are *Annual Reports* of the Medical Division of the United Fruit Company for the years 1913-1931 (Boston, 1914-1932), *Annual Reports* of the Rockefeller Foundation for 1913 to 1941 (New York, 1914-1942), and the various publications of the Pan American Sanitary Bureau located in Washington, D. C., a list of which may be obtained from the Bureau. With these materials and Charles Morrow Wilson's *Ambassadors in White* (New York, 1942) one may begin a thorough investigation of this important subject. Further information will be found in the medical and sanitary journals of the United States and Latin America. Data on the period before 1898 are widely scattered; letters from the consuls of the United States serving in various parts of Latin America are the most convenient and perhaps the best source.

CHAPTER XXII

The most useful sources for the investigation of the history of manufacturing in Latin America are *Consular Reports* (regular and special) of the United States, the various monographs published by the United States Department of Commerce (Bureau of Foreign and Domestic Commerce), the series issued annually by the British Foreign Office under the title of *Diplomatic and Consular Reports* (regular and special), and the monographs published by the British Department of Overseas Trade. Among secondary works in the English language, the best from the historical viewpoint are George Wythe's "The Rise of the Factory in Latin America" in *The Hispanic American Historical Review,* XXV (August, 1945), pp. 295-314, and *Industry in Latin America* (New York, 1945). Sources and secondary works published in Latin America, where much attention has been given to the subject of manufacturing in recent years, may be discovered by following Wythe's citations, which also include many specific references to publications by the United States Department of Commerce. See also J. Fred Rippy, "The Dawn of Manufacturing in Peru" in *The Pacific Historical Review*, XV (June, 1946), pp. 147-157, which contains many citations to Peruvian sources of information. In the 1940's the United States Tariff Commission began the publication of a series of useful processed monographs on the current state of the mining and manufacturing industries of the twenty Latin-American countries, and by 1947 most of the republics had been surveyed. Lloyd J. Hughlett's *Industrialization of Latin America* (New York, 1946) analyzes the present status of manufacturing, from the viewpoint of business leaders and technicians of the United States, in the main.

CHAPTER XXIII

William D. Pardridge, a graduate student at the University of Chicago, has given me much assistance in assembling bibliography for this chapter. Obviously the best source on aviation is the records of the commercial companies, but these have not been available. Another good source is the collections of Latin-American laws and official *diarios*, in which many of the regulations and contracts are published. The outstanding authority in the United States on aviation in Latin America is Anyda Marchant, a member of the staff of the Law Division of the Library of Congress, who is writing a series of articles on each of the countries. Those on Colombia, Chile, and Brazil have been published in *Air Law Review*, Vols. 9 and following. They also appeared as a pamphlet published by New York University Law School in 1939. Miss Marchant, however, gives main emphasis to legal phases of the subject. Perhaps the best guide to historical development is the index to New York *Times* from 1919 to date. The magazine *Fortune*, 1931 and following, contains several articles stressing promotion and competition. The *Bulletin* of the Pan American Union frequently deals with the subject—especially Vols. 55 (September, 1922), 66 (November, 1932), 69 (September, 1935), and 70 (April, 1936). Even more valuable are two items in *Foreign Affairs*, Vol. 16 (April, 1938) and 19 (January, 1941). *Geographical Review*, Vol. 20 (1930), contains a good sketch by H. Case Wilcox, who also has an article in *The Military Engineer*, Vol. 24 (1932). Members of the staff of the U. S. Bureau of Foreign and Domestic Commerce deal with airports in Latin America in *Trade Information Bulletin*, No. 696, published in 1930. See also *Aviation*, especially Vol. 39 (1940), *Pan American Magazine*, Vol. 43 (1930), *Living Age*, Vols. 336 (March, 1929) and 348 (July, 1935), and

Saturday Evening Post, Vol. 211 (December 3, 1938). Three suggestive books on the general history of aviation, with some attention to Latin America, are Robert Finch, *The World's Airways* (London, 1938), Elizabeth E. Freudenthal, *The Aviation Business* (New York, 1940), and Oliver J. Lissitzyn, *International Air Transport and National Policy* (New York, 1942). Lissitzyn often "elucidates the obvious," but his work is nevertheless important for the present volume because of its emphasis on Latin America and its bibliographical references. Strangely enough, he does not include *Air Law Review* in his list of periodicals nor reveal any evidence of acquaintance with the excellent contributions of Miss Marchant. William A. M. Burden's *The Struggle for Airways in Latin America* (New York, 1943) is a fairly satisfactory performance. Documents published in *U. S. Foreign Relations* for 1928 reveal the intimate connection between government and business in the drive for air-route concessions in Latin America.

CHAPTER XXIV

The summary of ownership in this essay is based upon Moody's manuals, mimeographed monographs of the Department of Commerce, and various bulletins of the Electrical Division of the Bureau of Foreign and Domestic Commerce, supplemented by such reports of the various corporations and the several Latin-American governments as were available, as well as by personal letters from numerous Latin-American officials. The percentages on ownership are estimates, of course; but it is believed that they are sufficiently accurate to be useful. See also the works listed for Chaps. XVIII and XX.

INDEX

Acapulco, Mexico, 22, 146, 147, 214
Acebedo, Arturo, 63
Acre Territory, 91
Adelphi Academy, 98
Aereomarine Airways, 250
Aerobrasil, 248
Aerolloyd Iguassú, 248
Aéropostale, 248
Africa, cable connections, 34, 37, 38
Agassiz, Louis, in Brazil, 96-97
Age of Reason, 11
Air France, 244
Airlines, Latin-American, 241-52. *See also* individual countries
Alajuela, Costa Rica, 118, 119, 120, 123
Alberdi, Juan B., 105, 107
Alfaro, América, 78
Alfaro, President Eloy, 78
All America Cables, 39
All America Cables and Radio, 187
Alta Vera Paz, Guatemala, 131
Alto de Raizal, Colombia, 59
Amagá Railway, 66
Amates, Guatemala, 135
Amazon Navigation and Commercial Company, 16
Amazon River, steamers on, 15-16. *See also* Madeira-Mamoré Railroad
Amazon Telegraph Company, Ltd., 33
Ambalema, Colombia, 64
Ambassadors in White, 218
Ambassadors of science and technology, in Brazil, 96-104
American and Foreign Power Company, 216, 255
American Antiquarian Society, 11
American Bell Telephone Company, 178, 181
American Export Airlines, 250
American Historical Association, 7
American Metal Company, 197
American Philosophical Society, 11
American Smelting and Refining Company, 197

American Telephone and Telegraph Company, 186
Anaconda Copper Mining Company, 197
Andes Agricultural Company, 131
Andes Mountains, 42, 58, 60, 68, 73, 75, 77
Anglo-Americans. *See* United States, citizens of
Anglo-Costa Rican Mining Company, 120
Anglo-Ecuadorian Oilfields, Ltd., 80
Anglo-Saxon countries, and Latin-American development, 253, 257-58. *See also* United States, British, English, Great Britain, etc.
Antioquia Railway, 63
Apure, steamer, 15
Arequipa to Puno Railway, 42-43, 47
Arequipa's conical peak (Misti), 47
Argentina, 4, 5; aviation in, 247, 248, 250; cable connections, 33, 37, 39; electricity in, 209, 210, 215-16, 255, 256; ice and refrigeration in, 213, 214; new technology in, 105-114; petroleum, 202, 203-04; railways of, 25-26, 107; steamers and steamship connections, 16-18, 111; the telegraph in, 30, 31, 32, 33; telephones in, 178-79, 185. *See also* Ownership
Arica-Tacna Railway, 23
Arillaga, Francisco, 22
Ariza, Juan A., 219
Armstrong, Frances, 109
Aroa copper mines, 27
Arteaga, Francisco, 146
Ashmead, P. H., 92-93
Aspinwall (Colón), Panama, 18, 23
Aspinwall, William H., 18, 23
Associated Telephone and Telegraph Company, 183, 256
Astronomical Journal, 110
Astronomical Observatory, in Córdoba, Argentina, 110, 112